The Crittenton Girls

Acknowledgements

Special thanks to my two book coaches, Kelly Hartog and Arra Boyles, who without their help, this book never would have been finished. Next, thanks to my family that has listened to me talk about this book for the last four years. Thanks to the members of my tribe, Marco Island Writers Inc. and W.F.W.A (Women's Fiction Writers Association) who have been my support and encouragement throughout my writing endeavors.

In addition, thank you to Shawn Fibkins and John Fernandez for talking so candidly about their experiences as either a kidney donor or a kidney recipient. No amount of research can compare with first-hand experience.

The Florence Crittenton Homes for Unwed Mothers, known as the Florence Crittenton Mission was a real place, founded by Charles N. Crittenton in 1896. It later became a part of the Child Welfare League of America.

In 2006, The National Florence Crittenton Mission adopted a new name: The National Crittenton Foundation. The organization separated from the Child Welfare League of America and returned to being a stand-alone organization affiliated with dozens of Crittenton-affiliated agencies around the country. The National Crittenton Foundation's headquarters are located in Portland, Oregon.

Dedicated to my children:

Candeus

Andrew

Amy

Terri

Joanne Simon Tailele

The Crittenton Girls

a novel

Joanne Simon Tailele

Simon Publishing LLC

Joanne Simon Tailele

Published by Simon Publishing LC
www.SimonPublishingLLC.com
Library of Congress Number: 2021909380
ISBN: 978-1-736-1881-6-3 Trade Paperback
        978-1-736-1881-7-0 eBook

2 0 2 1 0 5 0 5 8 2

One

2017

Mary Alice was no stranger to tears. She had been on this earth for seventy-five years. For fifty-nine of them, she loved one man. For fifty-seven, she nurtured three children. Being a mother fostered an ability to recognize the difference between crocodile tears and real pain. Sometimes it only took a hug, a whispered reassurance, occasionally a joke — or cookies. Maternal instinct. Practice. Tears were something that she could fix. Until today.

Bethany sat hunched over Mary Alice's kitchen table, arms wrapped around her head, muffled sobs heard through her arms. "Oh Gram" were the only words she'd muttered twenty minutes before dissolving into tears. Mary Alice stood behind her, arms limp and useless save for a box of tissues in one hand and a cookie tin in the other. Bethany hadn't spoken a word except to call her name. If only Mary Alice wasn't so out of practice.

She set the tissues and tin on the table next to Bethany's shaking arms. "Bethany." Mary Alice sucked in a breath. The air stilled. "Talk to Grandma, sweetie. Did somebody get hurt . . . or someone hurt you?"

Bethany didn't raise her head. Instead, she let out a long, shrill wail and curled in on herself.

Mary Alice's stomach squeezed like a fist. Words formed almost by their own volition. "I'm calling your Mom."

"Wait!" Bethany wailed. She sprang from her seat.

1

Before Mary Alice could reach the phone, Bethany's trembling arms were around her waist. With a suspended breath, Mary Alice lifted her granddaughter's red blotchy face. Bethany opened her mouth, and Mary Alice clenched her gut, hoping she was strong enough to hear whatever was going to come out of them.

"Gram . . . I'm . . . I'm pregnant!" The force of Bethany's cracking voice cut through the room.

Mary Alice blinked at her. *Pregnant*. Her vision blurred and her ears buzzed. An eeriness like déjà vu settled over her, paralyzing her muscles. She crumbled into her chair with a thud.

"Gram . . . shit." Bethany slapped a hand over her mouth. "Sorry, Gram, you okay?"

She was far, far away. Decades away. Snow blurred into her memory, car exhaust and gravel. Bethany touched her shoulder and she flinched before snapping back to the present, like someone sucked her back through a time capsule.

Mary Alice gave her the most convincing Gram-face she could muster. It felt like a poker face. "Sorry, sweetheart. I just felt dizzy there for a minute."

Bethany bought it. As Mary Alice patted her hand, Bethany's tears came back.

Pregnant. Something in Mary Alice stirred, dark and deep. She reeled herself above it. "Are you sure, sweetie? Periods can be late because of stress." She didn't believe that herself, but she had to say something.

"I took a pregnancy test."

Mary Alice glanced at Bethany's stomach. She was a little thicker around her middle, but she didn't *look* pregnant. "Have you seen a doctor?"

Another head shake. "I counted it out . . . from . . . you know. I'm three months along. I think the baby will come in May."

May. Bethany was sixteen. Life had a great way of making jokes. Mary Alice touched her own stomach, bile climbing her throat. She stood, wobbling on shaky legs toward the kitchen window, grabbing the counter for support.

2

"You're disgusted by me, aren't you Gram?"

Mary Alice whipped around. "Oh, no, no!" She grabbed Bethany's shoulders. She couldn't do much for her, but there was no way she was going to make her feel like that. "Sweetie, of course not. It's just a surprise. A bit of a shock. I could never be disgusted by you."

"That's why I told you first. Mom and Dad, on the other hand . . ."

"Your mom and dad love you. They'll be shocked, but they'll come around. Sometimes things happen." Her beloved husband, Charlie's words rang in her mind. *Life is messy.*

So, so very, unbelievably messy. More than she could tell her granddaughter right now. Or maybe ever. "What does . . . Trent, is that his name, say? Have you told him?"

Bethany wiped at her eyes and blew her nose on a crumpled tissue in her hand. She pulled away from Mary Alice's embrace and nodded. "I just came from his house. He's home from school this weekend. I told him we could make a little family. But . . . but . . . he was so *mean*, Gram. He wanted to know if I was sure the baby was his." Bethany's voice broke in ragged, staccato spurts.

What? How could he ever accuse Bethany of sleeping around? She was the most loyal, trusting child - yes, *child* - Mary Alice had ever known. How *dare* he?

"He thinks I should get . . ." Bethany's voice dropped to a whisper, "an abortion. I let him drive me there. . . to that place, the Planned Parenthood Clinic. He said he would pay. There were all these people out on the sidewalk holding signs that said 'Baby Killer' with pictures of tiny babies. I couldn't do it. I don't want to do it. I made him take me home. I can't have an abortion . . . It's wrong. . . but how . . . how can I . . . raise a baby?"

Mary Alice breathed a sigh of relief through her stiff lungs. Just saying the name of that place —thinking of Bethany near those signs sent a shiver down her back.

"Trent, how old is he again?" Mary Alice tried to remember the boy. She'd only met him once or twice.

"Eighteen. I know. He's too old for me. Mom already

told me that. But it's only two years. And we've been dating over a year since he was a senior in high school."

Oh goodness. Mary Alice could only imagine what would happen when Greg found out Trent was having sex with his sixteen-year-old daughter — that was considered statutory rape, even if she did consent.

Bethany's head bobbed. "He says a baby will ruin his whole career. He could lose his scholarship at Ohio State. Then he could never go pro. He says nobody can ever find out. His stupid football means more to him than me . . . or our baby." She drove her head into her hands.

She turned back to Bethany. "I know this is difficult. What do *you* want?"

"I don't know anymore. I didn't plan this — *any* of this. I thought I loved him, and he loved me too. I never would have done it with him if I didn't think so. He lied to me. He just wanted — you know — sex." A blush flushed her cheeks. "How could I have been so stupid?" Bethany twisted her napkin in spirals. "I hate him. How could he say such awful things to me?"

"It doesn't sound like Trent is ready to be a father." She looked away and closed her eyes, willing Trent to step up. Somehow, she doubted that. From what Bethany was saying, he didn't have that solidity of character, that dependability about him that Charlie had at his age. Charlie was a man, even at eighteen. Trent was a boy. Mary Alice exhaled. Men had it easy. They got to choose if they wanted to deal with the consequences of sex. But girls got the short end of the stick. Every. Single. Time.

"I'm only sixteen," said Bethany. "I had plans too. Maybe not like professional football. But I thought I'd go to college someday too." She dragged her fingers down her face, leaving red streaks where her cobalt blue nails pressed into her pale skin. "Maybe I should give the baby away. You know, for adoption."

Mary Alice's breath hitched. *No,no,no*, she wanted to scream. *You can't give your baby away. You will regret it your entire life*. But she didn't say it. Bethany had to make her own

4

decisions, not be pressured into a decision by anyone, grand-mothers included.

"You could raise him, or her, if that is what you want. I'm not saying it'll be easy, but your family would help." *Wouldn't they?* A longtime frustration started building inside her. Like an old friend, or enemy, she hadn't seen for a long time. "Sometimes people can be jerks. You're better off without them. But I can only imagine how much that must hurt. You don't deserve that."

Bethany looked up; her beautiful amber eyes rimmed in red.

Mary Alice took her hand. "You need to tell your mom and dad. This isn't something you can hide or avoid."

"Will you be there with me when I tell them?"

Mary Alice glanced at the box on the mantle that held Charlie's ashes. Some things, no matter how hard, had to be faced alone. This was one of them. "Ah, sweetie. I think this is something you need to do without me, but I promise I love you and will stick by you no matter what happens."

When Bethany left later that afternoon, the loneliness lingering in the house since Charlie died took on a whole new dimension. Restlessness had been building up in Mary Alice's chest since she'd heard Bethany utter the word 'pregnant.' She tried to put her mind to rest because Bethany's pregnancy didn't change anything for her. But her unsettled stomach disagreed.

She closed her eyes and Bethany's phantom wails, and her own, bounced through her memory. Mary Alice hadn't had anyone, not even Charlie until later. Bethany would have Ellie and Greg by her side, everything would work out fine. Bethany wasn't alone, and the mere thought of letting her believe so was almost too much.

Lying in bed, Mary Alice stared at the blank spi-ral-bound notebook she'd purchased two weeks before. Ever since Charlie died, she hadn't been able to get the what-ifs out of her head. What if she had been stronger? Used her voice. What if things had been different? She should write it down. And now . . . well, with Bethany, the memories kept crowding her skull, banging on the door of her mind's eye, screaming for her to look at them.

She didn't want to, and she did. It hurt to think about, but they were such precious memories. Life was short. Charlie's death had been testament to that. She should tell the family. Maybe let them read whatever she wrote. Even if no one knew until she was gone, someone should know the truth. But she'd made a promise to Charlie that she couldn't break. Mary Alice's fists twisted the blanket. She had stayed silent for almost sixty years, long enough for her to forget what the point was. Perhaps, now it was time.

"*Sweetheart, I know we agreed to never speak of it again. Please forgive me, but I need to put pen to paper.*"

Two

1963

My father dropped my ragged brown suitcase at my feet. His mammoth arms wrapped me in a quick hug, but his eyes never met mine. Last time he hugged me, I was seven and I broke my arm falling off my bike. I moved my arms to hug him back, or maybe to hold him in place, but he pulled away before I had a chance to try.

I brushed dust from my plaid, pleated skirt and raised my hand to wave, but Daddy's Chevy Impala was already peeling up gravel and dirt. By the time my arm was stretched high, he was gone.

He hadn't even waited to see if I got in all right. Daddy left me. He really left me. My heart pounded beneath my thin winter coat that didn't quite close in the middle anymore. I gulped back a sob and turned around to face the wrought-iron gate and a heavy iron plaque with chipped lettering.

The Florence Crittenton Home for Unwed Mothers, Established 1928

My knees gave way and I slid down onto my suitcase. How long would I be there? What had I done? I shivered. The chill came from inside.

I sat there until my hands and feet turned stiff and the tears froze on my face. I stuffed my hands in my coat pocket for my mittens. Nothing. I found the strength to stand and looked up the lonely street. No cars. Every home was tucked behind tall iron fences or stone walls. Not a person in sight.

I could just walk away. My belly felt light for a moment and then it sank again. I had no place to go. I turned back toward the gate.

My icy fingers trembled as I pressed the buzzer. I could do this. This was only temporary. Charlie would come for me.

A woman's scratchy voice crackled through the speaker below. "May I help you?"

I startled. "Um, yes Ma'am. I'm Mary Alice Cranston. My father called ahead."

"Mary Alice, yes. You're expected."

With a click, the gate swung inward to a long drive with brown grass wedged between uneven brick pavers. I picked up my worn suitcase and passed through. Behind me, the gate screeched and locked like a thunderclap. There was no turning back now.

I put one foot in front of the other and counted the steps in my mind: *fourteen, fifteen, sixteen . . . twenty-eight, twenty-nine.* I walked toward an enormous Victorian house with gargoyles standing vigilant at the foot of the steps and icicles hovering from bare trees like claws. Rows of green rhododendron tipped in ice framed clapboard rails across a long front porch. It might have been pretty once upon a time.

I plodded up the first stone step, my stomach somersaulting and my eyes cast down. Inching to the next step, I met a pair of black, laced-up shoes over heavy stockings like Gram used to wear. They peeked out from pleated folds of dark wool. My eyes moved upward and landed on a woman's face, surprisingly unwrinkled and smooth as Bavarian cream. A sleek cap of steely hair was pulled into a tight bun at the nape of her neck.

I extended a hand and a smile. I may have been in trouble, but I wouldn't forget my manners. "Hello, I'm Mary Alice Cranston."

The smile was not returned. A hand with long, thin fingers lacking any polish met mine. Her touch was warm and smooth, but firm and quick. "Our girls don't use last names here, for your own privacy, and your family's. I am Mrs.

8

Longsworth, the headmistress. Welcome to Crittenton. One of your roommates is here and we are expecting one other guest today. You will wait in the parlor until she arrives. No point in repeating myself thrice."

The headmistress turned and marched inside.

I picked up my bag and trailed behind. The house was drafty and I followed Mrs. Longsworth to a massive staircase with an exquisite banister. *Mahogany.* I appreciated beautiful woodwork. Charlie Goodson, the love of my life, was going to be a cabinet builder. He'd taught me all about different kinds of wood. I hoped our little surprise wouldn't curtail his plans.

"You may wait here." Mrs. Longsworth stood at the threshold of a little room and crossed her arms. Once I was inside, she turned on her heel and marched away.

I set my suitcase down by the arched doorway and ran my hand across a table next to a high back loveseat. *Maple.* Across the room, a tall armoire reached almost to the ceiling. *Walnut.* Charlie would be happy I could recognize the woods. When he came to take me home, I'd point them out to him.

I sat on a tufted horse-hair chair and ran my hands over ornate wooden arms. *Cherry.* I could almost hear my mother's words. 'Look, don't touch.' I pulled my hands into my lap and picked at my clear nail polish. Everything was pristine, salvaged from a more genteel time. It was like my grandparents' home. I'd only been there twice before they passed, but I remembered it vividly. It was vastly different from my home with an ultra-modern Scandinavian style.

A scent tickled my nose. Not dust, because not a speck was visible anywhere, but something . . . old. I stood and investigated the room. I pressed my nose against the leather-bound books in the armoire. Yes, the smell of old books, like Grandpapa's den.

Out the crisscrossed-leaded windows, the sun dipped behind a cloud, casting everything outside in an eerie, gothic glow. Snow would be nice. It would brighten things up.

An ancient grandfather clock, *oak*, chimed eleven times. My stomach rumbled. The atmosphere at home had erased my appetite and I hadn't eaten since dinner the night before. Mom hadn't stopped crying, wrapping me in hugs every time she got within arm's length.

"I don't know why you have to go away," my little brother Tommy said, which only sent Mom into another fit of tears. When he was old enough to understand, it would all be over.

My brother Paul pounded his fist into his palm. "I'm going to punch Charlie's lights out, nobody touches my little sister."

On the bright side, it was a relief to be away from it all.

I looked around. How long would it take to start missing them? They weren't perfect, but they were my family. They'd always been there, but now they were gone, and I had to be brave without them. It would only be for a little while. If only I could convince my pounding heart.

I peeled the polish from another nail.

A girl came in carrying a silver tray laden with short-bread cookies and a cup of tea. The freckles around her eyes were so dense it looked like she was wearing a mask. "Hi," she murmured. "Mrs. Longsworth told me to bring you this. She said you may have missed breakfast." She set the tray on the side table. *Maple.*

I smiled. Had Mrs. Longsworth read my mind and sent food? Maybe she was nicer than she first appeared. "Thank you, I'm Mary Alice. Do you live here too?"

The girl nodded. "At least for another three weeks. I'm Joanie." She patted her enormous belly. "It's not too bad here. You'll get used to it."

"Oh, I'm not staying. I'm getting married." I lifted a teacup and took a cookie with a smile.

The freckles above Joanie's eyes merged into one. "Don't count on it. We've all said that." She shook her head and muttered, "It would be nice if just once it was true."

Before I could respond, she smiled and left.

I frowned at the teacup. Charlie *was* coming. I was going to be Mrs. Charles Goodson. He wanted to marry me. He knew I was a good girl. If only we hadn't let things go so far, that one time. I wouldn't be here, and we'd be together. I nibbled on the

10

cookie and heard a pattering of wet snow against glass. I wandered to the window to watch it fall.

A police cruiser was idling in the drive right below my window. An officer held the back door open and a girl peered out. He reached toward her, but she jerked her arm away and climbed out by herself, lugging a dirty backpack. She stood there and looked around.

She was probably in her late teens, but maybe early twenties. She had blue-black hair. A tight mini-skirt barely covered her hips and emphasized her protruding belly. She wore a stained scoop-necked T-shirt and thigh-high stiletto boots. The top of her stockings had a tear disappearing into her boots, and red garters peeked from under her short skirt. No coat.

She flicked her hair over her shoulder and sauntered under the porch awning. The officer shook his head and followed her. Minutes later, clacking heels echoed in the foyer, punctuated by the clomp of Mrs. Longsworth's sensible shoes. I scrambled back to my seat and rearranged my skirt as if I'd been sitting there the whole time.

The headmistress entered, the girl dragging her feet behind her. "Mary Alice, this is Sophia."

She and I stared at one another. I suddenly felt younger than sixteen, a plain child next to this woman. Her black hair was long and glossy, her chest spilled out of her top; she had garters and stockings. I probably looked laughable to her with my mousey brown hair, flat chest hiding beneath a white Peter-Pan collared blouse, bobby socks and saddle shoes. Her miniskirt barely covered her privates while my skirt touched my knees. I felt ridiculous.

Without a word, Mrs. Longsworth left.

"Are you the other new *guest*?" Sophia scoffed.

I stood and extended a hand. It looked nondescript next to Sophia's red nails. "Yes, how do you do? I'm Mary Alice Cran . . . Mary Alice."

Sophia cackled. "Well, you can call me *gone*." She did not accept the extended hand.

I dropped my arm. "Oh, is your boyfriend coming for you too?"

She bellowed, spittle spraying across my face. "My *boy-friend*? Yeah. Sure." She stretched out *boyfriend*. "Classic. No, baby girl, I don't need no damn boyfriend to spring me. I'm outta here all by myself first chance I get." She plopped down on the loveseat and crisscrossed her legs.

I could feel heat rising to my cheeks and I tried not to stare. Hot pink lace flashed from underneath Sophia's skirt. My nail polish was gone, so I picked at my cuticles and grappled for something to say as I sat back down. Small talk was better than awkward silence, but what on earth did we have in common to talk about?

Sophia broke the uncomfortable quiet. "Damn, I sure could use a smoke." She chomped on her gum. "Got any on ya?"

My mouth dropped open and I shook my head. "Is that good for the baby?"

Sophia shrugged. "Why should I give a flying fuck? Giving the bastard away as soon as it pops — *if* it lives."

I choked at the F word. My parents would skin me alive if I ever said that word. And the way she said it; she couldn't *really* mean it; nobody was that heartless. "Oh, don't say that. You'll jinx him . . . or her."

Sophia's lips twitched and she opened her mouth to speak, but Mrs. Longsworth reappeared, her mouth as flat and apathetic as her voice.

"Follow me," she said, right before disappearing again.

Sophia rolled her eyes, popped her gum, then stomped out after her. I scurried to gather my suitcase and made it out in time to catch Mrs. Longsworth heading up the beautiful stair-case. It was too dim and too quiet for comfort in this house.

We followed behind like ducklings, our footsteps muf-fled by a threadbare carpet runner. I slid my hand over smooth, cool wood. *Mahogany*. We passed a few girls who nodded silently and slipped past us like ghosts.

We entered a small room on the second floor. A girl with warm terra-cotta skin was curled on the bed closest to us, and I gasped when I saw her. A wide, red scar ran from her ear to her jawline. Mini-craters, perfectly round and scabbed, dotted

12

across her cheeks and neck. Slapping my hand over my mouth, I muffled an apology. Sophia looked away.

Mrs. Longsworth glowered at me. "Well, now that we are all here, we shall begin." She gestured to the girl on the bed. "This is Gladys, she's been our guest for a few days now. Gladys, this is Mary Alice and Sophia."

I stood a little straighter and pulled my eyes away from her. Sophia cracked her gum and stared at Mrs. Longsworth with a defiant smirk. Gladys didn't budge.

Mrs. Longsworth cleared her throat. "The Florence Crittenton Home for Unwed Mothers has offered a haven for girls all over the United States since 1896. This establishment has been here since 1928. This is not a hotel. You are not here for a vacation."

No, this is where parents stashed their daughter when she disgraced them. When they no longer loved her. I bit my lip and tried not to think of Daddy's car peeling away from me like he couldn't leave fast enough.

"You will do your part around here. Everyone works, no exceptions. In return, you will have a safe place to live during the remainder of your condition, receive three balanced meals a day, and be transported to St. Elizabeth Hospital when the time comes. Girls are grouped by their due date, and the three of you will be sharing one room since you are all due in May. Normally, the house has twelve or fewer girls here at one time, but due to the rampant promiscuity these days."

My face burned and I tucked my ragged nails behind my back. Not me and Charlie. We were different. It was love and we were going to get married. I was a good girl, not a promiscuous one, and Mrs. Longsworth had no right to suggest otherwise. She didn't know me or Charlie. Instead of saying anything, I examined the ground. Consequences for speaking out were never worth it.

Mrs. Longsworth shook her head. "We are now up to nineteen girls, including the three of you. Breakfast is at seven, lunch at noon, and supper at six. If you miss mealtime, there will be no food until the next scheduled time. Lights are out at nine o'clock. Everyone is expected at Chapel on Sunday mornings at ten a.m. When you are not busy with your chores or in class, you are free to roam the grounds or visit with the other girls. Local calls are permitted on the house phone in the hall, but outgoing long-distance calls are forbidden. If you have long distance family, they may call you. No one leaves the premises without my authority." She crossed her arms across her bosom. "Any questions?"

The phone. I had to call Charlie right away. I raised my hand.

"This is not school, Mary Alice, no need to raise your hand outside of lesson time."

Sophia snorted.

I dropped my hand. "My boyfriend will be coming for me. Can I use the phone to call him now?"

Mrs. Longsworth's eyes narrowed. "You are a minor. Unless your parents give direct instructions to release you to someone else, you will be with us until you deliver."

My heart dropped. How could the father of my baby not have a right to get me? I'd have to persuade my mother to agree because Daddy hadn't looked at me since I'd confessed I was in trouble two weeks earlier. If only I'd had enough courage to stand up to them then, I would be with Charlie now. Then again, I would probably get the belt before either of them so much as acknowledged my presence.

No one else had any comments or questions.

I scanned the room. It was barely large enough for the three twin beds and three small chests of drawers squeezed inside. One bed had been angled to fit sideways. Each bed had identical cream-colored chenille bedspreads with flat pillows tucked neatly beneath them. Each dresser top held a King James Bible, an alarm clock, and a small lamp. The hardwood floors were bare except for a little braided rug. The walls were bare. One small window with a roll-up blind faced a wide expanse of tall oaks feathered in snowflakes.

I looked around and considered which bed to set my suitcase on, or if it even mattered. Everything looked so similar in this bland, gray room.

Mrs. Longsworth took a step forward and her shadow

crawled up the wall. I looked at the Bible, something comforting and familiar, but then I noticed deep gouges in the wood, *pine*, as if nails had clawed into the grain. My heart began to pound.

I couldn't do this. I didn't belong there. I needed to be home, in my cheery lilac room. I needed Elvis Presley and Bobby Vinton smiling down at me from posters taped above my bed. I needed Paul Anka crooning, *'and they called it puppy love.'* I needed my mementos tacked around my mirror; the wilting wrist corsage Charlie gave me for the Sweetheart Ball, a ticket stub from the elegant State Theater where we saw Music Man, the pencil sketch Charlie did of the house he'd build for us some day. I needed Charlie. Mom. Dad. Tommy. Paul. I chewed on another nail.

"The bathroom is down the hall," Mrs. Longsworth said. "You will share it with six other girls, so learn to take care of your personal business in an efficient and courteous manner."

Mrs. Longsworth leaned over Gladys, whispered something in her ear, patted her head, and glanced at her watch. "It's lunch time. I suggest you go down before it's all gone. Tomorrow I'll have your duty assignments ready." And she was gone.

Sophia tossed her backpack on the farthest bed and poked Gladys with a red-tipped finger. "Hey girl, wanna eat? You heard the old broad. Miss the chow line and you're out of luck."

"I think we should leave her alone. She'll eat when she's hungry enough," I said. I pressed a hand to my mouth, not quite believing what came out of it. Must have been my nerves.

"I mean . . ." I cleared my throat. "I'm starving. Shall we find where the food is?"

"Let's get one thing straight," Sophia crossed her arms. "I'm not your little girlfriend and I'm not going to hold your hand and skip down to lunch with you. Stay out of my way." She jerked her thumb at Gladys. "As for her, I don't give a shit what she does. Eat, don't eat. Live, die, I could care less."

She stared at me with hard eyes, and I didn't dare open my mouth to respond. I didn't move until Sophia pivoted and

15

stomped out.

I took a deep breath. *It's going to be fine. No one is going to hurt you. Just be nice and stay out of the way.* My stomach growled. I had to get to that phone and call Charlie. My parents had rushed me away before I'd even had a chance to talk to him. I needed to give him this address.

I laid my suitcase on the middle bed. There was an iron taste in my mouth. I wiped my lips with my hand. Blood. Everything was so foreign here. I focused on my suitcase latches instead of my jittering stomach. I kept unlocking them then locking them back.

Maybe Charlie would come for me right away. Tonight, even. Maybe tomorrow at the latest. Charlie would never leave me here. He'd have to borrow his father's car to come and get me. What if my parents had spoken to his and they were also trying to keep us apart? Where would we go when he came? We couldn't go back to my house. It was doubtful his parents would be very supportive either.

I flipped the latches again and sighed, leaning away from my suitcase. It didn't matter. We'd figure something out. We could move away, go to another town. Maybe Maryland. I'd heard you could get married there at sixteen without your parents' consent. Charlie could get a job as a carpenter. I could get a job at a restaurant. I didn't mind washing dishes. We'd make it work, as long as we were together. We *had* to make it work.

I sucked in a deep breath. It would all be fine as soon as we were together. He'd come for me. No question. My heartbeat returned to normal. Meanwhile, I had to take care of myself and our baby. My stomach rumbled again.

I tapped a finger against my suitcase. There was no reason to unpack. Maybe I could get Gladys to sit up and acknowledge me. I'd feel better if I had a friend, and it sure didn't appear to be Sophia.

I caressed my belly. *It's okay, baby. Everything will be fine.* Thank God I had Charlie. I'd never be able to get through this without him. Maybe that was Sophia's problem. She didn't have anyone to love her.

I pulled my purse from the suitcase and grabbed a snap-shot with scalloped edges, running my fingers over it. Even though it was black and white, I could picture Charlie's amber eyes, his curly chestnut hair, a farmer's tan on his strong arms. I glanced at Gladys and tucked the picture against my chest. If I showed it to her, it might make her feel worse than she already did. It didn't look like she had anyone to love her either. I didn't want to sound braggy.

I set the photograph against the lamp. I wanted, no, *needed*, to talk about him, but maybe it was best to wait. Gladys hadn't moved at all. Her open eyes looked far away, the scars on her face so ugly. She looked dead.

I looked at the clock. 12:25. I should leave, but it felt rude to leave Gladys alone. My mother would not approve of either leaving Gladys alone or being late for meals. She would say it was very un-Christian of me. But then, Mother wasn't here. She had abandoned me when I needed her most and hadn't said a word when Daddy took me away. I bit down on my lower lip and it bled again.

Of course, nobody ever stood up to Daddy. He was the boss. I should be grateful he didn't tan my hide when he found out. That had only happened once. I'd been ten years old and had climbed out my bedroom window to stay overnight at a friends after he'd vetoed it. There I was, hanging half inside and half out of my window when he caught me. When I'd climbed back in, he'd already whipped that belt from his waist. Five hard slaps across my backside. It hurt like crazy. He made me write the 5th commandment 100 times. *Honor your mother and father, that your days may be long in the land that the Lord your God is giving you.*

I did honor my parents, but I wasn't a child anymore. I had feelings and opinions. I had a right to be heard – to make decisions about my own body– my own *baby*. He had no right to deny me. If only he had heard what I screamed in my head, *please no, don't take my baby from me. I love him. I want my baby.* It wouldn't have changed anything, but at least he would have known what I felt. Conversations about my 'condition' were always between my parents, even with me in the room. No one

17

asked me what I wanted or even acknowledged my presence. I would never treat my children like that. No matter what they did, I'd support them.

Now, away from my father's thumb and my mother's submissive silence, I could both give and get some compassion. Starting with this poor girl, who looked like she was even more miserable than me. Up until this point I hadn't even thought it was possible. I wasn't the first girl to get pregnant out of wedlock, but I hadn't thought about how someone else might have it even worse.

"I'd like to stay here with you," I said as gently as I could to Gladys, "but I need to make a phone call and I'm hungry. I'll bring something back for you, okay?"

No answer.

I felt like curling into a ball too. But that wouldn't solve anything. I waited to see if she would answer, but she didn't, so I rushed downstairs, ignoring my growling stomach. I had to get to that phone.

Three

2017

Nobody would understand Mary Alice's predicament — *Bethany's* predicament — better than her two best friends. Mary Alice had been reluctant to call them so soon after they'd pieced her back together after Charlie died, but who could she call other than them?

Gladys put a kettle on and Sophia set three mugs on the table. Mary Alice observed them busying themselves around her kitchen, taking care of things — of her —and something in her unwound. Sophia reached for the infamous cookie tin, the one that was never empty, the one that shows up at every event, big or small. It was Mary Alice's mother's before her, and her grandmother's before that. Would it go to Ellie, then Bethany someday? Would it go to Bethany's baby? Would Bethany keep her baby? Surely Ellie and Greg would give her a choice, wouldn't they?

"So, what's going on?" Sophia handed Mary Alice a floral cloth napkin from the holder.

Mary Alice ran a hand through her hair and rubbed at her temples. "Bethy . . . Bethany is pregnant." There, she'd said it.

"Oh, Mary Alice, really?"

"Yes. I'm sure everything will be fine. Things are so different today from when it happened to us. Ellie and Greg won't abandon her." She hoped.

19

Gladys cocked her head to one side. "Of course, they won't. They're nothing like your parents."

Mary Alice nodded.

"Is she alright?" Sophia asked.

"She's stressed, rightly so, but I think physically she is fine. The boy is a piece of work. But she'll get through it."

Gladys reached out to squeeze her hand. "How did you find out?"

Sophia pulled off the cookie tin lid. "Yum, chocolate-chip."

Mary Alice snorted a laugh. "Go ahead, fresh yesterday."

Sophia pulled a few cookies out, placed two on a napkin, and took a big bite into a third. "Did Ellie tell you? I bet they're freaking out."

Mary Alice shook her head. "Bethany told me this morning. She was crying so hard I thought somebody died. She hadn't told Ellie and Greg yet."

"Uh oh, she came to you even before her mother? How is Ellie going to feel about that?" Gladys took a cookie off Sophia's napkin. "I'd hate to see Bethany go through what we did. She's a sweet kid."

Sophia playfully slapped Gladys' hand away from her cookies.

"I know. Bethany wanted me to go with her to tell her folks. I said no. I hope I did the right thing. She, Ellie, and Greg deserve a little privacy on this one. I simply need to be here for her."

"It's all you can do," Sophia said, "unless you want to slash the guy's tires too."

Gladys's blew on her tea and stared at Sophia through the steam with a raised eyebrow.

"*What*?" Sophia crossed her arms, "Some people deserve it."

Mary Alice stared into her mug and their banter faded into a quiet buzz. Ellie and Greg weren't like her parents, even Gladys said so. But what if they were? Mary Alice didn't know if she'd be able to take it. "There is something else I'm thinking about," her eyes darted between Gladys and Sophia.

"What?" Gladys asked.

20

Mary Alice ran her finger along her cup. "I'm writing a memoir. I'm going to tell all of it."

"Am I in it?" Sophia said through a full mouth.

Mary Alice's lips turned up. "You are, but I can change your names if you prefer."

"It's okay, I don't mind. But. . ." Sophia glanced at Gladys, then back at Mary Alice, "you and Charlie promised never to speak of it again, right?"

"Yes, but I feel like time is slipping away so fast. It feels wrong now. I'm not saying I need to tell them right now, but they can read it . . . later."

"You mean after you're dead. That's the chicken way out." Gladys said.

Who was she to talk? She didn't have any family to worry about. Maybe she was the one who took the chicken way out by keeping everyone at such a distance. Traveling around the world on her missions might look brave, but Gladys was running from any intimacy whatsoever.

Sophia on the other hand . . . she called it like it was. Mary Alice wished she could be like that, but there was too much at stake. If her kids hated her for keeping this secret for all these years, she wouldn't survive it.

"I don't know. Maybe. What do you think?"

"Where is all this memoir stuff coming from?" Sophia asked.

"I've been thinking about it ever since Charlie died. I bought a notebook to start writing in. But I hadn't done anything with it because of Charlie's promise. But now, with Bethany, it feels important. And it feels disloyal to my kids to take it to the grave. So . . . I started it."

Gladys laughed. "You are handwriting an entire memoir? Why aren't you using a computer?"

"You know I'm not good with that thing. Besides, words come easier with a pen and paper. I don't have to hunt for every letter."

Gladys and Sophia looked pointedly at her.

"I'm struggling whether I should tell Bethany," Mary Alice said. "Would it help her feel less alone? She'd know these things can happen to anyone, even her Grandma. When I . . . *we* . . . were her age, I felt completely alone, until I met you two. I have no idea how I would have coped without you."

Mary Alice stared into nothingness, caught in a memory. She looked at Sophia and Gladys and by their distant expressions, they were somewhere else too, maybe back at the home.

Gladys broke the silence. "Mary Alice. That was half a century ago."

Sophia shook her head. "Girl, I'm not sure it's a good idea. What would you accomplish by telling Bethany? You'll be opening a big can of whoop-ass. Maybe stick to the memoir."

"Language." Mary Alice glared at her, "and what do you mean? If it helps Bethany . . ."

"It *might* help Bethany," Sophia said, "but maybe not the rest of your family. What if she tells them before you finish your book?"

Sophia gave Gladys a slow grin, "What if she doesn't and Mary Alice makes it big time? Maybe a movie deal. Get some foxy broads to play us."

When Gladys and Sophia started laughing, Mary Alice couldn't help but laugh with them. Leave it to good friends to ease the tension. Charlie was the only other person who could ever do that.

Their laughter died down and silence took over again.

"Don't tell Bethany." Gladys said, breaking the bloated quiet.

"Well, besides telling her and writing, it's the only thing I know to do."

"That's not true and you know it. Be there for her, support her, that's all she needs. Think about the consequences, Mary Alice. Is it really worth it?"

Mary Alice looked down. Shame. Exactly what she had felt back then, and even now when the world wasn't as cruel, she still felt that way. She bit her lip to keep it from quivering.

There was truth in Gladys' words. Telling Bethany wouldn't change anything. Mary Alice was a coward on all counts. She let her family down by keeping her pregnancy a secret to begin with. She wanted to tell them, Bethany most of all, but what might come afterward wasn't worth the guilt she might shed.

An all too familiar emptiness filled her lungs, almost cutting off her breath as teardrops formed perfect little circles on the tablecloth. She wished, more than anything, she could go back to that time. She would have done things differently, then this wouldn't be a problem. She'd have four children instead of three and Bethany would know she wasn't alone.

"I could have, *should* have, fought harder. I didn't speak up for my baby, or for myself." Mary Alice pressed her palms into her eyes and took a deep breath. It was easier not to think about it when Charlie was around, when the past wasn't staring her in the face.

"It wasn't your fault, dear. Times were different. You didn't have a say. None of us did. But what's done is done, and your family shouldn't suffer for it now." Gladys smiled, watery and weak, wrinkles forming around the scars below her eyes. "So, write your book and let Ellie and Greg handle Bethany. You said it yourself. They aren't like your parents. They'll do fine by her. Some secrets are best left buried."

Mary Alice stretched across her king-sized bed and ran her hand over Charlie's cool, empty pillow. "Darling, I know what we promised. To never talk about it again. But I have to at least write it down, even if I never mention it to a soul. Please forgive me."

Mar, Charlie's voice filled her mind. *We agreed. I don't want you to get hurt. You'll be shaking up that Coke can, Mar. It might explode. Ready for that?*

"*I think I'm telling you I'm doing this, writing this memoir, not asking your permission. But I would like your blessing.*"

She wrapped the comforter tighter around herself. She missed him, the warmth of his arms around her, the way he made her laugh. They said he suffered no pain, but how could they know? What did a massive stroke *actually* feel like?

"*Well, Charlie?*"

Nothing.

"*Now you decide to be silent? You disapprove?*" The only

sound was her own ragged breath and the tick-tock of the old cuckoo-clock, *maple*, in the hall. Charlie had given her that clock on their 51st wedding anniversary last June. He'd only been gone a month. Everything still reminded her of him: the empty spot beside the bed where he left his dirty socks, the toothpaste cap neatly screwed on instead of left off, his sawdust-covered boots, now clean and put away in the closet. Everything was too neat.

She rolled over to his side of the bed and wrapped her arms around his pillow. Even though she'd washed the sheets, she hadn't washed his pillowcase, still hoping for a whiff of his scent. It was almost gone.

"Charlie," she whispered. "What am I supposed to do without you?" The lawn needed mowing. The bills had stacked up in his study. She'd never written a check her entire life. Why had she been so content to let him handle everything? She was practically paralyzed. She had to learn to take care of these things, and soon. And now this.

She flopped onto her back with the pillow still encased in her arms, watching the lights from passing cars slide across the dark wall.

"Oh Charlie, poor Bethy. I can never let her go through what we did. I can't let her be railroaded into a decision like we were, afraid to even have her own say in her life, or her baby's. If sharing what happened to me makes her feel less alone, less ashamed; if it gives her the strength to stand up for herself, I should do it, right?"

A calmness wrapped around her.

Mar, just take care of Bethany. It is all that is expected of you. Make sure she knows she is loved, no matter what. Ellie and Greg will do right by her.

Mary Alice wanted to be comforted, but she wasn't. *Will they?*

She picked up her notebook and tapped her pen against her chin.

Four

1963

Prior to the Home, I had high hopes for the future of our new family. I knew my parents would be upset, but it was what it was, and I thought they liked Charlie enough to give us their blessing. A small part of me doubted it. Very small, but still there. As I sat on my bed, my heart pounding so hard I wondered if I was going to have a heart attack. Keeping it a secret was impossible. I waited until Daddy was engrossed in the Ed Sullivan's Show on late-night TV. The sound of the water running in the bathroom had stopped and Mother's bedroom door opened then closed. Watching the numbers flip down as they rotated on the clock beside my bed, I waited fifteen minutes before I conjured up enough bravery to tap on her door.

"Mom? Are you sleeping?" I opened her door. I saw her reach for the light.

"Don't," I said.

"Mary Alice? What's the matter dear?" She sat up in bed.

I sat beside her on the edge of the mattress, my hands clasped together to keep them from shaking. "I . . ." The words wouldn't come out. "Um, you know how much I love Charlie, don't you?"

"Of course, dear. Has something happened between you two? Did he break up with you?"

"No, no, nothing like that. It's . . .it's . . . we want to get married." The last words tumbled from my mouth fast.

25

I heard more than I saw her shake her head. "You're children. If you are still together when you are grown, we'd be happy to see you married. Charlie's a nice boy. But don't you think you should get through high school first?"

I pressed my hands tighter together until my nails dug into my palms. The pain was somehow comforting. "We can't wait . . . I'm going to have a baby."

The silence cut the room like a knife. If she was breathing, I couldn't hear it.

"Mom? Say something."

Finally, she said, "I see."

The two feet between us felt cavernous. If only she would wrap her arms around me, tell me everything would be okay. But we just sat there in the dark, in the silence.

The TV turned off in the living room. Mother fidgeted with the blankets on her lap. "Okay then, your father and I will figure this out. You go back to bed now."

I was being dismissed, but since I didn't want to face Daddy anyhow, I quickly retreated to my room.

I climbed in my bed and pulled the covers up to my neck. My hands reached under my nightgown and I caressed the slight mound I thought I felt. My baby. I was having a baby. It didn't feel real until I'd spoken it out loud.

Murmurs echoed through the wall between my parent's room and mine. A loud thud made me jump as something hit the wall. Then a door slammed. A creak of the garage door opening and a car peeling out the drive.

Then silence. Only more silence.

Five

2017

Ellie's smiling face appeared on Mary Alice's calling ID. A smile she was most likely not wearing today. A knot twisted in Mary Alice's gut. She was pleased Bethany felt close enough to confide in her, but if she were in Ellie's shoes, it would hurt. A mother expects a daughter to come to her first with big stuff, but Bethany went to her grandmother. Mary Alice swallowed thickly. Ellie had bigger things to worry about, and so did Mary Alice. "Hi, Sweetheart."

"She said she told you already."

Mary Alice gulped. "I'm sorry. She should have come to you first."

"No, it's fine," Ellie said. But it sounded like it was anything but fine. Not a good start.

"Are you okay, sweetheart?"

"Ah Mom, I don't know," Ellie groaned. "How could this happen? I'm so disappointed. She had so much going for her."

Words too familiar, words told to her. A chill prickled at the base of Mary Alice's neck and traveled down her spine. "She still does, Elinor. Pregnancy doesn't have to alter all her plans, just side-step them a little."

Ellie's voice rose an octave. "How can you say that? Everything is different. Her life is ruined."

Mary Alice clenched her jaw. Her own mother had

uttered those exact same words to her fifty-four years ago. Untrue words. Her life was not ruined. She'd had a good life. Even if it was wrought with guilt. A guilt she wouldn't have had if her parents hadn't straightened everything out for her. "Now listen here, you must never let Bethany hear you say things like that. She needs your support, not your judgment."

"I know Mom, but it's so overwhelming. I thought things would be different for her. I gave up everything to have her . . . and not that I'd change it for a second, but I wanted . . . more for Bethany. I was much older than her and I thought I had my life all worked out but having a baby changed everything. At her age? She has no idea."

Mary Alice shook her head, even though Ellie couldn't see her through the phone. It was true. Ellie had an upward mobile position in a small law firm. She could have made partner if she hadn't dropped it all to get pregnant. Neither pregnancy nor life as a stay-at-home mom was an easy one for her. "Has Bethy told you what she wants to do?"

"Not really. It was all pretty emotional. I can't say we ever asked."

And therein lies the problem. Nobody asked the one person who should have a voice. "You've always been pragmatic, Ellie. Unlike your pie-in-the-sky brother and doomsday sister, you are the one who can handle this. God only gives you what you can handle. You and Greg can do this." She hoped it came across with more confidence than she felt.

"Greg," Ellie moaned. "He's beside himself. She's his baby girl. You know how he is with her. I'm afraid of what he's going to do to Trent."

"What do you mean, do to him? You think he'd hurt him?" It would only make things worse. She'd seen glimpses of his temper, although he usually held it in check around her.

"I don't know. He's losing it. He stormed out of here last night after Bethany talked to us. I haven't seen him since and he's not answering his cell."

"Oh no. That can't be good." *Like my father.*

"Bethany texted Trent in case Greg showed up there, but so far, it appears not. He probably got drunk and is sleep-

28

ing it off somewhere. Truthfully, I'm glad he's not here. I have enough on my plate trying to calm Bethany down. I don't need someone else to take care of."

"How is Bethany? She told both of you together?"

"Yes. She's barely short of hysterical. She feels ashamed and betrayed by Trent. I tried to be positive, but I'm afraid I didn't handle it as well as I should have either. I said some things I shouldn't have. It was such a shock. Of all the news she could hand me, this would have been last on my list. I know other teenage girls are having sex these days, but I guess I was one of those naive mothers who thought 'not my daughter'."

Mary Alice opened her mouth to speak but nothing came out. What could she say? Teens and sex were hardly anything new. When Ellie got her first steady boyfriend, Mary Alice hadn't thought about whether or not Ellie was the type, she knew she didn't want her daughter to go through the same thing she did, no matter how improbable, so she got her on birth control. Maybe she should have talked to Ellie about getting Bethany on it before, but what was done was done. They were here now and all they could do was look to the future. "At least you didn't run out on her. And you've got some time to figure this out. I'm sure you'll do the right thing."

Ellie's voice caught, coming out in small sound bites. "And . . . what . . . is the right thing, Mom? . . . I can't . . . even think straight."

Neither could Mary Alice. Things looked so different from this side, her mother's, Ellie's. Her stomach twisted like she was going to be sick. "Well, the first thing you need to do is to make sure she understands you love her. She was sure you would hate her. Which can't be farther from the truth." Mary Alice could hear soft weeping sounds from Ellie's end. "Honey?"

"Yes, but Mom — "

"I know this is hard. But you'll get through it. It's not a death sentence."

"Are you sure? It feels like it."

"Of course not. It will all work out fine." She hoped she was right.

"You seem awfully calm about this. Do you have some insight into this kind of stuff?"

Mary Alice's heart stopped. "Nope, but I know you. Teenagers have been getting pregnant since the stone age and you're not alone in your feelings. You're a great Mom. You'll figure it out."

Ellie gave a small chuckle. "I guess I needed to hear that. When did you get so smart? What would we all do without you?"

"Your father was the smart one, not me."

"Why do you do that? You never give yourself enough credit. You show your strength in a quieter way. Being different from Dad didn't make you wrong and him right."

Was that true? Did she have a quiet strength? It didn't feel that way, especially without Charlie. But this wasn't about Mary Alice; this was about Bethany. "Are you going to tell Evan and Charlene? You can hardly keep it a secret."

"Yes, of course. But we need to work this out between the three of us first. We need some sort of plan. Greg's got to come home so we can talk this out. When he stormed out, all conversation stopped. This is a nightmare I can't wake up from."

Had her own mother felt that same pain? Maybe she had struggled over what to do. Then again, maybe her father had decided everything and disregarded her mother's thoughts. Mary Alice pressed a palm to her forehead, trying to remember her mother's face. It was so long ago, images and memories blurred, making what was real and what was imagined hard to separate. It didn't matter now. Her mother was dead, but Bethany wasn't.

"Well, when you do, we can call a family meeting," said Mary Alice.

"A family meeting? We haven't had one of those since . . ." *since Charlie's stroke.* "Do we need to make it official? I was thinking more like phone calls."

"Bethany's going to need the whole family's support, and the sooner the better. Say the word and I'll make brunch. Unless you really don't want your siblings to know yet."

"Well, we can't hide it for long. Might as well get it out

30

in the open. I'll let you know."

You could try to hide it like my parents did. "I'll wait for your call. Ellie, you've got this."

Mary Alice pulled a fresh tray of snickerdoodles from the oven when the phone rang. Dropping the potholder on the counter, she scanned the caller ID. The Struthers Police Department. *What the heck?*

"Hello?"

"Mrs. Goodson?"

"Yes?" Mary Alice's heart began to pound. She mentally did a headcount. Where was everyone? Ellie should be at home with Bethany. Evan was on tour with the symphony. Charlene would be teaching at Ohio State. Something bad must have happened to one of them. Police did not call to chit-chat.

"We are putting a call through to you. Hold please." The voice disappeared. Mary Alice waited, holding her breath until her chest felt like it was going to explode and she was forced to exhale.

"Mary Alice?"

The deep voice was familiar, and she was momentarily stunned. "Greg?"

"Yeah. Um . . . I'm sorry to call you, but I can't face Ellie right now."

"Greg, what are you doing at the police station? Were you in an accident? Are you hurt?" She heard a deep sigh through the line and the background noises of phones and muffled voices.

"No, I'm not hurt. I'm sorry to have to call you."

And?

"I've been arrested. I need someone to make my bail. I was hoping—"

"Arrested, whatever for?"

"Assault." Greg's voice dropped almost to a whisper. Mary Alice pressed the phone tighter against her ear to hear over the other noise.

"I went to have a few drinks. To cool off. I . . . I only wanted to talk to him. Talk some sense into him, but then he said Bethy wasn't going to ruin his life."

"Ah, Trent."

"Uh, huh. I saw red. Next thing I knew he was on the ground, and someone was pulling me off him, his face a bloody mess. I guess I did a number on him."

"Oh boy. Is he pressing charges?"

"Probably. I don't know. For now, I need to get out of here. My hearing isn't for two weeks. If I can make bail . . ."

"Okay," Mary Alice hesitated. "How much? Don't you think you should call your wife?"

"I can't ask her. I only need ten percent of my bail if I do an appearance bond, which I can do because I'm a first-time offender and not a flight risk. I've never done anything like this before."

Mary Alice had never even met anyone who had been arrested. This was like learning to speak a new language on demand. *Bail, bond, flight-risk, offender.* "Do you need an attorney?"

"Probably. I didn't have one for the bond hearing this morning. I'm so sorry to have to ask you this. I didn't know who else to call . . . besides Ellie, who I can't face right now."

"How much, Greg?"

"Bail was set at $75,000, so ten percent is $7,500. I'll pay it back; I swear I will."

He sounded so pathetic. It's not like she didn't like Greg. He was nice enough, although he did have a short fuse. But he'd never laid a hand on Ellie or Bethany, so she minded her own business. Perhaps she had thought Ellie could have done better than an auto mechanic, but she never expected this. Who was she to judge? Charlie had been a carpenter. But, she had expected Ellie to find someone at law school, someone more on her intellectual level. Mary Alice looked at the clock. After five. The bank would be closed. She remembered Charlie said she could only get two hundred at a time from the ATM. Where would she get $7,500 at this time of night?

"Greg, I'm not sure I can help you right now. I don't have that kind of money on hand and the banks are closed. What do you want me to do?"

"Oh," Greg said, clearly disappointed.

"Times up." A voice sounded on the line.

"Wait, wait you —," Greg said.

"I'll help you Greg, but it won't be until tomorrow. And I can't keep this from Ellie."

Six

2017

Before Mary Alice drew money from the joint checking account, she had to talk to Ellie. If Greg didn't have the nerve to talk to her, then she would have to do it. True to her word, she was not keeping this from her daughter. She pulled on her lined trench coat and hooked her handbag over her arm. It was getting late, and Ellie had to be getting worried about Greg by now. She couldn't let Ellie go a second night without knowing where her husband was.

As she pulled into traffic, she was mindful she had her lights on, seatbelt fastened, and was paying attention. It had been ages since she'd driven a car. Charlie had been the primary driver and for the past month, one of the kids always seemed to be hovering, making sure she was everywhere she needed to be. As she settled into the routine, it was like riding a bike. Not that she thought it was a true reference. She hadn't been on a bicycle in thirty years, at least. But the independence felt good. *I can do this.* She smiled as she pictured a little blue engine climbing a hill on the cover of a picture book. *I think I can. I think I can.* The children had loved that book, especially Evan. Hopefully, she could read it to Bethany's baby, to her first great grandbaby.

Before Mary Alice knew it, she was pulling into Ellie's driveway. She hadn't even remembered the drive. Was that good or bad?

She rapped lightly on the front door and tried the knob. It was unlocked, so she let herself in. "Ellie, are you here? It's Mom."

Ellie came from the laundry room, her arms full of fresh linens. "Mom, what are you doing here?" She looked out the window at the dark sky. "Did you drive here? By yourself?"

"Of course, I drove here. I am not an invalid, you know. I can take care of myself." Boy, that felt good. She dropped her handbag on the kitchen counter and slipped out of her coat.

"O. . . kay," Ellie said, dropping her bundle on the counter. "Is everything alright?"

"I'm fine," Mary Alice said. "But I needed to tell you something and thought it should be in person." She was grateful Ellie and Greg had bought a home a few blocks away.

Ellie slipped onto a high bar stool. "You're scaring me, Mom. Do I need Greg here? He hasn't come home yet . . . or called me." She brushed a dark lock away from her face. Her clothes were wrinkled. She had a big stain, perhaps coffee, across her chest. Old, smudged, mascara lines still streaked her face. This was not the immaculate daughter Mary Alice was used to seeing.

"That's why I'm here. Greg called me."

Ellie's mouth dropped open. "You. Why would he call you? I don't understand."

Mary Alice slipped onto a stool beside her daughter and took her smooth hand into her wrinkled, age-spotted one. "Greg called me from jail. He was arrested after fighting with Trent. Something about a bond. He'll be back home soon, but I thought you should know."

"Oh my God." Ellie's worried face turned to anger. "Of all the asinine things to do. And then to call you instead of me. I'm so sorry Mom. He shouldn't have involved you. How much money does he need?"

"Seventy-five hundred. But he said he'll pay me back."

Ellie's face dropped. "We don't have $7,500 cash. And our credit cards are pretty maxed out. Maybe if I take a little from one and a little from another . . ."

"No," Mary Alice placed a hand over Ellie's. "I'll do it. I

told him I'd bring him the money tomorrow. I'll get it out of the bank in the morning and take it straight down there. He didn't want me to tell you, but I was not going to keep this from you and I told him so. A marriage can't have secrets like this. And you'll need to stick together right now for Bethy's sake."

Ellie pulled her hand away and dropped her head into her hands. "Bethany. I wonder if Trent told her." She rose wearily from the stool and dragged her feet across the floor to the bottom of the stairs. "Bethany?" She called up the stairs. "Gram's here. Can you come down a minute?"

They waited, but no sounds came from upstairs.

"Maybe she's already in bed?"

Bethany appeared at the top of the steps. She was holding her phone in her hands, a look of shock on her face. She knew.

"Mom," Bethany said, not even acknowledging her grandmother. She held up her phone. "Trent texted me. He said Dad beat him up. He's in the hospital." Each sentence came out a little louder and a little higher. "Is this for real?"

Bethany trudged down the stairs and Ellie wrapped an arm around her before leading her to the sofa in the living room. Mary Alice followed and perched on the arm of a chair.

"Yes," Ellie said. "Gram came to tell us. Your dad has been arrested for assaulting Trent."

Bethany looked up at her grandmother as if she just realized she was there. Her head spun back to look at her mother, her mouth dropped open in a perfect O. "What? Arrested?" Without warning, she burst into tears. "It's all my fault. I'm having a baby and Dad is in jail and Trent is in the hospital. I'm sorry. I'm sorry. Mom, make it all go away." She looked up at Ellie as if she could somehow miraculously fix all this.

"No, sweetie," Mary Alice said. "This is not your fault. Your dad shouldn't have gone after Trent. And his arrest and Trent's injury is not your doing. Did he say if he was hurt badly?" *Please let it be nothing more than a black eye.*

Bethany stared at the screenshot of his face on her phone. "Cut on his forehead and eyebrow, black eye, two teeth knocked out. He says he's going to sue."

Mary Alice bristled. Trent deserved to be punched out, even if it was a stupid thing for Greg to do, but the last thing they needed was a lawsuit. "Let's not get ahead of ourselves. I'll bring your dad home tomorrow and we'll call Mr. Johnson, the attorney who did Papa's will. We'll get this all straightened out. Right now, we need to stay calm and take care of you and your baby."

The next day, Mary Alice's heels clicked on the black and white marble floor of the bank lobby. Around her, people were dressed in jeans, or worse, sweatpants. Did no one dress up to go to town anymore? Only the tellers were dressed in business attire.

"Good morning. May I help you?" A young girl with shiny black hair falling to her waist greeted her from behind the high counter. A silver name tag pinned to her sapphire blue sweater identified her as 'Jasmine.'

"Yes, thank you. I need to make a cash withdrawal."

"My pleasure. Will you be writing a check, or can I help you with a withdrawal slip?"

Oh, dear. Mary Alice had not remembered to bring the checkbook from Charlie's desk. "A withdrawal slip is fine, please."

Jasmine smiled, showing a silver line of metal across her teeth. "Will you be withdrawing from your checking or savings? Do you have your account number?"

"Um . . . I'm sorry. I forgot to bring it with me. Can you look it up for me? Goodson, Charles and Mary Alice Goodson."

Jasmine nodded and her fingers flew over the keys in front of her. "Yes, I have your accounts right here. I know your husband. I haven't seen Mr. Goodson in a few weeks. How is he?"

Mary Alice's heart dropped in her chest. "He . . . he passed away four weeks ago," she said, barely above a whisper.

Jasmine's smile vanished, and her fingers paused in mid-air. "Oh, I am so sorry. Please accept my condolences. He was such a nice man." She pulled her eyes away from Mary Alice and concentrated on the monitor. "Let me fill out this withdrawal slip for you. Did you say checking or savings?"

"Um . . . checking."

"Okay. Amount?" Jasmine picked up a pen to write in the amount.

"$7,500," said Mary Alice.

Jasmine frowned at her monitor. "I'm sorry. Mrs. Goodson. Your checking account does not have the funds for that withdrawal." She slid a piece of paper with the balance toward Mary Alice. "Shall we try your savings? Also, it's a large sum. Would you prefer a cashier's check?"

Mary Alice looked at the little white piece of paper. $836.15. That was all? Where was all their money? Charlie must have kept it all in the savings account. She breathed a little easier. Of course, he did. That would be his way, frugal man that he was. "Savings is fine then."

Jasmine tapped a few more keys and a new white slip printed out. "Here is your balance from your savings account."

Mary Alice stared down at the paper and felt her jaw slacken. This couldn't be right. She looked up. "This is all?" Their entire life's savings, their whole retirement, should be in there, yet the paper read $9,567.23. "Is there another account? Maybe a retirement account? CD's?"

The girl tapped on the keyboard and shook her head. "No Ma'am. Only the two accounts. One checking and one savings."

"I . . . I don't understand. Maybe another bank?"

Jasmine shrugged. "Possibly. Would you like copies of the last few months' bank statements? I don't see any large withdrawals, only transfers from the savings to the checking on a regular basis."

"Yes . . . yes please." Mary Alice fumbled with the clasp on her purse and knocked over a small tray of business cards, sending them splaying everywhere. "Oh dear, I'm sorry." She stooped to start picking them up when a gentleman swept in and did it instead.

"I've got this. No problem Ma'am," he said.

Mary Alice tried to regain her composure. There had to be another account somewhere else. As soon as she got home, she'd hunt through Charlie's desk. For now, she had business to take care of. "I'll make the withdrawal from the savings," she said to Jasmine, attempting a smile that probably looked as awkward and forced as it felt.

Jasmine nodded as the young man set the business cards back on the counter beside Mary Alice. She moved them farther away from her arm and handbag.

"Cashier's check, then?" Jasmine asked.

Mary Alice had no idea if the jail would accept a cashier's check. "No, cash please." She almost explained why before she caught herself. Bailing someone out of jail was not the kind of thing you shared with strangers.

Jasmine raised a perfectly arched eyebrow. "I will need an ID, Mrs. Goodson. Bank policy with withdrawals."

"Of course." Mary Alice dug into her handbag and withdrew her wallet with her Ohio driver's license. "Will this do?"

Jasmine glanced at it and handed it back. "Of course. Do you have a preference in bills?"

So many questions. Why did a trip to the bank seem like such an ordeal? No wonder Charlie insisted on handling everything. "No preference."

Jasmine handed Mary Alice the withdrawal slip and pointed to the bottom line. "I need your signature here."

Mary Alice obliged and watched as Jasmine counted out seventy-five one-hundred-dollar bills onto the counter. She slipped them into a bank envelope and handed it to Mary Alice.

"Thank you."

"Bank statements," Jasmine said. "How many months back do you want? You can also access them online for twelve months back. Farther, and we can pull them from the archives."

"I don't know, six?"

Jasmine tapped some more keys and waited as the papers printed out. She folded and handed them to Mary Alice. "Here you go, Mrs. Goodson. And again, I am so sorry for your loss."

Mary Alice nodded, swallowing a lump lodged in the back of her throat. She couldn't get out of there fast enough.

Back in her car, she rested her head against the seat and closed her eyes. She knew they were not wealthy, but money hadn't been a concern for them since the children were young. There was never a question of funds for their college educations, or vacations, as few and far between as they had been. There had always been savings. Surely Charlie had a reason to move the funds to another bank, she had to track it down to help with . . . oh yes, Greg. The money situation had completely thrown her off focus. She needed to get Greg out of jail, *then* worry about the other account. She put the car in gear and steered it in the direction of the Struthers Courthouse and Jail on 6 Elm Street.

Mary Alice parked in the diagonal spaces beside the banal gray two-story building. She climbed the long, wide steps to the entrance, passed through security scanners, and was directed to the jail at the rear of the building. A burly corrections officer offered one-word directions to the correct barred window.

On the other side of the window, a cluster of uniformed officers sat around gray metal desks in the center of the room. "I'm here to make bail for Greg Proctor," Mary Alice said.

A female corrections officer, tall and rail-thin, looked up from her desk. She made brief eye contact and went back to the monitor on her desk. No one hurried to the window to assist.

"Excuse me," Mary Alice said a little louder. "Can someone help me?"

Officer Tall-and-Skinny took a bite of a huge bear claw and washed it down with whatever was in the white mug stenciled with the seal of the city of Struthers. With about as much urgency as a fly to flypaper, she moseyed over to the window. "Name?"

"Proctor, Gregory Proctor. I believe he came in two days ago."

The officer went back to her desk without uttering another word and sat down with a thud. She typed something into her computer and took another bite of her bear claw. The sound of a printer echoed through the window as Mary Alice tried to tamp down her impatience. Finally, the woman returned with a small stack of papers. "ID," she said.

"I don't have Greg's ID with me. He should have had it

40

on him when he was arres—"

"Yours," said Officer Tall-and-Skinny.

"Oh, of course." Mary Alice rifled around in her purse for her wallet. Why did everything end up at the bottom where she couldn't reach it? The officer harrumphed as she fumbled with her license inside the plastic insert.

Papers were pushed through the slot under the metal bars. "Sign here. You are accepting responsibility for him as a flight risk. His court date and information about his hearing are attached."

Mary Alice quickly glanced over the papers. She didn't take the time to read the fine print. She wanted out of the dreary place almost as much as Greg probably did. She signed and dated on the correct lines and passed the papers back through the slot.

"The funds?"

"Oh, of course." Mary Alice pulled the bank envelope from her purse and passed it over.

The officer opened the envelope and slowly counted out the bills. She handed Mary Alice a carbon copy receipt. "Wait there." She nodded her head at a line of metal chairs against the marred gray wall. Across the room stood two men in cheap business suits, bail bondsmen or attorneys, probably. One scraggly blond-haired girl who was very pregnant and with a child of about two-years-old attached to her bare breast stared back at Mary Alice with a bored, been-here-before look.

The air whooshed through the cracks of the green pleather cushion as Mary Alice took a seat between the girl and the men, unconsciously trying to offer some privacy to the girl's bare breast. She checked her watch. 9:20 a.m.

She waited. A skinny young man with dreadlocks down to the middle of his back came through a metal door and left with one of the men in suits. 10:05 a.m. The door opened again, and a woman dressed provocatively appeared and left with the other man. The young pregnant girl pulled her stained sweater over her chest and hefted the now sleeping child onto her hip and stood. She waddled to the window and rattled the bars. "Hey," she hollered. "What the fuck is takin' so long?" The

41

child bobbed his head, then settled back on her shoulder.

A new face appeared on the other side of the window. "Ain't my job to hurry 'em up. Hold your horses."

"Bitch," the girl murmured as she retook her seat. "This place is the shits," she said, making eye contact with Mary Alice.

Mary Alice nodded silently. *Please get me out of here.*

At 10:46 the door opened, and Greg stepped out. His dark hair looked unwashed and a two-day growth of salt and pepper stubble covered his chin. A purplish ring circled his left eye.

"Hey," he said, not looking up from his shoes. "Thanks."

"Let's go home, Greg," said Mary Alice. She hurried to keep up as Greg's long strides exited the building and bee-lined to her car parked right out front.

The car ride home was mostly silent. "Are you all right?"

"Yes."

"Do you need to see a doctor about that eye?"

"No."

Mary Alice's mind raced ahead. She didn't know if Ellie was even going to let him back in the house. She was pretty angry. But they had to work this out, for Bethany's sake as well as for their marriage.

"I told Ellie I was bailing you out. She's pretty upset."

Greg nodded his head like a reticent child. "I'll pay you back, I promise."

Mary Alice waved a hand in the air. "Of course, you will. Right now, you need to fix things at home. Talk to your wife and daughter. They need you. Don't let them, or me, down. You are a better man than this, Greg."

Another nod and Greg turned his face toward the passenger side window, shoulders rolled in on himself. Was that a sob he was choking back? They drove the rest of the way in silence, and she dropped him off in the driveway of his home. Mary Alice rolled the window down and poked her head out as Greg lumbered up the walk. "I'm glad you're okay, Greg. We'll get through this . . .together."

He raised a hand in a limp wave and disappeared behind the green front door.

Mary Alice waited impatiently for a call from Ellie. Three times over the next two days she reached for the phone to call. No, they needed this alone time. They were working this out, talking to Bethany. Mary Alice needed to stay out of it. Bethany was the one and only focus here. Mary Alice looked at the mobile phone. She wished she knew how to do that texting thing all the kids were doing now so she could at least check on Bethany. Unable to sit and do nothing, she made a fresh batch of chocolate-chip cookies.

On day four, Ellie called. "Well, I didn't kill him."

"Ellie, what about Bethany? Has he talked to her?"

"Yes, we both did. He apologized to her for his behavior and assured her he still loved her. I guess it's time to tell the rest of the family."

"Good. Bethany needs our support. Do you want me to plan brunch at my place on Saturday?"

"Yes. Let's get this over with."

Seven

2017

Saturday swept in on Mary Alice like an impending tornado. Would gray skies pass over or would the storm crash them to bits? Butterflies hatched in her stomach and tried to force their way up her throat. It was all she could do to prepare the meal and not forget any ingredients. She didn't know why she was so nervous. Her decision was made. There was no reason to tell the family her secret. This was about Bethany, not her. The family would find out someday, when the memoir was done, or after she was gone too, but for now, she'd keep their secret. A pang seized her heart. How dare he leave her now . . . again . . . when she... the whole family needed him so much? Her gut unclenched and she bit her lip. He didn't want to leave them, then or now, she was sure.

Evan arrived first, his eyes swollen and red. "What's this special meeting all about? Are you sick? Please, tell me fast, so I can get a grip on it before Ellie and her family arrive."

"No, baby, nobody's sick. Nobody is dying."

Evan exhaled and his stiff stance relaxed.

Mary Alice reached up and pulled his six-foot frame down by the crisp blue collar so his face met hers. A musky scent pervaded her nostrils. She planted a kiss on his freshly shaved cheek. He looked so much like his father.

Evan stood and stretched his long slender torso, as if releasing some built-up tension.

"Where's Ricky?" Mary Alice asked, looking toward the door.

"You sounded so serious on the phone and I didn't know how you felt about an outsider being here."

Mary Alice shook her head. "Ricky's not an outsider. He's family, just like Greg."

"Thanks, Mom. I wasn't sure I could deal with additional drama from Char, either. It's best if he's home. So, what is going on?" His face still registered concern, brows knitted, lips pinched together.

Mary Alice held her ground "No, you have to wait for the others. Here, have some quiche." She scooped a mammoth portion of her signature bacon and cheese quiche onto his favorite orange Fiestaware® dinner plate. Each child had their special-colored plate ever since they were little.

Multiple car doors slammed. Ellie and Greg let themselves in through the side kitchen door. Bethany dragged herself behind them, shoulders turned in, her chestnut hair curtaining her face, looking as if she wanted to disappear.

"Hi, Mom." Ellie planted a kiss on her mother's cheek. Her normally smiling face was fraught with worry lines.

"Ah, it's the Proctor gang." Mary Alice tried to encompass them all in a sweep of her arm, the way Charlie used to do. It wasn't the same.

Greg slipped past her with his head down, rushing straight for the living room.

She made eye contact with Ellie who raised one shoulder in a shrug.

"Hi, Gram," Bethany said, her voice barely above a whisper.

Mary Alice wiped her hands on a dishcloth and wrapped an arm around her granddaughter, kissing her temple. "It's going to be okay," she said so only Bethany could hear.

Tears rimmed Bethany's amber eyes. Charlie's eyes.

Mary Alice straightened. "Let's eat first before we start anything else."

She handed Ellie her yellow plate and winked. She set Char's blue plate aside and let the rest pull from the pile on the

45

counter. "It's buffet style this morning. Don't expect me to wait on you."

"You waited on me." Evan laughed as he took a huge bite.

"Because you're Mom's favorite," Ellie chided.

Mary Alice balked. "I do not have favorites!"

"Where's Aunt Char?" From her seat at the small kitchen table by the window, Bethany spread the blinds so she could see out to the driveway.

Mary Alice gave her a sympathetic look. She knew telling Aunt Char would be difficult, and Bethany, like herself, went out of her way to appease everyone. Confrontations weren't easy for either of them. Perhaps that is how she got into this situation with Trent. Someday she'd have to learn to stand up for herself. Let's hope she didn't take half a century like her Gram.

Evan scoffed, oblivious to his niece's discomfort. "Aunt Char is always late for everything. On time for her is if she gets here by the time we are done eating. I wouldn't be surprised if she's late for heaven and they shut the gate." He scooped up a forkful of quiche and stuffed it into his mouth. He didn't seem to notice the quiet way Bethany picked at the sleeves of her sweater and chewed on her lip.

"I thought," Bethany's voice cracked, and she sat a little straighter, "punctuality was next to godliness . . . Wouldn't that be Aunt Char's thing?"

"That's cleanliness, and your room could use a bit of that. Your mother is not your maid, you know," Greg snapped as he stepped back into the kitchen and picked up a plate.

Ellie's head whipped around at the tone to her husband's voice, and she leveled him with a hard, flat stare. Greg used to be so patient and gentle with Bethany. An edge as sharp as a razor surrounded him now. The tiny smile on Bethany's face dropped, and she turned her face toward the window again, but not fast enough to hide the way she had to bite her lip to keep it from wobbling.

A Lexus squealed into the drive, turning Ellie's attention toward her sister. "And there she is now, Mother Theresa Charlene."

Mary Alice gave Ellie a stern look. This family meeting was already too charged.

Charlene swept through the door, her mobile phone affixed to her ear, one finger raised to request everyone's patience as she rattled on about something to do with side-tracking a syllabus, whatever that was. "Sorry I'm late," she said as she hung up. "What?" she said in response to Evan's shaking head.

Once everyone was present, they carried their plates into the dining room. Brunch started off without a hitch once Char finished her five-minute blessing. Ellie and Greg tried to steer the conversation toward Evan's recent tour through Europe with his orchestra group and Char's new theology class at The Ohio State University in Columbus.

Evan kept staring at the now-yellow ring around Greg's eye. Mary Alice was glad he held his tongue and refrained from inquiring about it.

"And how're things going with you, Bethany?" Evan looked over at his niece. Bethany's face turned scarlet before she burst into tears and ran from the room. Charlene's brows knitted together as her eyes followed Bethany's hasty exit.

Evan frowned. "Did I say something wrong?"

"Not your fault man," Greg said. "Hormones. Be glad you don't have teenage girls."

Ellie pinched her lips together.

"What happened to you?" Charlene wagged her fork in Greg's direction.

Greg glanced at Ellie, then Mary Alice before speaking. "Nothing for you to worry about."

"What does that mean?" Char rebutted.

Mary Alice cleared her throat and stood. "If everyone's done, let's get this cleaned up and go into the other room." She started gathering plates, rinsing and stacking them in the dishwasher. There was no more putting it off. Mary Alice sucked in her breath and exhaled.

"Ellie, can you see if Bethany is ready to join us?"

Ellie wiped her mouth and scooted her chair back. She tossed her napkin down and it landed on Greg's plate, rattling his silverware. Before Greg could so much as frown, Ellie had already marched from the dining room. Nobody said anything, not even Greg. Mary Alice cleared her throat and walked to the living room and heard the soft footfalls of her children falling in behind her like ducklings.

Ellie returned with Bethany, red-faced with swollen and watery eyes. Char and Evan had claimed the comfy overstuffed chairs, Ellie and Greg took the sofa, and Bethany sunk to the floor at their feet. It didn't escape Mary Alice's notice that Greg kept his eyes focused on the floor. Served him right for snapping at a time like that.

Mary Alice eased into her favorite double recliner. A little threadbare, but she loved how she could get her weary legs up and still hold her darling's hand, even if only in her mind now. She brushed her fingers across the empty space on Charlie's side.

The room was too quiet. Even their old black lab, Brutus, was coiled as small as his ninety-pound body could go and was asleep on his plaid doggie bed in the corner.

"Ellie's family has some exciting news to share with the rest of you." Mary Alice nodded at Ellie.

"Yes." Ellie leaned down and wrapped an arm around Bethany's shoulder. Bethany was staring at the floor, picking at a loop of carpet.

"It seems like I . . . we," she nodded at Greg, ". . . are going to be grandparents. Bethany is going to have a baby." She gave Bethany's shoulder a squeeze, and a tear rolled down her daughter's cheek.

Silence swept over the room. All eyes trained on Bethany.

Evan clapped his hands over his cheeks. "Oh my. . . are congratulations in order?"

Bethany attempted a smile, but it didn't meet her eyes.

Dear, sweet Evan, always the optimist. Evan the sensitive, Ellie the practical, and Charlene the zealot. What a mix of temperaments from the same loins. Charlene strummed her fingers on the leg of her pants as her foot bounced up and down. Mary Alice watched her face contort into a grimace. A storm was brewing.

"Congratulations? Hardly." Char snapped, jumping to her feet. "A sixteen-year-old having a baby out of wedlock? It's sinful."

Mary Alice's blood pressure began to rise. She opened her mouth to speak when Evan stood to face his sister. "Stop it, Char. You're not helping."

Mary Alice stared up at Charlene. If only she wasn't so predictable — exactly what Bethany was worried about. She forced the words out. "Whatever she decides, we will *all* support her in it." She almost didn't recognize the sound of her own voice when it thundered from her. It felt good. Mary Alice lifted her chin and glanced at Bethany, who was cradling her face in her hands.

"Of course," Evan said. "I was afraid you'd all disown me when I finally came out, but you've all been great."

The corner of Ellie's lips turned up in a smile. "It wasn't a surprise to any of us. I think we knew you were gay before you did."

Evan's eyes bored into Char. "Everyone wasn't okay with it."

Charlene looked wide-eyed and innocent. "What do you mean, Evan? You know I love Ricky." Mary Alice did not miss the obvious eye roll.

"Now," said Evan, turning back to Bethany. "Have you made any decisions yet?"

"I don't know what to do," Bethany's voice was muffled and thin against her palms. She didn't look up.

"Of course you don't," Char said. She squatted down and stroked Bethany's head in a rare show of tenderness. "You're a child."

"I don't love Trent," Bethany's body slumped lower into the floor. "I thought I did, but now I realize I don't want to be married to him for the rest of my life. I wanted to go to college, I wanted to be someone." Her shoulders began to shake, and she curled in on herself.

"Well, you can't keep it." Char said, plopping back down onto the armchair. "What would people think? You'll have to put it up for adoption."

49

Mary Alice watched how Ellie looked toward Greg for guidance, the gap between them suddenly gone.

"She doesn't need to. Right, Greg?" Ellie asked.

Greg didn't answer.

Ellie cleared her throat and sat a little taller. "We appreciate all your concern, but we didn't mean to imply any of you had a say in what she does. We thought you should know." She rubbed Bethany's back in small comforting circles.

Mary Alice felt something beginning to erupt inside of her. Ellie seemed to be deferring the decision to Greg. Did Bethany not have a say either? Greg had not answered Ellie's question. It wasn't even his question to answer. Bethany could not be forced to give up her baby. This thing could not be happening . . . again.

"We're looking at all options," Greg said. "Trying to figure out what is best for Bethany. She is so young. She has her whole future ahead of her. We don't want her to drop out of school."

"I thought you two were going to start traveling once Bethany was in college," Char spat. "It's all you've talked about for years. You can't do that if you are raising another child."

Ellie glared at her older sister. "Well, things change."

Greg stood and towered over his sister-in-law. "Char, we have not made a final decision on this yet. We came here for your support, not your judgement. If you can't support us on this, then perhaps we should part ways."

"Is that how you got that shiner? Defending your daughter's honor? The Lord will forgive her, she needs to . . ."

Ellie jumped up next to her husband. "Stop! Not another word."

Brutus jumped too. Bethany sprang up and ran from the room.

Now Mary Alice's blood pressure reached a boiling point. She struggled out of the cushiony recliner and spun to face first Charlene, then Ellie and Greg. "This baby is a gift from God. Bethany is the only one with a right to choose, and whatever she decides, it will be the right one."

Evan covered his mouth. Charlene's eyes widened, and

the sneer disappeared from her face. Ellie stared at Mary Alice, mouth agape and Greg took an unconscious step away.

"Ah . . .we—" Greg ran a hand through his hair and looked from Ellie to Mary Alice, but Mary Alice lifted a hand to stop his objections. A fire burned in her now, one she couldn't stomp out or smother. She crossed her arms over her chest. "If you're going to judge Bethany, then you need to judge me too." The words were out before she had time to think them through. She had to protect her granddaughter, her great-grandchild, no matter the cost. Mary Alice would not let this happen again: she would die first.

"What are you talking about Mom?" Evan asked.

She pressed her hands together as if in prayer. But this was not a prayer. It was a confession. Deep breaths.

Charlie's voice echoed in her mind. *Don't do it, Mar.*

Mary Alice's heart felt as though it was going to pound right out of her chest, but the words spilled from her mouth, almost without her volition. "Papa and I have kept a secret from all of you for a long time. I'm sorry." She squinted her eyes shut and waited for the repercussions. Nothing. She opened first one eye, then the other and surveyed the faces of her family. Char was poised on the edge of her chair like she was ready to bolt. Evan's eyes were as round as Frisbees. Ellie chewed on her lower lip. Bethany stepped back in the room, her mouth gaping open. No one said a word, so she inhaled a deep breath and continued.

"Three years before Char was born, when we were both sixteen, Papa and I had a baby. A baby girl." There, she'd said it. Exhale. For a brief second, the weight was lifted off her shoulders, the weight of carrying this secret for half a century. But it was replaced with fear: fear of rejection, fear of judgment, fear of scorn.

Silence. The cuckoo clock chimed once, and everyone jumped. Bethany sucked in her breath, clasped her hands over her mouth and sunk into the sofa next to her mother.

Mary Alice rushed to fill the space. "Things were different back then. It was 1963. My parents did what they thought was the best thing for me, and I believe they thought it was the

51

right thing for the baby too." A lump formed in her throat. Did she really believe that? Well, that was the story and she was sticking to it. No good came from speaking evil of the dead. She swallowed hard several times trying to find the words to go on. "Papa's parents felt the same way."

Bethany's voice cracked. "What . . . what did they do?"

"I was sent away . . . to The Florence Crittenton Home for Unwed Mothers. There were lots of girls like me there."

The siblings exchanged bewildered glances.

"Were they nice to you?" Bethany asked.

"Well, it was clean. We were fed well and had school lessons, but they kept reminding us what bad girls we were and how the only right thing to do was to give our babies away." That was a gross understatement. The memories of those days, how she was treated, and the horrible day she finally gave in to the pressure haunted her to this day. But she couldn't allow herself to even go there. It was too raw, painfully erupted from someplace buried deep in her soul. Mary Alice inhaled and tried to calm her beating heart. It did little to help.

Bethany's face pinched and she wrapped her arms around her stomach. "Terrible. Gram, but what happened to the baby?"

Mary Alice wished she didn't have to answer, but the secret was out now and they deserved the truth. No matter how hard this was, there was no turning back now. "Adopted. I got to hold her for five minutes. I never saw her again after I signed the papers." A tear trickled down her face. She could still see the rise and fall of the fontanelle under the soft cap of light brown curls, the tiny turned-up nose, the perfect eyelashes brushing her cheeks as she slept.

Evan shook his head and held up a narrow index finger. "Wait. You're telling us somewhere out there is a full-blooded sister who our grandparents forced you to give away? That doesn't sound like Grandma and Grandpa at all." He had been especially close to his grandmother. It was hard for anyone to have their idol fall off the pedestal, so Mary Alice wasn't surprised by his reaction.

She glanced up at the box on the mantle. "Your father

and I wanted you to love and respect your grandparents. It was our decision not to tell you, not theirs."

Ellie's face was drained of all color. "Mom, why haven't you tried to find her?"

"We did. The adoption was closed. Papa and I tried right after we were married but the records were sealed; there was nothing we could do. She would have been almost three years old by then."

Char's mouth was set in a tight line. "I can't believe this." Her short blond hair swished back and forth as she shook her head. "You had an illegitimate child? A bastard? You've lied to us all these years?"

The truth stabbed Mary Alice in the heart. Such an ugly word, bastard, coming from her own daughter. Her baby was never a b... that word. . . to Mary Alice or Charlie. The words, the accusations, the judgement she had listened to every day when at the home echoed in her mind. A familiar helplessness settled in her stomach. What was the use? The names she had been called, the things she told herself– they were all true. Even after all these years, the shame still swept over her. Shame for getting pregnant out of wedlock, shame for giving her child away, shame for keeping the truth a secret. All the strength she'd mustered to tell the truth seeped out of her like a leaky teacup. Instead, she bowed her head, noticing the linen napkin balled in her fist. She straightened it across her lap. How did they keep a secret like that all those years? What kind of parent does that to their children?

"Is that why you always seemed too preoccupied to give us the time of day? You were thinking about her?" Char's words bit into Mary Alice like shark's teeth.

Mary Alice's head jerked up. It wasn't true. She wasn't preoccupied. She hadn't ignored her children, even though Char was the type of child who demanded non-stop attention. Maybe she hadn't spent as much time as she would have liked with her children. There had been a household to run, meals to be made, laundry, cleaning, running everyone to doctor appointments and ballet and soft ball, cheerleading and more. Any mother of three children would have done the same.

Wouldn't they?

"That's not fair, Char," Ellie said.

Evan ran a hand down his face. "Give it a rest, Char." He turned to his mother. "Why didn't you get married right then? Wouldn't that have solved the problem?"

"Our parents wouldn't allow it. We were minors, still in high school. Your grandparents forced Papa to enlist in the Navy to get away from it all . . . from me. It was not a happy time for either of us."

Char stood and paced the room, muttering to herself, praying or losing it — Mary Alice wasn't sure which.

"Why now? Why tell us now, after all this time?" Char glared at her. "Are you looking for redemption? Well, it's too late." She began quoting scripture: "Visiting the iniquity of the fathers upon the children, and upon the children's children."

Brutus moved alongside Mary Alice's chair. Mary Alice patted his head. "It's okay, boy." Mary Alice and Charlie hadn't brought up Char – of any of them – to be so judgmental. True, they hadn't gone back to the church after the baby was given away, but they still believed in the merciful God that had forgiven them. Char took God and twisted him into a warlord. They raised the children to be kind and to live by the Golden Rule: *Do unto others as you would have them do unto you.* And they had taught them decent manners. How had Charlene turned into a religious bigot? When did that happen? It seemed like a long time. But not as a child. She was impulsive and strong-willed, but she was kind back then. Mary Alice bit her tongue and turned away from Char.

"Bethany." Mary Alice stated, finding strength in her granddaughter's name. "She is why I decided to tell you about this now . . . because I know exactly what she is going through. I understand all the fear and anxiety. She needs the whole family's support in this, Char."

Mary Alice watched Ellie nod her agreement. Did she really understand what Bethany was going through? She seemed more interested in following Greg's lead on this, taking over all decisions for Bethany. Did she believe she was doing the best for her daughter? Mary Alice wasn't so sure.

Charlene grabbed her purse and it opened, spilling the contents all over the floor. Bethany reached for the tube of lipstick rolling toward her, but Char grabbed it first and scooped up pens and pencils, a prescription bottle and comb, and shoved them back in her bag and stormed out, not even bothering to say goodbye to anyone.

Greg announced gruffly it was time to go. Ellie dutifully gathered up her daughter and wrapped her mother in a warm embrace. Their eyes met and Mary Alice tried to interpret the sadness in her daughter's eyes. Was it over Bethany or about the news of a sister she never knew existed? Was she judging Mary Alice too? This conversation was far from over as Ellie and Bethany followed Greg to the car.

Mary Alice leaned against the counter and watched as Greg's car backed out of the driveway. She didn't realize she was staring out at nothingness. She was floating, pushing memories away and wishing for them all at once. Now she understood why Charlie made her promise to never bring it up again. Now she couldn't stop thinking about it. The baby's first cry, the warmth of her skin, the smell of her hair. The surge of falling so deeply in love; it was impossible to explain. She couldn't live in the past like this, chasing a ghost. It would have killed her then, just as it would kill her now. She couldn't let it happen again, not to her and not to Bethany.

"Mom?"

Mary Alice's shoulders sagged, and she wiped her eyes with the back of her hand. She let go of the counter and turned to face her son who was leaning against the kitchen table. She'd forgotten Evan was still there. She met his eyes with the most convincing smile she could muster.

"Mom, we can find her. If we try to —"

Her shoulders slumped. "Oh Evan, don't get your hopes up. We tried. We really did. We had to let her go or we would have driven ourselves crazy." Mary Alice couldn't say she had to go into survival mode. She couldn't say first, her parents, then Charlie had watched her like a hawk, afraid to leave her alone, concerned she might do something to herself. She couldn't say she had to bury it deep, deep down to find a way to go on . . . to accept her baby was gone for good. But she had never let her go. She couldn't say any of it, because if she did, then she would have to accept it all over again, and she was too weary to have to shatter her own heart once more.

When everyone left, the house was finally quiet. Too quiet. This was not the way it was supposed to be, the family leaving with hard feelings between them. Charlie would have handled this so much better. He would have prevented the blow-up between them. She and Char, Char and Evan, Char and Greg. Always Char. *Had I, had Charlie, done something to make our child so bitter, so cruel to lash out like that?* It was a concept she'd never considered before. Was there some truth to it?
"*I messed this up so badly, Charlie.*"
Mary Alice hoped she hadn't irrevocably severed her family's ties. She couldn't live with that. How would that help Bethany? And she still didn't know how they would feel once they had a chance to calm down and digest it. It was a lot to handle in one blow. Charlene made her feelings quite obvious and reacted just as she had feared. Evan seemed onboard, maybe too much so. But what about Ellie? Char's reaction had tempered any further discussion. This subject was far from over.
The cuckoo clock chimed four times. Mary Alice was tempted to pitch it out the window.
"*Why Charlie? Why did you have to leave us now?*"
I'm here Mar. I've always been here.

Eight

2017

It had been two days since the big blow-up. Thanksgiving was in four days. What kind of Thanksgiving would this be if no one was talking to each other? As Mary Alice threw a load of clothes into the washer, she was surprised by a knock on the front door. No one had called to say they were coming. The neighbors' handouts had finally stopped after four weeks, and she wasn't expecting any deliveries. Sophia and Gladys rarely stopped by without calling first. The one technology Mary Alice had mastered in the last few weeks was ordering online with the tablet the children had bought her last year but had never used until recently. She could even order groceries online. It became practically an obsession. The postman made deliveries so often, Mary Alice often had a cool drink and a bag of cookies to offer him.

The knock came louder and more urgently.

Mary Alice peered through the side lights of the massive front door, *birch*, Charlie had built with his own two hands. She swung the door open. It was unusual for family to use the front door.

"Bethy, what a pleasant surprise. Did you call and I missed it?"

Bethany gave her a subdued smile and planted a kiss on her cheek. "No, Gram, I didn't call. Is it a bad time?" Her eyes clouded over, and she dropped her gaze.

"No, no, never for you. How about some hot cocoa?"

Bethany nodded and followed Mary Alice into the sunny kitchen. She dropped into a chair at the table. "Gram, I can't stop thinking about you having a baby at my age. I can hardly believe it . . . wow. What was it like for you when you found out you were pregnant?"

Mary Alice sucked in her breath. No small talk about school or parents. So much like her grandfather. Where to begin?

"Confusing is the best word. My parents whisked me away to the Florence Crittenton Home before I understood what was happening."

"Were you scared?" The way she was picking at the loose thread of the tablecloth made Mary Alice wonder if she was also scared. She had to be.

"Not scared so much as bewildered and ridiculously optimistic. I'd had an easy childhood: safe, happy, secure, albeit strict, so anything short of that was not imaginable to me. Back then, the thing to do was hide girls away and pretend it never happened."

Bethany shrugged one shoulder. "We have some pregnant girls in our school now. It doesn't seem to be much of a big deal. But everyone still talks about them."

"Well, it was a big deal then. You weren't allowed to go to school once you were showing. It was like you were contagious. Even the word 'pregnant' was considered too vulgar to say out loud. We weren't pregnant, we were in the family way."

Bethany dropped some mini marshmallows into her mug. "I think it's easier now, but I still feel weird." She looked down at her stomach. "I don't even have a belly yet, but I already feel like everyone is staring at me. What if Trent told his friends he isn't the father? Everyone will think I slept around."

Mary Alice reached over and took her hand. "Bethy, your friends know better and the others aren't worth their salt."

Bethany's shoulders slumped "I don't have many friends anymore. I had to drop out of cheerleading and soccer. Even my BFF who said she'd stick by me has gone incognito. And Mom and Dad are acting so weird. You are all I've got."

Mary Alice remembered the silence in her own house after her big announcement. When her father wouldn't look her in the eye. She remembered how her school friends abandoned her like she was a leper. But that was a long time ago. Things were different now, weren't they?

"Your mom and dad love you. You know they do. It hurts them to know you're going through a hard time. Nobody likes to see their child hurting. I wasn't planning on telling any of you about my baby, but when Char got so judgmental of you, I lost it. I hoped it would help, and maybe take some of the pressure off you. Your whole family is here to support you."

"It only seemed to make Aunt Char angry."

"For now, but it also let her and everyone else know I'm beside you all the way. My oldest brother, Paul, and I were never close again. Only your great-uncle Tommy has always been there for me."

Bethany ran her palms down the outside of her mug, warming her hands on the sides. "Tell me what it was like for you there."

Mary Alice sighed. "At the home? This could take awhile. But if you want to know, I'll tell you everything." She poured herself a fresh cup of tea and took a seat. She'd just written this part in her journal. It still sat open on her bed upstairs, but she didn't need to see the pages to tell the story. Try as she might, she could never forget those days. At least the bad memories had a better purpose to exist now.

Nine

1963

All I wanted was to get to the phone and call Charlie. I looked both ways down the hall at the bottom of the steps and wandered farther down toward the main living room. The phone was tucked behind a plant on a side table in the hall. *Oak.* I wished it were someplace more private. A tablet sat by the phone along with a pencil. Other names were listed with dates and times and who had called whom. I penciled in my name and Charlie's with the date and time. I picked up the avocado-colored receiver and dialed the numbers, watching the dial rotate back in place after each number.

"Goodson residence."

"Hello, Mrs. Goodson? This is Mary Alice. May I please speak to Charlie?"

Silence.

I could hear Mrs. Goodson breathing. "Mrs. Goodson? Is Charlie there?"

Mrs. Goodson cleared her throat. "Charles is not available to speak to you. We would appreciate it if you didn't call here again."

The line went dead.

I stared at the receiver in my hand. Tears threatened to fall. I gulped for air. No, no, no. This couldn't be happening. I dialed the number back. It rang and rang and rang. Finally, someone must have lifted the receiver and dropped it back into the cradle. Mrs. Goodson had always been so nice to me. Had it all been fake? I thought about the lovely scarf she had given to me last Christmas. I thought she saw me as her future daughter. How wrong I could be. Losing grace in her eyes hurt almost as much as not finding Charlie.

How was I going to get out of there if I couldn't reach Charlie? My hand shook as I rested the receiver back on the cradle. I sank to the floor. What now? I'd keep trying. of course. Sooner or later, he'd have to pick up himself, wouldn't he? What if he didn't? What if they convinced him he was better off without me? What if they told him this baby wasn't his problem? He could walk away. I'd be all alone. What then? I wrapped my arms around my knees and dropped my head into my arms, fighting back the angry tears threatening to fall. No, I was not going to cry. I could not let them win. I had to stay strong. I pounded a fist on the carpeted floor.

"Hey."

I looked up to see Joanie sliding down the wall alongside me.

"Are you okay? What's the matter?"

I shook my head. "They won't let me talk to Charlie."

"Oh," Joanie said. "That sucks." She wrapped an arm around my shoulder.

"I'm not giving up. I'll keep calling and calling until he answers."

She gave my shoulder a squeeze. "That's the spirit. Keep trying. Or write him a letter. And if he doesn't come, you'll still be okay. We all will. You'll see."

No, no. Staying was not an option. I wouldn't be okay. I couldn't do this without Charlie. We sat on the floor, side-by-side, neither saying a word. I had no idea how much time had passed but at some point, Mrs. Longsworth came along.

"Get up girls," she said not too kindly. "No dawdling in the halls. Lunch is almost over. You'd better hurry if you want to eat."

"Yes Ma'am," Joanie said, clumsily trying to get to her feet with the large bundle under her blouse impeding her action.

"Mary Alice, this is a warning. Stay clear of the halls.

61

Someone could trip and get hurt."

Couldn't she see I was upset? Couldn't she offer me a little kindness? I had to get out of there. Slowly, I rolled onto my knees, then used the wall to lift myself up. At six months along, my belly was beginning to hinder my flexibility. I followed Joanie into the dining room. I spotted Sophia sitting alone at a folding table at the back of the dining room. About a dozen girls were sitting at a long, rectangular table. *Oak.* Other folding tables and chairs were scattered around the perimeter of the room. Heeding Sophia's warning, I shadowed Joanie to the large center table.

"Hey." Joanie swept an arm wide to introduce her. "This is Mary Alice, our newest 'promiscuous guest.'"

I felt heat rise to my face.

"Hey," "Hi," "Pleasure to meet you," "Welcome," came from around the table.

"So, tell us, Mary Alice, where did you come from?" Joanie sat and passed a platter of baked ham my way.

I eyed the mounds of mashed potatoes, baked ham, steamed brussels sprouts and cauliflower. It was more food than I'd seen since the Christmas buffet at our Baptist church back home. Meals at home were adequate but hardly spreads like this. Daddy didn't believe in gluttony. "Umm, I thought we weren't supposed to tell our personal stories. Aren't we supposed to stay incognito?"

The girls exchanged smiles. "Only in front of Mrs. Longsworth," one of them replied. "Did they think we weren't going to talk? They used to give the girls fake first names too, but when nobody answered to them, they gave up and let us keep our own."

"I'm from Cincinnati," Joanie confessed. "My baby's daddy is in the Army."

"Mine's a truck driver. Last time I saw him was the night he knocked me up in the cab of his truck," said a girl sitting kitty-corner from me.

"Knock it off, Sheila," Joanie said. "You don't have a clue who your baby's daddy is."

Were all these girls as promiscuous as Mrs. Longsworth

62

said? Or did they have stories not so different from mine? Except for Joanie, who was pleasant with her freckled-mask face, everyone looked so sad. And guilty. That was it. Everyone looked like they were being punished. Were they? Was I? Did I deserve that too? Yes, Charlie and I had committed a sin of having sex before marriage, but I didn't feel like a terrible person. We were in love. The other girls probably felt the same way.

"Where did you say you were from?" Sheila asked.

I hadn't. "Struthers," I said. "The east side."

All the girls at the table nodded. One of them mumbled between bites, "Does your baby's daddy work in the mill?"

I shook my head. "No, but my father does." And my uncles, and my cousins, and my future father-in-law. Almost all the men in Struthers, the blue-collar suburb of Youngstown, worked in the dirty steel mills along the boiling, highly polluted Mahoning River. "Charlie's in high school, like me, but someday he's going to be a cabinet maker."

The girls nodded, but by the expression on their faces, I got the feeling they weren't convinced. Almost all the men ended up at the mill sooner or later unless they went off to college or got drafted.

"I'm calling him to come and get me."

"Yeah, well good luck," one of the girls said. "Most of us thought our boyfriends would spring us too, but as you see, we're all still here."

"Not Charlie. He'll come."

The girls offered weak smiles and changed the subject to the latest dance move by Annette Funicello on American Bandstand. After lunch, they scattered in different directions. Some headed into the kitchen to clean up the dishes. Others went to the laundry, and I saw others dusting and vacuuming the lavish house. I grabbed a few dinner rolls for Gladys.

I glared at the phone on my way back to my room. I tried again. This time there was no answer. Ah. Why wouldn't they let us be together? NO. I would not let them get the best of me. I could still write.

I climbed the stairs, running my hand over the beautiful banister and made my way to my room. Sitting on my bed, I composed a letter to Charlie. If his parents wouldn't allow him to talk to me, would a letter get through? Would it be read or censored here before being mailed? They didn't have any right to prohibit me from writing, did they? To be safe, I kept the letter short and sweet, assuring Charlie I was safe but anxiously awaiting his arrival. I wanted to say, *Get me the hell out of here,* but of course I couldn't. You can take a Baptist out of the church, but you can't take the church out of a Baptist. Sometimes I wished I could be more like Sophia. I'd write every day until we could be together again. I wrote the address of the home in big, bold letters at the bottom of the stationery and again on the return address of the envelope before licking and sealing it.

Sophia came in, smelling of cigarette smoke, and plopped down on her bed. "This place ain't so bad. Three squares a day, free smokes, no bars on the windows or doors. All good, as long as I don't get slop duty."

"They gave you cigarettes?"

"Naw, but some of the girls had some."

"What's slop duty?"

"Cleaning the johns. I ain't cleaning up piss and crap for anybody."

"I hope she gives me polishing the furniture." I glanced over at the small chest, *Pine*, and smiled to myself. An image of Charlie in his undershirt, suspenders hanging around his waist, popped into my head. He was sliding the plane across a fresh-cut piece of wood, perspiration shimmering on his bare forearms and down his long, thin neck. My face flamed.

The next day I caught Mrs. Longsworth in the living room. I had to try again to get through to Charlie. "Ma'am," I ventured. "I've tried calling my boyfriend, but his parents tell me he's not home. I must talk to him. I need a pass to go home for a few days." Or forever.

Mrs. Longsworth stiffened and shook her head. "I have no instructions from your parents allowing that. You may write to him, but I do not get involved in your girls' problems." She dismissed me with a wave of her hand and turned away.

I gulped down the baseball-sized lump lodged in my throat and slumped onto the sofa. Maybe I could run away. Call Charlie from a payphone somewhere. No, the gate was locked. I was trapped. My body began to shake uncontrollably. I couldn't stay here. I couldn't leave. My heart pounded wildly in my chest. I wanted to go home with Charlie and the baby. If I couldn't, then . . . no . . . I couldn't even think that. I had to keep faith and try harder. I couldn't fall apart. I had to stay strong. For Charlie. For the baby. For myself.

Joanie sat down next to me. "You okay?"

I shrugged, took a deep breath and fisted my hands in my lap to keep them from shaking. My nails bit into my palms. The pain was somehow a welcome release. "I thought Mrs. Longsworth might let me go home for a day or two. I need to find my boyfriend."

"The old battle ax ain't gonna let anyone outta here except on the arm of a parent. It's hopeless to ask."

"But I thought . . ."

Joanie shook her head. "I wouldn't count on her to help you."

I still had to try. I couldn't give up.

At least Mrs. Longsworth let me write to Charlie. After two weeks, I finally received a response from him promising he was coming for me on Sunday at 8 a.m. Would he remember the letter of permission from my parents? I'd been very clear in my letters I needed it. What if they wouldn't agree? Maybe he'd forge their signatures. Would Mrs. Longsworth call to make sure it was legitimate? Of course, she would. Please God, let them give permission.

On Saturday night, I folded the clothes I had finally relinquished to the dresser and packed them neatly in my brown suitcase. My stomach fluttered at the thought of being Charlie's wife, raising our baby together. Where would we live? Would Charlie be making cabinets right away? What about finishing high school? He must have it all worked out. All I needed was to keep faith in him.

At a seven thirty on Sunday morning, I crept out the front door and made my way to the end of the long driveway. I sat on my suitcase inside the gate, waiting for him. I'd been up since five, primping in the small bathroom mirror, trying to make myself as pretty as possible. I skipped breakfast to wait for him. He'd have to ring the buzzer to open the gate. Would Mrs. Longsworth let him in? I pulled my coat tighter around me against the early March winds. March didn't come in like a lamb, more like a polar bear. The temperature dipped below freezing and the wind chill sliced through me. I waited.

Hearing crunching over the icy pavers, I turned to see Sophia stomping down the driveway, her chenille bedspread wrapped around her shoulders, the ends flapping in the bitter air. "What the hell do you think you're doing out here? Old lady Longsworth was looking for you at breakfast. I told her you were having stomach problems and was in the bathroom. But she'll come looking for you soon. Besides, you're going to freeze to death out here."

"Charlie's coming any minute. He can't be much longer now." I said through chattering teeth. I hoped I sounded braver than I felt. An uneasiness in my stomach told me I was a fool, he wasn't coming after all and even if he did, the locked gate would not open for him. But I couldn't believe that. He'd promised, and Charlie never lied.

"Listen, you've been out here for two hours. Go back to bed. I'll cover for you at Chapel." Sophia said rubbing her arms with her hands. "If he's coming, he'll be here whether you are outside in this crap or inside where it's warm. Longsworth ain't gonna open those gates until he brings permission from your parents. Besides, how's he gonna feel if you catch pneumonia and die waiting for him out here?"

Sophia had a point. He wouldn't be happy if I caused any harm to myself or our baby. "I . . . I was so excited to go home with him. I guess you're right. He'll come up to the house when he gets here. And I am awfully cold."

Sophia pulled me to a standing position, a difficult feat with my legs frozen from sitting on the suitcase for so long and my seven-month belly weighing me down. "Come on, it's ten

66

o-clock. Let's go inside." She swept the bedspread off her own shoulders and wrapped it around me.

Why was Sophia being so kind? Sophia wasn't kind to anyone, least of all her roommates. Maybe there was a speck of goodness in her too. Pastor Wrigley was right. Everyone was born with goodness in them. Sometimes you had to look a little harder to find it. The halls were quiet with everyone at Chapel. Back in our room, I climbed into bed and tried to warm up. I was frozen to the bone. My eyes closed. The next time I opened them, the clock by my bed said noon. I watched the minutes tick by, *please come Charlie, please*, until the warmth of the bed forced my eyes to close.

Two hours later, I awoke with a start. Two fifteen. Had he come and Mrs. Longsworth sent him away? I never should have closed my eyes. I glanced over at Gladys who lay curled on her bed, eyes wide open watching me but not saying a word. "Did Mrs. Longsworth come looking for me? Was Charlie here?" She stared, non-blinking without answering. I jumped from my bed and hurried from the room and down the stairs. I ran into Mrs. Longsworth in the parlor.

"Ah, Mary Alice. Are you feeling better? Sophia said you may have a stomach bug?"

My stomach lurched. I might be sick, but not from a bug. "Did anyone come to see me?" I sucked in my breath, already pretty sure of the answer.

"No, no visitors. You should take it easy the rest of the day and stay away from the rest of the girls if you do have a bug. Go back to bed, Mary Alice. I'll have someone bring you some chicken soup and ginger ale for dinner a little later."

I nodded and plodded back up the stairs. I was glad to have the alone time, except for Gladys who wasn't talking anyhow. Someone must have stopped Charlie from coming. His parents maybe. Mrs. Goodson hanging up on me spelled it out pretty clear. But he wouldn't have not shown up. Even if he had to sneak out, he would have come. Did something else happen to him? My heart raced at the thought. A car crash? Was he in a hospital somewhere wanting to come to me and unable? Or something worse. Tears stung my eyes at the thought. No,

I couldn't think that. I had to stay positive. He'd come, he'd promised, he had to be okay. I watched the small round dial on the clock beside my bed. Five o'clock, Six, Seven. If only I could be sure he was safe. If only he would keep his promise. The soup brought up to me sat untouched. Joanie arrived and silently took it away, her eyes filled with sorrow. Sophia grumbled something about men being worthless and not trustworthy. But she didn't know my Charlie. He was different.

Charlie didn't come that day, or the next, or the day after that. The following Sunday, Mrs. Longsworth said I had a visitor.

Charlie! Finally! I ran a comb through my curls and smoothed the borrowed dress over my belly. I liked the green gingham-checked smocked dress I'd found in the donation closet. Charlie would be surprised how much I was showing. I hurried into the living room to meet him.

But it wasn't Charlie. Instead, standing beside a high wing-backed chair was my mother. I felt the smile wash away from my face and a shiver run down my back. Something was wrong. Maybe my worries had been right. Maybe Charlie was hurt. The baby gave a swift kick to my side. I know, baby. Where is your Daddy? A prickly feeling ran up my arm. This was not good. I could feel it.

Mother slapped both gloved hands to her cheeks when she saw my belly. What did she expect? For my belly to be getting smaller? Of course, I was showing. Why was she here? Something told me this was not a social visit.

"Mom." I planted a kiss on her cheek. "What are you doing here?" Instantly I regretted my words. I'd been raised better. "Not that I don't love seeing you. How's Daddy? Is everything all right with Tommy and Paul?" Small talk. I couldn't care less what Tommy and Paul were doing. Charlie was all I cared about. What about Charlie? Why wasn't he there? Remorse immediately enveloped me like a wet blanket. What if something had happened to one of them? Wouldn't that be bad too? It wasn't like me to be so self-absorbed.

"Everyone is fine Mary Alice. I've . . . um . . . I've come

to talk to you."

I tried to smile. Remembering my manners was hard under the circumstances, but Mrs. Cranston hadn't raised an ungrateful child. Even if she hadn't stood up for me against Daddy. From the way things had transpired back at the house, I didn't expect a visit from my mother. "Of course. Let's sit over by the window." I gestured to a small round table with two chairs in the corner of the room far away from the TV and the girls swooning over Dick Clark reruns. I couldn't hold back my question any longer.

"I've been expecting Charlie. He said he was coming for me. Did you give him permission to come and get me?"

Mother sat on the edge of the chair, pillbox hat on her permanently curled hair, her hands folded on the table. "Mary Alice, I hate to be the one to tell you this, but Charlie's not coming." She pulled the gloves from her hands, one finger at a time and folded them neatly on her black patent leather handbag.

It felt like someone had punched me in the gut. I grabbed at my stomach. "He's hurt, isn't he? Oh, please tell me he is okay. What happened to him?"

Her perfectly shaped eyebrows pinch together. "No, he is not hurt. Where did you get that idea?"

"He was supposed to come for me last Sunday. And I didn't hear from him all week. He was bringing permission from you . . ." Then it occurred to me. "Did Daddy refuse to let him come? What did he do?" I felt the panic rising in my throat.

Mother's red and wrinkled hand reached out and enveloped mine. I stared down at them, showing years of hard work, despite her buffed nails and clear polish. I knew how important it was to my mother that a woman always look her best. Keeping up appearances was what it was all about. In contrast, my hands were milky white and smooth, with ragged nails from biting them and gnawing on the cuticles.

I pulled my hand from her's and tucked them under the table. Charlie would make sure I never had to work as hard as my mother had. I'd have a better life, an easier life. Myself, Charlie, and our baby.

"Darling, Charlie's gone," Mother said. "The Goodsons didn't want their son saddled with a wife and baby at his age. They convinced him to enlist in the Navy."

I jumped up, nearly knocking the table over. "No, that can't be right. I have a letter from him. He's coming for me." I trembled. An anger I never even knew existed bubbled up inside me. "What did you do? What did Daddy do? He did this, didn't he? Well, he can't stop us. Charlie's coming for me. He is . . . he is . . . he is." With each word, my anger crumbled more into despair. I sank back into the chair.

Mother's voice was soft but resolved. "Mary Alice, I'm sorry. I watched him board the Greyhound bus myself last Saturday. Perhaps it's for the best. His parents didn't have the means to support a whole new family. If they think . . ."

"NO! No, they don't know what's best. That's why he didn't come? Because he had already left . . .they had sent him away?" I slapped my hand over my mouth, sure I was going to be sick. "You can't possibly agree with them," I mumbled through my palm. "The Goodsons are wrong. You're wrong. Me, Charlie, and our baby are meant to be together. Charlie wouldn't do that to me . . . to us." Tears poured down my face. "He wouldn't," I whispered. "He couldn't. He loves me."

Mother set a linen handkerchief from her handbag on the table and wrapped an arm around my shoulder. "Shh, shh, it'll be all right. You'll see." Her arms felt foreign around me.

I stared at the pure white handkerchief. I didn't pick it up, instead wiping my eyes with the back of my hand. But it wouldn't be all right. Not without Charlie. Without him, I was like every other girl here, a pathetic unwed mother with no hope and nowhere to turn.

"Your father and I have been talking. We agree with the Goodsons. This is for the best." She motioned to my stomach. "After this is over, you can go back to your life. You can be back at school for your junior year. You'll graduate with your class, like nothing ever happened. We've told our friends and the people at church you went to stay with your aunt in Colorado for a few months to help her since she was ill."

I sunk lower into the chair, incredulous. "I don't have an

aunt in Colorado."

Mother pinched her lips together and leaned in as if to whisper. "Nobody knows that. Nobody needs to ever know about your situation. Life can go back to normal."

Who was she kidding? Everyone already knew. Just because no one spoke of it out loud didn't mean they didn't know. No doubt I was already the talk of the town. Everyone at Struthers High School knew. The few friends I had abandoned me the minute I told them. They couldn't risk a bad reputation hanging around with me.

"Mom, I'm having a baby. Charlie's baby. How do you expect me to ever go back to what you call normal? I'll have a baby to take care of."

Mother's back stiffened. "Not if you give it up. Think about the child, Mary Alice. What kind of life do you think you can give it as a sixteen-year-old mother? How would you support it, feed it, raise it to be a good member of society?"

Give it up? How could she even say a thing like that? I could never . . . Charlie could never . . . this was our baby, OUR BABY. I jumped back up, this time the chair crashing to the floor behind me. I swiped away the angry tears with the back of my hand.

"You mean like you, Mom? What you're saying?" I could feel the blood pulsing at my temples. "That I need to be a 'good' mother like you? A good Baptist girl that obeys her mother and father? Did you do that Mom? When you married Daddy so young? Did Grandma and Grandpapa approve? You expect me to be a 'good girl,' never speak up for what I want or believe. Are you embarrassed that your bridge club friends will find out I'm pregnant? Do you think you can hide me away in here and nobody will ever know?"

Never in my sixteen years had I ever spoken to my mother that way. Never had I raised my voice to anyone, least of all a parent. My mother winced, as if I had physically slapped her. I'd hurt her but I didn't care.

Mother looked toward the ceiling and blinked hard. "No, Mary Alice. Better than me. It's true. I had you too young. And Grandpapa did not approve. I had Paul when I was only eighteen, you a year later, and Tommy only two years after that. Is it so bad I want something more for my children? More of a life than dirty diapers and meals and housework?" She tried to reach for my hand again, but I pulled away. Mother pulled some papers from her handbag and set them on the table. "Your father and I have already signed these. We're giving consent for you to put the child up for adoption as soon as it's born."

I watched her swallow hard several times and her stiff back slumped a little. There was a catch in her voice I'd never heard before. "It's for the best, Mary Alice. It's best for you and for the baby. Think of him or her. Doesn't he deserve a family with a mother and a father, a mature family with means to take care of him?" Her voice dropped to a whisper. "Do the right thing, Mary Alice. Sign the papers."

Cold slithered down my spine. How could I give away my baby? Never. They couldn't make me do it. Could they? Charlie and I had our whole life planned out. We'd marry. We'd have a beautiful baby. Charlie would make furniture out in the garage until we could afford a real shop. I'd bring his lunch out to him every day while the baby napped. We were going to have the happily-ever-after. Give away our baby? No, no, this couldn't be happening. Not to me. Not to us. I closed my eyes and pictured our life together. If I could visualize it, it could come true.

When I refused to respond or acknowledge the conversation any further, my mother straightened her back, slipped her gloves back on, hooked her handbag over her arm and stood.

"I'll come by to pick you up . . . when it's all over. Mrs. Longsworth will notify me. Take care of yourself Mary Alice."

I watched the perfectly aligned seams of her stockings as she left. The adrenaline rush seeped out of me as quickly as it came, leaving me as deflated as a three-day-old balloon. Numb, I pushed at the papers with my index finger. Closer, closer to the edge of the table, until I watched them flutter to the floor. I couldn't wrap my mind around it. Charlie was really gone. I was expected to give away our baby. No questions. Facts. How could I have been so naive, so stupid? Why had I thought I'd have the happily-ever-after? Of course, I wouldn't. Girls like me, like the rest of the girls here, never got the happily-ever-after.

Ten

2017

"Oh Gram," said Bethany. "That's terrible. How could they do that to you?"

"It was a different time. They did what they thought was best. The important thing is things will be different for you. You'll be fine. You have your whole family supporting you."

Bethany picked at the cuticle on one of her fingernails until it bled. "Not Aunt Char."

"Not true. No matter what she says, I know she loves you, and she loves her brother and sister. You have to take Char with a grain of salt. She's a little intense, but she'll come around. She's finally accepted Uncle Evan and Ricky, at least as best we can ever expect from her. You need to understand she's been through some tough times too, and that's why she is the way she is. She means well."

Bethany kept picking at her nails and didn't look up. Mary Alice glanced up at the box on the mantle in the living room. *"Oh Charlie, think how different things would have been. Maybe Char would have felt more secure and never lost her way if I had spent more time with her, or if we had more support from our parents. Bethany doesn't know how good she has it. We wouldn't have wasted those three years apart. We'd still have our daughter. I know, woulda-coulda-shoulda doesn't get us anywhere. It's so hard not to compare. Or wonder what if."*

"Have you tried the internet to find your baby?"

Mary Alice looked away from the box and gave Bethany a weak smile. If only it was that easy. "She's hardly a baby anymore. I don't know anything about that internet thing. Your Papa was the one that used it. I simply dust it and let it be. It's too much for an old woman like me. I'm doing good to order food on that tablet thingy the kids bought for me."

"It's not hard Gram. I can show you. There is so much information you get on the web these days. And ...," she looked up hopefully, "if you find her, I can ask her what it's like to be adopted."

Mary Alice's heart skipped a beat. "Why? Are you thinking about putting your baby up for adoption?" *Please say no, please.*

"Yes . . . no . . . I don't know. Dad seems to think it's best."

Greg. Of course, Greg. "Sweetie, ultimately, it has to be your decision. It's something you have to live with the rest of your life . . . either way. Like me. And now? I wouldn't even know where to start looking."

"What about the home they sent you to? Have you tried to see if it still exists? Maybe they have records."

"I told you. Papa and I tried. They said the records were sealed."

Bethany stood and headed for the den. "Come on, Gram. Let's start with the home. See what we can find. What could it hurt?"

Heartache, lots of heartache. Opening these old wounds was a bad idea. Mentioning the place made the memories come swimming back to her. Mary Alice could almost see the little room she'd shared with Gladys and Sophia. She could smell the lemon polish she'd used on the furniture. Was Bethany right? Was there a chance now? Even Gladys had said the laws had changed since 1967, since she and Charlie had last tried to find their daughter. If the place still existed, would it mean girls were still being sent there and being forced to give up their babies? Did they still have records of all the births and adoptions? Did she dare hope there was still a chance to find her?

By the time Mary Alice reached the doorway to the den,

Bethany was already sitting in Charlie's chair behind the desk. Charlie's desk. *Pine*. She brushed her fingers across the wood. She rarely went in there anymore, except to dust and vacuum. His memory was so painful and fresh in there. She touched the arm of the chair where Bethany sat. She was drawn to his chair, the one place she could still smell him.

Bethany pressed the button on the computer tower at her feet. The screen began to spring to life. A blinking icon asked for a username. "What's the username, Gram?"

"I have no idea. Try his name. Charles Goodson." Accepted. The next screen asked for a password. What was it? Charlie's initials and birth date. Wrong. Mary Alice's initials and birth date. Wrong. They tried every combination they could think of: the kids' names, the kids' birthdays, they even tried Brutus' name and birthday. All wrong.

"I don't think we'll ever get it," Mary Alice sank into a straight chair beside Bethany, then leaned closer and breathed in the scent of Charlie's chair. *"Help me out here Charlie. What would you have used?"* The only person left to try was the baby. "Try BabyGirlMay271963"

The screen flashed to life. Bethany let out a little squeal. "Bingo!"

Out of all the passwords he could have picked, it was that one. What were the odds she would have the password in the right order? There must be hundreds of combinations that would convey the same thing. Maybe it was meant to be.

Mary Alice wiped at the corners of her eyes and watched as Bethany's fingers flew across the keyboard. She typed the words 'Florence Crittenton Home,' and dozens of links appeared on the screen. The top one was the national website.

"Wow. Look, Gram. They still exist."

Mary Alice moved closer so she could see the screen more clearly through her bifocals. The first thing that struck her was the smiling face of a young mother with her baby. The tag line read, "Changing lives, two at a time." Bethany clicked through to the history of the Home.

Charles Crittenton, the founder, had intended the homes to be a safe haven for girls and a place for them to learn to take care of their young.

Mary Alice sucked in a breath and blinked at the screen. Certainly not what they told her when she was there. How had things gone so astray from his purpose, so judgmental in the fifties and sixties? Mr. Crittenton's mission was back to its intended use. The smiling faces of young mothers with their babies gave testament to that.

"Look Gram, they've got homes all over the country."

Mary Alice bit her lip. All over the country. Hundreds, no, thousands of girls and their babies. Were they staying together? Happy? It was a good, beautiful thing. She was happy for them. Her stomach felt empty.

"Where was the home you were at?" Bethany asked.

"Right here." Mary Alice's knuckles ached as she unclenched her fists. "In Youngstown."

Bethany typed in "The Florence Crittenton Home for Unwed Mothers, Youngstown Ohio." A link opened, showing a view of the austere old Victorian building.

"Is that it, Gram?"

And there it was. Mary Alice closed her eyes. There was the black iron gate, the blades of grass poking through the uneven pavers, the austere Victorian house with gargoyles standing guard. She shook her head to come back to the present. She looked again at the structure on the screen. It didn't seem as foreboding and daunting. There was a playground in the background. A playground.

"Yes," she nodded. "But it looks so different." Bethany clicked through to read more. The About Us page boldly proclaimed they were 'giving young women and their children the tools to succeed.'

They clicked through the testimonials. Over and over, the mantra was the same.

'If I hadn't found Crittenton, I wouldn't be where I am today. They gave me a future and, most importantly, they gave my son a future too.' There was a picture below the testimonial of a young woman in her late twenties and a teenaged boy. The woman was holding up her degree with one hand, while the other held her smiling son close. They both looked so happy. A feeling a little like hope began to spring up in her, shoving past the cold decades of resentment.

"You should go there," Bethany said. "It looks so cool. Not at all like what you said. Can I go with you?"

Go there? To the one place that ruined her life? Why? They couldn't tell her where her child was. The records had been sealed. Unless Evan and Gladys were right, unless it wasn't too late.

"I don't know Bethany. This is a lot to think about."

Bethany's face dropped. "You still want to find her, don't you?"

"Always." Mary Alice answered breathlessly. She needed to get a better perspective on this. She needed her friends. "I'll think about it, Bethy, but I'm not making any promises."

"But why? I don't understand. It's a great idea. And there are other ways too."

Mary Alice looked at her granddaughter and let out a big sigh.

"Okay, Gram, but you can't give up on her."

Mary Alice could explain how so many things could go wrong. They could not have any information. Or they could and they weren't allowed to release them. Or they could try to connect them, and her daughter would reject her. How it would destroy her. She could tell her, but she wouldn't. She couldn't burden Bethany with her own problems.

Bethany stood and headed for the door. She rubbed her hand across her middle. "Think about it, promise?"

"I promise." Mary Alice kissed her cheek.

"Gotta run, Gram. Love ya."

Eleven

1963

As I polished the beautiful stair rail, *mahogany*, in the foyer, something in the front window caught my eye. The wrought-iron gate keeping people out, or people in, opened and a yellow school bus wound up the drive. We'd been told visitors were coming, this must be them. A whole load of them.

The bus came to a stop and the door opened. I couldn't believe my eyes. A group of young girls clad in green skirts and white blouses filed out of the bus and gathered in front of their leader. They wore sashes full of badges across their budding little chests. *Girl Scouts.*

Mrs. Longsworth met them at the door as I scooted past her toward the living room. I heard them shuffling through the hallway.

"Girls, this is the living room where our guests congregate," Mrs. Longsworth said. "We take great pride in making everyone as comfortable as possible. The Crittenton Home is the best solution for girls finding themselves in the family way without a husband."

I grabbed an out-of-date Life magazine from February with Alfred Hitchcock on the cover, pulled it close to my face, and hunkered down. From the corner of the magazine, I saw the other girls sitting around the TV had turned their backs to the scouts as well.

"Can we talk to them?" one of the girls asked.

"Shh, shh," their leader said. "These unfortunate young girls are not here for your entertainment."

That was for sure. The question was, why were they here? If this was going to be a sideshow of don't-do-what-these-girls-did, I didn't want any part of it. Mrs. Longsworth didn't even have the decency to let us know ahead of time we were the main attraction. It was humiliating. The girls were whispering among themselves and some even pointed at us. My ears burned and I slunk lower in the chair. I had to get out of there. There was no escape without heading straight into them in the hall. How was it this place could make me feel so bad about myself and my baby?

"Do they get to keep their babies?" another girl asked.

"It's in the child's best interest to put it up for adoption at birth," Mrs. Longsworth said.

I cringed at her calling my baby an 'it.' I wanted to scream. He's not an "it", he's a baby.

Mrs. Longsworth continued. "If these girls had husbands at home to support them, they wouldn't be in this situation. A child deserves a Christian, moral home with both a mother and a father."

"What if they are Jewish?"

"Well, the Crittenton home is a Christian home, but we do our best to find a suitable Jewish family if the birth mother's parents' wishes. Now, let's move on to the kitchen, then to the guest rooms."

The parents' wishes? What about the birth mother's wishes?

I breathed a sigh of relief when they finally left. "What was that all about?" I asked the girls around the television. "Does this happen all the time?"

Sheila shook her head. "First for us. But I heard from one of the girls sometimes they 'put us on display.' I guess this is what she meant."

One of the girls beside the television burst into tears. "How dare they do that to us? We're not animals in a zoo for them to gawk at."

Another girl laughed. "I wonder what type of badge

79

they earn for that? A virgin badge, for learning how not to end up like us?"

"What would that badge look like?" Sophia asked. "V for virgin or virtuous or vagina? I bet the badge would have a V with a red slash through it, like a no crossing sign." Sophia crossed the V on her left hand with a slash with an index finger on her right and burst into laughter.

My face flamed and I dropped my gaze while the other girls bowled over laughing.

Everyone made the sign with their own hands. Everyone except me. I glanced over my shoulder as if my mother or father were there. Of course, they weren't. But they'd definitely not approve.

Truthfully, I wanted to embrace the girls' new-found symbol of defiance, but sixteen years of training in submissiveness made it almost unthinkable. "My mother's hair would turn pure white from shock if she heard us talk like this. She'd call it heresy or sacrilegious." I giggled into my hand. "Might be kind of funny to see it though."

"Well, well," Sophia said. "Is Little-Miss-Goody-Two-Shoes finally going to admit she is just as knocked-up as the rest of us? You dropped your drawers like everyone else here."

My ears burned and I chewed on a cuticle. "Um, I never meant to . . ."

"We know," Sheila said. "Don't let her get to you," nodding toward Sophia, "We understand exactly how you feel. Most of us never dreamed we'd end up here."

No matter how nicely Sheila tried to smooth things over, Sophia didn't lie. Who did I think I was kidding? What made me any different from the other girls here? Maybe I had Charlie, but that didn't mean I was any better than them. The shame of my judgement of these girls settled in my gut. "Sophia is right. I'm no better than any of you. And I apologize if I came across that way. This is all so new to me."

I caught Sophia smiling from the other side of the room, not laughing at me, but with me. I raised my hands and gave her the V sign, even as I felt my cheeks flush.

Twelve

2017

Mary Alice smoothed her hair in the rearview mirror before she turned the ignition and pulled the car from the garage.

Breathe. Mar, you can do this.

"I'm going, I'm going."

Mary Alice pointed her car north. She passed through downtown Youngstown, which was attempting yet another revitalization. She continued up Wick Avenue past the shiny new-looking Youngstown University. At the right turn onto McGuffey Road, her chest constricted. She gripped the steering wheel to stop her hands from trembling. When that didn't work, she pulled off to the side of the road and parked. She didn't want to be sick. Deep breaths, Gladys would say. She closed her eyes. Inhale, one, two, three. Hold, one, two, three. Exhale, one, two, three.

It didn't help much, but at least she wasn't afraid of losing her breakfast anymore. She looked around at the neighborhood. Elegant homes, mansions really, stood quiet and ghost-like, captured in a time long past. Some had boarded windows, and some were obviously converted into apartments. A few had huge Greek symbols on the front lawn. All the big executives that lived in this neighborhood were long gone. First the closing of the steel mills, then later, the car plant, had turned Youngstown's economy upside down. Only the university, which grew from a small community college to a state university, kept the town alive now.

Go ahead, Mar. You'll be fine.

She turned into the drive and stopped at the wrought-iron fence around the property. It was the same as she remembered, but the gate at the entrance was missing. She hadn't noticed on the website. No locks to keep people in or out. The sign on the fence had changed as well. In big, bold letters, it read, 'The Florence Crittenton Home, Founded in 1928.' No mention of unwed mothers. Different from the sign she had seen when she and Charlie had come back looking for answers in 1967.

Mary Alice put the car in park at the edge of the drive and stared through the pillars that once held the heavy gates. Her entire life had changed because of this place. She didn't know how to feel; angry, sad, or grateful her parents hadn't thrown her out into the street with nowhere to turn.

Then I'd have had Charlie, her heart said.

Not necessarily, her brain argued. They could have still sent him away.

She stared past the drive to the Home. It could hold all her answers. Was she ready to find out?

"*Charlie, are you ready?*" She maneuvered the car up the drive, heart pounding in her ears.

The pavers had been replaced with stamped concrete, the direction now curvy and inviting. It led to a spacious parking lot full of cars, a bike rack with shiny new bicycles, some with baby seats attached. She recognized the playground from the pictures on the website. It was full of small children. Mary Alice pulled into an empty spot marked Visitor. The sign was like a slap to the face. She watched the children, counting them and then recounting them as they shrieked and ran around. Was she stalling? Probably.

This didn't seem like such a good idea anymore. Especially without making an appointment. Pulling down the visor mirror, she patted at her hair. She wasn't decent enough to do this. She should have had her hair done. She looked down at her dress. It was all wrong. She placed her hands on the steering wheel to back out of the drive.

Mary Alice breathed deeply and let go of the wheel. No,

she wouldn't leave, she needed a minute.

The ever-trusty spiral notebook appeared from her bag. She read over her last entry, stalling or trying to find strength in it. The words blurred on the page and she took a deep, shuddering breath. No. She wouldn't procrastinate, she wouldn't find her bravery in the pages. If she didn't get out the car right now, she might drive away. Now or never.

Don't quit now Mar. You've come this far. Do it.

Mary Alice tucked the notebook back in her bag.

She stepped from the car, steadied herself for a moment, then placed one foot in front of the other. She made her way up the drive, pulling her coat tighter around her. The gargoyles that had set on either side of the expansive steps had been replaced with cherubs. Good. Those awful things probably would have scared the dickens out of children.

She climbed the stairs, half expecting Mrs. Longsworth to be standing at the top, arms crossed over her bosom, mouth pinched in disapproval. Instead, the door opened to a smiling teenage girl in jeans with a chubby, round infant on her hip. "Hi. Are you looking for someone?"

What an understatement. She'd been looking for fifty-four years. "Um, yes, I mean no. Not someone who would be here now." That had come out all wrong. "I'm looking for information."

The girl nodded. "Come on in. I'll find you Estelle." Mary Alice followed her in.

The girl pointed to the room to the right of the hall. "You can wait in here if you like." She ran a hand over the toddler's blond curls. "Want to go for a walk with Mommy? Let's go find Auntie Stelly." She set the child down and took his hand as he toddled away with her.

Mary Alice took three steps onto the long Aubusson carpet runner in the hall, her eyes immediately drawn to the beautiful staircase, *mahogany*. She stepped into the room, holding her purse in a death-grip. The very same room she had been deposited in on the first day she'd arrived. Naturally, the furniture had changed after all this time, all but the old armoire in the corner, *walnut*, as beautiful as ever. The room had a comfortable, lived-in feel now. It was a happy room with soft colors and fabrics, framed photos of mothers and babies, and a toy box nestled in the corner.

"Hello," a voice came from behind her. "I'm Estelle Zellers. May I help you?"

Mary Alice turned. Estelle Zellers was no Mrs. Longsworth. Her dark hair was pulled loosely into a low pony-tail. She had creamy mocha skin with a hint of gloss on her lips and long, shapely legs in cream capris over knee-high brown leather boots. She wore a gauzy blouse of periwinkle blue. She extended a slender hand and a warm smile.

Mary Alice caught herself staring. "I'm sorry. You're not what . . . I mean, you're not who . . . oh dear. I must sound like a bumbling idiot."

"Phf. Don't worry about it. You wouldn't believe the state I've seen women in when they arrive here. I'm the house mother. Can I get you a cool drink or some coffee?" Estelle glanced over to a small fridge next to a bookcase filled with picture books.

"No, no thank you." She'd had it all planned out, exactly what she was going to say. She had practiced it over and over again in her mind. Now it was completely blank.

Estelle raised a perfectly shaped eyebrow. "Mrs. . . . Mrs. I didn't get your name."

"Goodson. Mary Alice Goodson." She felt heat rise to her cheeks. She was acting like an old fool.

"Well, Mrs. Goodson. Please have a seat, and you can call me Estelle." Estelle breezed across the room and sat in an overstuffed chair, the air whooshing out of it when she sat. She nodded toward the high-back sofa.

"Mary Alice. You can call me Mary Alice." Thank God, she at least knew her name. She sat on the edge of the cushion; hands pressed together in her lap. "Um, Estelle, I wanted to know . . . I mean I wanted to find out . . . ugh, is it possible to find . . ."

"Find?" Estelle's face brightened. "So, you're trying to find someone? Do you have a relative, perhaps a daughter or granddaughter here?"

Mary Alice thought of Bethany. Bethany could be here, but Mary Alice would never allow that. No matter how improved the place appeared now.

"No, someone from a long time ago."

Estelle nodded, the smile slipping from her face. "Mary Alice, may I be so bold as to ask if you were a guest here at one time? It's not unusual to have past guests show up here looking for answers."

Did it show? Did she have some sort of invisible imprint marking her as an unwed mother? She thought of the V symbol. Did she act guilty? She nodded, ever so slightly. The all too familiar knot settled in her stomach. She never should have let it happen, let them take her baby. It was all her fault. She could have, should have fought harder, stood up to her parents, to her in-laws-to-be, to the pressures from this home.

"Ah," Estelle nodded. "I thought so. What year were you here?"

"1963."

Estelle's glossed lips turned down. "Oh my. I wasn't even born then, but I know the history of this place. As I recall, the fifties and sixties were a rather dark time here. A very puritanical and judgmental part of our history which we would rather forget."

All Mary Alice could do was nod. The room was instantly warm. Perspiration broke out on her lip and ran down the back of her dress. She sucked in a deep breath. Don't get sick. Don't pass out.

"Mrs. Goodson . . . Mary Alice, are you all right? You seem flushed." Estelle stood and reached into the fridge, bringing out a bottle of water. "Here, have some of this."

Mary Alice accepted the water and took a small sip, hoping it would make it past the huge lump in her throat.

"Things are very different here now," Estelle said. "I've been the house mother here for about ten years. We have some amazing programs for our girls. Skills training, not only in motherhood, but job skills, and self-worth. So many of our girls come here thinking it's the end of their lives, that they'd ruined any chance of a happy future. I take it as my personal responsibility they leave here happy, healthy, and ready to take on the world."

Her prattling gave Mary Alice the break she needed to get a grip on her emotions. "Yes, I can see that, even at first glance." Then in a softer voice, "much, much different."

"Well," Estelle brightened. "I'm proud to say those days are in the past. Girls today get every opportunity to succeed, as parents and young adults."

Mary Alice nodded and scrambled to find something to say. Could she actually find her daughter? Probably not. It could still be like last time.

Silence stretched between them before Estelle cleared her throat.

How rude. Mary Alice didn't mean to drop the conversation so suddenly. Her father would have been appalled at the behavior. She dabbed at her forehead with a tissue. Her mind was like a page full of indecipherable scribbles. Had Estelle been talking and she missed it all? "Excuse me?" she finally squeaked out.

"Mary Alice." Estelle had the kindest smile, "Would you like a tour?"

A tour? Yes, she would like a tour. Maybe the ghosts would disappear if she faced them head on.

Estelle stood. "Okay then, let's do this. Let's start outside." She grabbed a wool plaid poncho off a peg and slipped it over her head.

Mary Alice followed her out the massive front door, *oak*, and around the wrap-around porch to a new set of stairs, leading into the playground.

"Many of our moms have jobs, and finding affordable daycare is near impossible for entry level employees. We offer free daycare to any of our mothers until the kiddos reach school age, or until they don't need us anymore. It's hard enough to get a start without worrying about who's taking care of your child and if they are safe."

Four little boys chased each other around, laughing and trying to tag each other with a big red rubber ball. Two little girls sat on a blanket under a maple tree, Barbie dolls and clothes scattered about. Others played on the swings or in the sand box. The cool weather did not seem to deter the children from having fun. Off in the corner, three teens bounced babies on their laps, like any happy playground anywhere in town.

"Do the mothers stay here after their babies are born?"

"A few. Most of them don't stay here at all. A larger percentage stay at home with their parents and come here for school, counseling, skills training, and daycare."

Mary Alice followed Estelle back inside and found herself in the old living room. A memory of her mother sitting at the round table, hands folded on top of her white gloves and patent leather handbag, telling her to give up her child, flashed before her eyes. She searched for the round table, *oak*, by the window they had sat at. To her surprise, it was still there, but now it was covered in white butcher paper, little handprints streaked across it in red, blue, and green. The paint reached the elbows of a little boy with flaming curls covered by a paper Indian headdress. He smiled and waved. A teen with the same fiery locks grinned as she leaned over the child.

"Auntie Stelly, look, look what I'm making."

Estelle walked over and admired the artwork. "Great job, Casey. Is that a turkey?"

He grinned and nodded, the paper headdress slipping down over his eyes.

Estelle smiled at the teen. "How's it going today, Jenny?" She tipped her head toward Mary Alice. "Jenny, I'd like you to meet a new friend of mine. This is Mrs. Goodson."

Jenny wiped her hand on a damp cloth and offered it to shake.

"Call me Mary Alice."

"Mary Alice used to live here when she was about your age, and I'm giving her a tour."

Jenny's eyes traveled up and down Mary Alice's body and her mouth dropped open. Mary Alice could almost see her trying to calculate her age.

"Seriously? Cool."

Wasn't so cool then. "Well, that was a long time ago. You've got a nice setup here now."

"You bet. I don't know what I would have done without the FC," said Jenny.

"FC?"

"Florence Crittenton," Estelle explained. "You've got to learn the lingo to keep up around here. It's like Morse code."

Mary Alice laughed. She could almost see the street-wise young Sophia making the V sign, their own code back then too. "I understand. I have two daughters and a son, and one teenage granddaughter. They're even teaching me to text."

Estelle shook her head, her dark eyes dancing with laughter. Her ponytail swished across her shoulders. "New way of communication, but it's instant and successful. Best invention since the telephone." She waved her mobile phone in the air. She slipped her poncho off and led Mary Alice to the stairs.

Charlie never did get to see that spectacular piece of wood. Magnificent detail. Same shiny banister. *Mahogany*.

They reached the top of the stairs and turned right, toward the East room: the room she shared with Sophia and Gladys. Her heart picked up its pace. If she looked in that room, would she see the stain of blood on the wood floor where Gladys tried to kill herself? Hopefully, it would only remind her of the place she found her best friends.

Estelle opened the door but didn't step into the room. She gestured for Mary Alice to lean in and peek. The walls were lined with desks holding an array of laptops and tablets. Six chairs graced either side of the room. Two girls were busy pecking away on keyboards and didn't look up. They were both wearing headsets and couldn't quite pull their chairs up to the counter due to mounds around their middles.

"This is our computer lab, and that's Crystal and Amy. They're taking online courses so they can graduate with their class. They are residents here. I'd rather not disturb them."

The room she'd occupied with Sophia and Gladys for three long months was gone. The only thing recognizable was the small window too high to look out of. She tried to picture the bland room with the three narrow beds and tiny dressers. It was a blur. It was much better this way. The butterflies in her stomach disappeared. Mary Alice nodded, and they proceeded down the hall. They passed some open doorways that looked more like dorm rooms from the local college. Each was bright and sunny, with loads of personal belongings hanging on walls, stuffed onto dressers, dropped on the floor.

Another couple of rooms had beds and cribs in them. Mary Alice admired the soft colors, the rocking chair in the corner, the changing table by the door. "This looks like a lovely place to live."

"We try. Some of our girls come from some pretty rough places. Not every parent can accept their daughter is about to become a mother."

You can say that again.

"For those girls, they come here. They can stay as long as they want, though our goal is to make them self-sustaining young adults within a year or two after their baby's birth."

Estelle took Mary Alice back downstairs and led her into her office. The same office Mrs. Longsworth had occupied. This room hadn't changed much except for the construction paper handprint turkeys gracing the walls. Same desk, *oak*, in the middle of the room, same grey metal file cabinets against one wall.

Mary Alice's eyes fixed on the metal drawers.

"Your answers aren't in there," Estelle said sorrowfully.

"Excuse me?"

Estelle pointed to the cabinet. "In there. What you came here for is not in there."

Mary Alice sank into one of the chairs. "They're not?" All her hopes and dreams were dashed in those few little words. A heaviness settled in her stomach. She would never know.

"I failed, Charlie. I'm sorry."

Estelle handed her a box of tissues. Until that moment, Mary Alice hadn't realized she was crying. "Those records only go back to 1975. The year before, a vandal, or one of the girls, who knows — someone made a bonfire of all the files. From what I heard, what wasn't destroyed by fire was ruined by water when the fire department showed up."

It was then Mary Alice noticed part of a black charred floor peeking out from under a new modern rug. She stood on trembling legs. She shouldn't have bothered. She wouldn't find her baby. "I'm sorry to have bothered you. Thank you for the tour."

"Wait, there is still hope. Have you checked the state adoption agency? Court records?"

"We, my husband and I, tried the court records about three years after . . ." Her words trailed off. "We were told the adoption was sealed and there was nothing we could do about it. I was hoping . . ."

She couldn't grasp the right words. There was nothing she could say that would make her any less of a horrible mother. She shouldn't be there with all of those happy children and the mothers that made the right choices. Her lip started to tremble. Mary Alice didn't bother explaining or asking Estelle what she meant, she knew she had to get out of there. She turned and headed for the door, pushing herself to make it to the car before she lost all control.

"Don't give up, Mary Alice. Try the Ohio Adoption Agency. There are new rules. I'm not sure what they can do, but it's worth a try."

"Thank you," Mary Alice managed in a whisper.

She crumbled the minute she made it to the car. Her body convulsed with wracking sobs. She wanted to scream but her throat felt strangled. Why had they waited so long? Why did they let this happen? *Where was her daughter?*

Thirteen

2017

Estelle's words stuck in Mary Alice's mind, *try the Ohio Adoption Agency*. She'd been mulling it over for two days. She'd talked herself in and out of it a dozen times. Each time she was convinced it was too late and would only open old wounds, but a niggling in her soul told her it wasn't. What was the worst that could happen? She'd be exactly where she was now. If she ever wanted to get some sleep, she had to try. But she had no idea how to begin. The computer still loomed as big as the Pacific Ocean, of which she had never seen but imagined so massive it was incomprehensible. Cautiously, almost as if it was going to attack, Mary Alice approached the computer on Charlie's desk. Her finger lingered over the On button on the tower. Taking a deep breath, she pressed it and waited for the screen to pop up with a landscape of some unknown place.

The center screen blinked with a bar asking for the password. BabyGirlMay271963. She smiled to herself and poked at the letters and numbers on the keyboard with her index finger. The cursor blinked at the top of the screen. Her fingers felt foreign on the keypad. She told herself it was no different than a typewriter, which she hadn't used in more time than she could remember. Her fingers hovered over the letters and she slowly began to type 'Ohio Adoption Agency.' Several options appeared on the screen. She clicked on the first one. Ugh. It brought up another list of optional sites. So confusing. One read

'Adoption Agency in Ohio - Free Application.' The second read 'Private Adoption Agency, Explore All Options.' The third, 'Birth Mother Adoption Program.' None of them looked like what she needed. They all appeared to be private sites, not one central agency she was hoping to find.

An hour into the search and frustrated beyond belief, she finally stumbled on the Ohio Department of Health. A page took her to an overview of what records were available divided by years: 1996 to Present, 1964-1996, and prior to 1964. She clicked on the last. As she read, her heart slowed. In the case of adoption, the child (now adult) or his or her descendants could request copies of the birth certificate. No mention of the birth mother being able to request the information. She clicked on the form. Same thing. It appeared only the adopted child had any right to the birth certificate, not the birth parents. There was a form the birth parents could submit allowing the state to release his or her contact information with the child, but it required a name. That was the point — she didn't have a name. There was a phone number to call at the bottom of the screen. (555) 466-2531. The cuckoo clock chimed. Mary Alice looked up. Where had the time gone? She scratched the number onto the back envelope of a past due bill and turned off the computer. If she didn't hurry, she'd be late for her lunch date with Ellie and her family.

Mary Alice arrived at the Elmton on 5th Street before the Proctors. Known for the best pizza in Struthers, she enjoyed the sweet aroma of the rising bread, the tang of the garlic in the tomato sauce. The place was far from fancy, and it only had room for about a dozen tables, but it was close, the food was excellent, and the atmosphere, casual and friendly. She took a table for four by the window and watched the foot travelers bundled in winter garb. Fall had only begun and even if the calendar claimed it to be so, Mother Nature was notoriously unpredictable in Ohio. The server had set a warm mug of hot chocolate in front of her when the Proctors arrived.

"Hey, Mom." Ellie leaned in, gave Mary Alice a peck on the cheek, and slipped into a chair across from her. Mary

Alice observed the small family dynamic. Ellie's face was fixed with determination. She had something on her mind to discuss. Bethany only briefly made eye contact with a weak hello to her grandmother before she busied herself with her cell phone. Greg offered a perfunctory squeeze to her shoulder before taking his seat. He ordered beers for himself and Ellie and a Coke for Bethany.

"It's been a while," Mary Alice started. "Everything okay?"

"Better than okay," Ellie said. "We spoke to —"

"Can we at least order first?" Greg interrupted, frowning at his wife. He turned to Bethany. "And put that thing away. No electronics at the table, you know that."

Bethany grunted without answering and stuck her phone into her jeans pocket.

Okay. Mary Alice sensed a little tension. The server took their order for two large pizzas, one pepperoni and sausage, and one white. She looked across the table at Ellie. "Have you heard from your sister? She's been especially quiet since our family meeting. I haven't heard a word. Of course, it's not unusual for her to go weeks without calling me. But I thought the two of you . . ."

Bethany looked up from the slice of pizza on her plate she was picking at and grimaced.

"No," Ellie said. "Not a word. I guess she is still upset with all the news." She made air quotes around the word. "Speaking of which, we have some good news to share."

Greg chugged his beer and Bethany resorted to dissecting her pizza like a surgeon.

"We met with the Myers — you know, Trent's parents."

Mary Alice raised an eyebrow in response and bit into her pizza to keep from interrupting, a bad habit the whole family seemed to adhere to.

"Trent's dad was one of those guys laid off at the Lordstown plant. Things are tight for them. They can't afford the expense of a child, or an attorney for a lawsuit against Greg. They are putting all their hopes into Trent getting a pro football contract after college. They can't risk him losing his scholarship at OSU over a scandal."

Mary Alice nodded. "So, what about Bethany? He should show some responsibility with child support, even if he is barely an adult."

"We . . .," Ellie looked across over at Greg. "We felt it was a fair trade off if they agreed to drop the charges against Greg and have Trent give up his parental rights to the baby. Then we would not pursue child support. A win-win for everyone."

Bethany slunk lower in her seat. "Except my baby . . .who now has no daddy and no money. They sold us out to keep Trent quiet about Dad punching him."

"Bethy," Ellie said with that mother-tone everyone recognized so well. "We've talked about this. If Greg isn't ready to be a father, then this is the right course of action. Now *you* can make all the decisions on our baby."

Bethany bristled. "Our baby? Since when did he become our baby? Seems to me you weren't even sure if I should keep him. Me, make decisions? Since when? I haven't made one decision. It's all been you and Dad. Does anyone even care what I think?"

Before anyone could answer, Mary Alice's phone rang in her purse. She ignored the ring. Bethany was taking a stand for herself. Mary Alice wanted to cheer.

The table went quiet. Greg's pizza was halfway to his mouth. Ellie looked like she could be knocked over by a feather.

"Bethany —" Ellie started.

"No!" Bethany shouted. People were staring now. "*You* don't get to decide." She jumped up, knocking over the chair before storming off to the bathroom.

The ring resounded again in Mary Alice's purse, rattling her nerves and vibrating from her handbag. She couldn't ignore this. It had to be an emergency. She looked first at Ellie, then to Greg. "I'm sorry," she said while reaching for the phone. She raised a finger to indicate, just-a-minute, and walked away from the table to a small hall leading to the kitchen.

"Hello?"

"Mrs. Goodson, this is Steve Willoughby. I am . . . er . . . was Charlie's accountant. I've been putting together the paperwork to file the quarterly taxes on the business and . . . well . . . I have some things I think I should discuss with you."

"Things?" Mary Alice knew nothing about the financial aspect of the business. Her mind raced back to the bleak checking and saving account. "What kinds of things?"

"Can we schedule an appointment for one day week after next? At my office?" Mr. Willoughby sounded as anxious to end this conversation as she was.

"Certainly. What about the Wednesday after Thanksgiving?"

"Fine. Ten o'clock then?"

"Mr. Willoughby? Your address?" It was embarrassing to admit she didn't know the address of the man who had more knowledge of her personal finances than she did.

"Oh, I'm sorry. I thought . . . oh, never mind. My office is in the City Center in Youngstown, 25 W. Boardman Street, Unit 412."

"Oh, yes, of course, it must have slipped my mind. Thank you. See you then. And Happy Thanksgiving." Mary Alice hit the disconnect button and stared at the phone. She was sure she had never been to Mr. Willoughby's office in her life. This had to have something to do with the missing money. Thank God, he'd be able to explain it. Surely there was a simple answer. Why had she never asked a single thing about their finances? She'd blindly gone along, totally trusting in Charlie to handle everything. Well, she needn't worry. She made her way back to the table.

"Everything all right?" Ellie asked, eyes narrowing toward her mother.

"Um . . . I think so. That was Steve Willoughby, your dad's accountant. He said there are some things he needs to discuss with me about the business."

"Like what?"

"Something about quarterly taxes. I made an appointment with him for the Wednesday after Thanksgiving."

"Do you want me to go with you? Drive you?" Ellie said.

"No, no. I can drive myself." Mary Alice looked down at the now cold piece of pizza, practically untouched on her plate.

Joanne Simon Tailele

Her mind buzzed with unanswered questions. Between Trent Myers and Mr. Willoughby, her head was pounding. "You know, I've lost my appetite. Is there more we need to discuss?" She glanced toward the bathroom where Bethany still had not appeared.

Ellie shook her head. "No, we'll handle Bethany. We . . . I thought this was going to be a pleasant lunch over good news. Maybe I underestimated her." Her eyes followed Mary Alice's to the bathroom door.

"Okay then." Mary Alice rose. "I think I'll go." It was nice of them to update her on the situation with the Myers, but really, she had no say in any of it anyway.

Mary Alice saw Bethany returning to the table, her eyes red and swollen. "Well, I am glad Trent dropped the charges. None of us need more drama." Ellie rose and gave her a kiss on the cheek.

Mary Alice passed Bethany by the door. "It's going to be fine, sweetie. Come over soon and we'll bake cookies together. Or maybe you can teach me how to do that texting thing, or how to use the interface better."

A slight smile spread across Bethany's face. "Internet, Gram, not interface. I'll see you soon."

Fourteen

2017

Bethany had become a regular visitor at her house, clearly more comfortable around Mary Alice than her parents. The company was nice, and it filled the silent house with noise, but Charlie's voice was still distinctly absent.

"Gram," Bethany said over marble cake and a huge glass of milk. "What do you think about me staying home after the baby is born? Not go back to school."

Had she made the decision to keep the baby? Good. Was that her decision or Ellie and Greg's? Mary Alice wasn't sure. "Where else would you go, sweetie? And you'll need an education."

Bethany's face darkened. "I don't know. I could get a job, get an apartment, take care of the baby by myself."

"That's one idea." Mary Alice had to tread lightly so she didn't lose the confidence Bethany now had in her. "How do you see that working? Who would watch the baby while you worked or went to school?" She sounded like her parents, fifty years ago.

If it was possible for Bethany's shoulders to droop lower, they did. "I don't know."

"I'm sure your mom and dad are willing to help you. It's a lot of work taking care of a baby. You still need to finish school so you can go to college."

"Do you really think I'll be able to go to college someday? Mom acts like I'm nothing but a loser now, even though she says all the right things. And Dad doesn't talk to me at all. I know they are disappointed in me. I've ruined all their plans, and mine."

The last thing Mary Alice wanted was to get between her daughter and her granddaughter, but she would not stand by and let Bethany be bullied into what Greg felt was best. She hoped Ellie was strong enough to stand up to him. "Sweetie, plans change. That's life. Nobody's life goes exactly as planned. You have to go with the flow. Your mom and dad will be fine, and you'll be glad to have them around when the time comes."

Bethany leaned her chin on the palm of her hand, elbows resting on the kitchen table. "I see it already. They've already made all the decisions about me and they'll make all the decisions about the baby. Nobody asks me what I want. I won't have any say at all after the baby is born. What if I want to raise him differently than they raised me? What if I have my own ideas? They'll never treat me like an adult."

What she said was probably true. In Ellie and Greg's eyes, Bethany would always be their baby. It would be a long time before they would be able to see her for the young adult she was turning into.

Bethany looked at her with sorrowful, but hopeful eyes. "I wish I could stay here with you after the baby is born."

Whoa. As much as Mary Alice loved Bethany, she was pushing seventy. How could she help raise a baby? Pure nonsense. On the other hand, she couldn't turn her back on her either. She'd promised to stick by her. If she turned her away, it would sound like a rejection. She thought about the girls at the Crittenton home with their headsets on, leaning over computers. They were getting an education. And the children had daycare after the girls gave birth. Would Bethany consider this? Was she really considering sending her granddaughter to the place she gave up her child? *But it wasn't the same place*, she argued with herself.

"Um . . . Bethany. I was going to tell you. I went to the Crittenton Home."

Bethany's eyes got large. "You did? Without me? I

thought I was going to go with you."

"I thought it was best if I took a look on my own first. You know Honey, the girls there were studying for their diplomas, and some who already had their babies were preparing for jobs so they could take care of them on their own."

She scrunched up her nose. "Gram, are you saying you want me to go there? I don't need to go to school. I can be a mom without that, and I can get a job too. Why would you want to send me someplace you hated? Because you don't want me either?" Her face dropped and she blinked away tears.

Mary Alice put a hand on her shoulder. "Of course not, I am not trying to get rid of you. I love you. But I saw wonderful opportunities there, opportunities that did not exist when I was there. It's not the same place at all. Trust me, you do need a diploma at the very least. Perhaps you should discuss it with your parents. Go and take a look at the place yourself. I was very impressed."

"I don't know. Seems like they are just more people telling me what to do."

Mary Alice smiled. "Advice is not a bad thing. You admitted not too long ago that you did not know what to do. At least look at all your options before you make any decision, especially like dropping out of school."

"Okay, Gram. I'll think about it. I'll see you on Thanksgiving." She closed the door a little too hard as she left.

Mary Alice watched the little red pickup truck speed away. Oh boy. She hoped Bethany made the right choice. Dropping out wasn't the answer, and neither was living with Mary Alice.

Fifteen

Thanksgiving, 2017

Mary Alice was up at five a.m. to get the turkey stuffed and in the oven for Thanksgiving dinner. After she slid it in to bake, she sat at the kitchen table drinking a cup of tea and thinking about past holidays.

By an hour past noon, the food was almost done and the house smelled divine. The roasted turkey was still in the oven and the pumpkin pies were cooling on the counter.

When the phone rang, Mary Alice glanced at the caller ID and smiled when her granddaughter's name flashed across the screen.

"Happy Thanksgiving, Gram," her voice was cheerful when Mary Alice answered. "Can we come over a little early? I've thought about it and I want to tell Mom and Dad about the Crittenton home. But I need you with me. You can tell them what you saw."

Mary Alice looked at the clock on the stove. "Sure, sweetie. Dinner is at four. You can all come over anytime you want. Most of the work is done, but I can use your and your mom's help with the last-minute items anyway."

"Cool," Bethany said. She sounded upbeat and excited. Mary Alice hoped she meant she'd decided to stay in school one way or another.

The Proctors arrived around one and they gathered around the kitchen table. Greg appeared agitated, twirling a pencil between his fingers. From her conversations with Bethany, it appeared he still was not talking to her. He couldn't keep avoiding her, he was her father.

Mary Alice placed coffee cups in front of the adults and a soda can in front of Bethany. Ellie nodded at her daughter. "Okay, Bethany, we're all here. What is it you wanted to talk about?" Mary Alice gave Bethany an encouraging nod.

"Well, I'm a little worried about how things would work if I stay home and have the baby."

"As if you have any other options," Greg scoffed.

Bethany shot Mary Alice a look that read, *see what I mean?*

"Greg," Ellie cautioned, "give Bethany a chance to talk."

"Well, Gram gave me another idea." All heads turned to look at Mary Alice.

"Gram said I could go to school at the Crittenton home with other girls like me."

Ellie's mouth dropped open. "That place where you gave up your baby? Mom, what are you thinking? Are you implying Bethany should give —"

"No, no," Mary Alice protested. "You see." She fiddled with a napkin. "I went to the Home last week. To see if I could get any new information . . . about your sister."

"And did you?"

"No, but that's not the point here. What I saw was a lot of young girls in the same situation as Bethany. They were attending school there and getting job training and childcare."

"Yea," interrupted Bethany. "And I looked it up online. It's pretty cool. I know you don't want me to drop out of school —"

"Not an option," Greg said gruffly.

"Sooo," Bethany continued. "I'd like you to go with me to check it out. See what you think." She looked over at Ellie. "How about it, Mom?"

Greg harrumphed. "I don't want our daughter in an institution. This is absurd."

Ellie looked at Mary Alice. "Would she have to live there? I'm not sure about that. What about the baby?" Her eyes went to Greg. "I thought we decided to keep the baby."

"*I* am keeping the baby—not you!" Bethany pounded a fist on the table. "And no, I do not have to live there, but can if I want to."

Mary Alice needed the tone to simmer down. "It is only an option. I am for anything Bethany agrees to, especially if it keeps her in school."

Ellie nodded. "Well, I guess we could at least look at it. Right Greg?"

Greg mumbled something unintelligible but gave a reluctant shrug.

"Great," said Bethany, suddenly back to smiling. "We can set up an appointment on Monday."

Mary Alice breathed a sigh of relief. At least one hurdle over. What they decided to do as a family was up to them. "So, how about some help with mashing the potatoes?"

Her house smelled just as it should, the scent of cloves, nutmeg, pumpkin, and roasting turkey. Ellie and Bethany had helped Mary Alice set the table, and it was exquisite: autumn colored tablecloths, gleaming china and crystal.

Mary Alice swallowed a lump the size of a turkey leg when she viewed the seating arrangement around the formal dining room table. She'd been avoiding it since this morning. There was a chair on one end and four others on each side. The chair on the far end was conspicuously missing. Charlie's spot. Everything felt wrong. Charlie missing. Maybe Char, too. She hadn't called Mary Alice back since Bethany made the announcement. They should all be around her table, with Charlie in the kitchen sampling everything. *Get out of the way,* she should be saying, *you're going to burn your fingers sticking it in the gravy like that.* But there was no Charlie to shoo out of her kitchen, no Papa to beat the girls in a game of chess, no number eleven to tickle the back of her neck with a kiss when her hands were too occupied to swat him away. How was she ever going to get through this first holiday without him? Or the next, or the next?

The doorbell rang, interrupting the moment.

"I'll get it," Ellie patted Mary Alice's hands and stood before striding out of the dining room. Maybe it was Char.

Instead, Mary Alice heard the sound of her son's voice bouncing through the house and her shoulders dropped. Charlie was already missing, and the thought of having another empty chair for dinner made everything feel even more wrong.

She'll come, Mar.

Charlie was right. She would never miss a holiday, even if she was angry. She was running late, that was all.

Mary Alice wiped her eyes with her palms and patted her cheeks to bring some color back into them. Regardless of who was and wasn't here yet, she wouldn't be a neglectful hostess to the rest of her family. Mary Alice stood, forcing a smile she didn't feel as she walked into the kitchen. Ellie and Evan were facing the counter, away from Mary Alice. Evan was loaded down with apple crumb cake, green bean casserole, and a tin of Snickerdoodles.

"Happy Thanksgiving!" He wrapped his long arms around Mary Alice and she held onto him. "Rough day, I hear." He muttered, so quiet only she could hear him. Mary Alice patted his arm and pulled away from the hug, "Not anymore, now get out of the kitchen and go wait patiently for dinner."

Evan bent down and kissed her cheek before he sidled out of the room, headed for the living room to watch the football game, no doubt. Mary Alice heard Ricky whoop from somewhere in that general direction. As quiet as that boy was, he sure did get animated when it came to football.

"Looks like everyone is here." Ellie said. She was implying they start dinner, Mary Alice could hear it in her voice.

"Not Char. I've texted and called her. No answer. We haven't spoken since last week at the family meeting." Mary Alice sat at the kitchen table to finish folding her napkins. Ellie sighed and sat down with Mary Alice, picking up her own napkin to begin folding as well. "I don't understand her. What is so bad about having a sister? It's not like her existence is bothering Char."

Mary Alice's hands stopped and rested on her pile. "I'm not entirely sure it was my baby she's angry about."

Sixteen

2017

It had been three days since Thanksgiving and still no word from Char. Mary Alice found herself drifting from hurt to worry whenever her mind wandered to her second-born, but she could find out nothing when Char refused to take calls. Maybe Mary Alice should go to the university to talk to her daughter in person. Or maybe that would only push Char further away. Charlie used to say she was like a cat — she would do something when she was good and ready, and their job was to wait patiently for that time.

Luckily, Bethany came over almost every day. It helped to keep Mary Alice's mind off her wayward daughter. Yesterday, she and her parents had toured the Florence Crittenton home, and Bethany would be attending her first day that coming Monday.

Bethany sat at the kitchen table with Mary Alice, her brows knit tightly as she stared at the cross-stitch in her hands. She was trying, bless her, but Bethany was like Char — she couldn't make a straight stitch to save her life. Still, she wanted to do it. Whatever she made would be for the baby, and even if it wasn't the most beautiful thing, the child would surely treasure it.

"Gram, did you call the Adoption Agency yet? I can't stop thinking about your baby. I'm dying to know what she is like." She missed a stitch and cussed under her breath.

104

Mary Alice didn't meet her eyes. "I looked them up online and got the information. I even wrote down the number, but I haven't had time to call them yet."

"Gram, you're home every day, how can you not have time?"

Mary Alice twisted the thread of the cross-stitch. "It's complicated."

"How?"

"Only the child can request the records to be unsealed. The best I can do is fill out a form stating when I had a child and where. I've reached a dead end . . . again."

Bethany wrinkled her nose, a habit Mary Alice had noticed she did whenever she was displeased about something. She tossed her work down on the table, her wide eyes pinning Mary Alice as a big grin spread across her face. "Well, no biggie, my idea is way better than the adoption agency. There are a lot more current ways to search for lost people in the 21st century, you know."

"Is that so? And what would this new 21st century method be?" *She really does think I'm ancient.* They abandoned the cross-stitch when the timer went off on the stove. Mary Alice pulled a fresh tray of ginger snaps from the oven and set it on a wire rack to cool. She wiped her face with a linen dish cloth.

Bethany stood and stretched, her hand rubbing her lower back. She reached for a hot cookie from the tray and pulled back, licking her finger. "Social media. She might be a Facebook follower. Did you know there is a Florence Crittenton Reunion Page? We could run a post, see what we get. I can set it up for you."

It was good to see Bethany so light-hearted and optimistic. Maybe too optimistic. "I don't know anything about book facing."

Bethany's amber eyes twinkled in the morning sunlight streaming through the kitchen window. Charlie's eyes. "Facebook, Gram, not book facing. Even Mom and Dad use Facebook. Actually, most of us have moved off it because all the old people are on it now."

105

Mary Alice raised her eyebrows. "Old people, huh, like your parents. Then what am I? A dinosaur?"

Bethany rolled her eyes. "V-e-r-y old. No offense, Gram."

"None taken, sweetie. I am a dinosaur. What makes you think this thing would work? How would this face book," she said the words slowly and separately, "help me find my missing daughter?" A twist in her gut made her doubt the outcome.

"I was looking at the Facebook FC reunion page. Lots of people are looking for mothers and daughters, or brothers and sisters given up for adoption. If she is looking for you, she might look there. A lot of people on there say they've taken those DNA tests. All you would have to do is get one of those tests, then we'll create a Facebook page for you and post something about you on the FC Reunion page. You know the date, and the hospital, right? If she also took a DNA test, the company would send her an email when they found a match."

"Then we ask everyone we know to share it since it is a public site. Hundreds, no, thousands of people will see it. Somebody must know where she is. Or maybe she'll see the post herself. And it's free."

"And if she didn't already have the test?" Mary Alice asked.

"Then maybe the post would encourage her to do it - especially if the birthdate and hospital match."

Mary Alice sank into a chair across from her granddaughter. Could something like that work? It couldn't be that simple. What if no one responded? This would only open old wounds. She recalled the hopefulness when she and Charlie first started looking. And the despair when it stopped at a dead end. Then the flip-flop of hopefulness and despair when she went to the Florence Crittenton Home, only to see the scarred remains of the records in the burn mark on the floor. Then one more time with the adoption agency, when in less than five minutes on the phone, Mary Alice had been rebuffed. Time and time again, she failed to find her daughter, and if she took a chance on Bethany's way, it would probably happen again.

Mar, it could work. You should do it.

"Charlie, do you really think so?"

106

"Come on." Bethany slid out of the chair and went to Charlie's den, probably to get on the internet. Mary Alice stood up without a word and followed Bethany, halfway scared of looking at the computer, and halfway scared to not look. Bethany booted the computer up and after a few mouse clicks, the Florence Crittenton Reunion Page appeared on the screen. "See Gram. Look at all these people. Look how many already have their DNA. There might even be a post from her on here already."

"Okay," Mary Alice said slowly. "If I did agree to this Facebook thing, what would I have to do? I don't think I want my name plastered all over the internet. Or my face. What would everyone think? Your parents, your aunt and uncle?"

Bethany was practically bouncing in her chair now. "No, we don't do anything like that. I'll set up a homepage for you. You can use whatever name you want. A first name is fine. But it needs a picture of some kind for the cover page. And we'll put a post on the reunion page. And we could even use an Avatar for your picture."

"A what?"

"Avatar - kind of like a cartoon. We'll say you were a resident at FC and were forced to give up your baby girl. We'll give the birthdate and name the hospital. We'll ask if anyone knows of an adopted woman born that year in that hospital to PM you."

Mary Alice shook her head. "PM? Are you even talking English?"

Bethany's eyes danced. "Private message. That way, she can send you a note. From there, you can figure out if she is someone you want to meet."

"Bethany, you don't meet strangers like this do you? How do you know they aren't stalkers or pedophiles?"

"Ew, Gram." Bethany wrinkled her nose. "No. I only PM with my friends."

"How can I be sure I won't meet a predator?"

"Maybe you set up a public meeting place, like Starbucks. Anyway, some place where you can see her first. Maybe see if she looks like Mom, or Aunt Char, or Uncle Evan. Some hint she is the right person. Then, you introduce yourself. And BAM, you've got your daughter back."

If only it was that simple. How would Mary Alice know if her daughter even wanted to meet her? What if she only wanted to tell her how messed up her life was thanks to her? She could hate Mary Alice.

"What would I have to do?" Her heart pounded in her chest. Was she really going to do this?

"I'll set up the Facebook post. You should probably go ahead and get the DNA test. Then . . . w-h-e-n she answers your post, you will have the information to make the match." Bethany's fingers were already flying across the keys.

Mary Alice took a deep breath. She hoped she was doing the right thing. "Okay, I'll do it. How do I get one of those DNA kits?"

"Awesome Gram. Let's see what the people on Facebook use, and we'll go with that."

"O-k-a-y." Mary Alice dragged out.

Bethany laughed. "Don't worry about it, Gram. I'll show you. Let's log onto the Facebook Reunion page and look at the posts. What was the birth date and the name of the hospital?"

Mary Alice sucked in a big breath of air. This was moving so fast. "May 25, 1963. St. Elizabeth Hospital in Youngstown."

"Cool. This is going to work, Gram. I know it."

Mary Alice was taking matters into her own hands, standing up for herself and her daughter. It felt good. Mary Alice stared at Charlie's picture. Our daughter. *Happy now?*

"It looks like most of the people on the Reunion page did an at-home test from a company called DDC, at least first." Bethany said, scrolling through the posts of the Crittenton Home Facebook Reunion Page. "Wouldn't it be rad if she already took the test?"

"Rad, sure."

Mary Alice placed the order for the in-home test. The website said it would arrive in three to five business days. Her stomach did a somersault.

Mary Alice tried to get the hang of Facebook. With

Bethany's help, she scrolled through family posts, mostly of Ellie and Evan. Even Charlene had a Facebook account.

Bethany posted on the reunion page:

> Mother seeking lost daughter. Lived at the Florence Crittenton Home, Youngstown Ohio from February to May,1963. Baby girl born May 25,1963, St. Elizabeth Hospital, Youngstown Ohio. Put up for adoption at birth. If you think you are my missing daughter, please PM me. I've always loved you. In process of getting DNA test now. Please share.

On her personal page, she only identified herself as Mary Alice, no last name. Bethany put a cartoon of a woman holding a baby where a photo was supposed to go and reposted the same message there as she posted on the reunion page.

Mary Alice stared at the plain brown wrapper. This could change her whole life.

"Charlie, I'm afraid."

Afraid of what? Getting our daughter back? There isn't a downside to this.

"But there is, Charlie. What if I find her and she doesn't want me? I don't know if I could handle losing her all over again."

If she is our daughter, she won't do that. She'll want to be a part of our family. You'll see.

"And what about Char? She won't be happy."

She's not happy now. She'll have to work through it.

Mary Alice read the directions three times. She rinsed her mouth out a half dozen times to make sure there wasn't anything that could mess up the results, like toothpaste, or the tuna salad she'd had for lunch. Finally, she swabbed the inside of her mouth, and careful not to touch it on anything else, she slipped it into the sleeve provided. A form accompanying the kit asked for personal information, name, address, phone, email. Date of birth. City of birth. Her hand trembled as she wrote. Slipping the card in the return envelope with the sleeve sample, she sealed it.

She placed extra stamps on the envelope and set it on the counter to take out to the mailbox. The tea kettle whistled and made her jump. She was as nervous as when she went to the doctor at sixteen to find out if she was pregnant. Sitting at the table, she tried to sip her tea and calm her nerves, but her gaze continuously fell on the obscure envelope on the counter. How could something so innocent looking carry such life altering results?

Just do it, Mar. Mail it.

"*Okay, Charlie, okay. I will.*" She rose and marched all the way from the kitchen to the mailbox at the end of the drive. Once she slipped the envelope in, she marched right back to the kitchen and sat down at the table once more. *"There, are you happy?"*

A week later there were still no responses from the Facebook posts, but Bethany pointed to the screen. "Look, the post had been shared over fifty times on the reunion page, and almost all of them shared it to their personal pages. That's good, Gram. She'll see it. Try to be patient."

Patient? Mrs. Longsworth had told her once never to pray for patience. The only way to learn it was to wait. She'd been doing that for fifty-four years.

On day eight Mary Alice opened her computer and found an email message from the DDC. She sucked in her breath. She clicked on the message.

"Your DNA maternity test is now on file with the DDC. Interested parties must first obtain written permission from you before they would reveal any matches." They were halfway to finding answers. If her daughter was even looking.

Bethany arrived after a day in school at the Home and tossed her backpack on the chair. She headed straight to the cookie tin and a glass for some milk.

"I've got some news, Bethy. I received an email from the DDC. The DNA results are in."

"Awesome, Gram. Let me update the reunion page so she knows you have the DNA results."

As Mary Alice and Bethany sat at Charlie's desk and scrolled through the posts, a notification of a post on her personal page popped up in the lower right-hand corner of the screen. Bethany reduced the reunion page and opened Mary Alice's page.

Contact me to find your daughter. ABC Private Investigator.

Another comment suddenly popped up below:

Don't do it. He's a scam artist.

Oh dear. What had she gotten into?

Two more comments appeared on her personal page.

My mother was adopted and her birthday is the same. I'll ask her. I hope you are my Grandma.

Mary Alice's heart skipped a beat. Wow. What if this is another granddaughter?

"Oh, Gram," Bethany squealed. "That could be my cousin."

"Or maybe not. Let's not get ahead of ourselves." She sounded much calmer than her pounding heart attested.

Another comment popped up and Mary Alice's breath hitched.

If you hadn't been a slut in 1963, you wouldn't need to be looking for your daughter. She's better off without you. You'll rot in hell for what you did.

Mary Alice pulled her hands away from the keyboard. Who would say such terrible things? She didn't even know this person. Char's words flashed through her mind—*bastard*. She had been just as critical. In fact, she could have written that comment. Maybe this was a bad idea. Why was she subjecting herself to this abuse? What were the odds of ever finding her daughter anyway? She noticed Bethany watching her reaction. The red splotches on her face were probably a good give away.

Bethany switched to some of the other personal pages from women also on the reunion page. "Gram, some people like to be mean. We call them trolls. And you have to ignore them."

A private message popped up in the bottom right-hand corner of the screen. A trickle of perspiration formed on Mary Alice's upper lip. Her mouth went dry. Was this her? Mary Alice tapped on the message.

> Hi. A friend of mine forwarded your post to me. I was born on May 25, 1963 in St. Elizabeth Hospital. I don't

know where my mother lived at the time of my birth, but I was put up for adoption. However, I was never adopted and was in and out of foster homes all my life. Still, I consider myself a success story. If you'd like to meet, I live in Girard, Ohio. My name is Constance Green. Here is my Facebook page. I haven't taken a DNA test yet, but I am willing to.

She provided a link.

Mary Alice's heart thumped in her ears. She hesitated, her finger lingering over the keyboard. Why? What was she afraid of?

She got up and paced the small den. This one little click could change her whole world. Was she ready? She went to the kitchen and made herself a cup of green tea and carried it back to the den. She stared at the words on the screen. Here is my Facebook page. She could see her face, learn things about her. Constance Green. What a nice name. Was she her daughter? All she had to do was click on one little link to find out.

"What are you waiting for Gram? Click on it."

Mary Alice mouthed a silent prayer and placed her index finger over the mouse. The blinking black cursor hovered over the link. She closed her eyes and clicked.

Opening one eye, her heart dropped. The woman in the picture was definitely not her daughter. She had a large head, hair cropped close to her scalp, huge big brown eyes, and skin a dark mocha. She scrolled through the pictures of family and friends, a diploma from the University of Michigan, her husband's Medal of Honor. This woman had a good life. Mary Alice was happy for her. But she was not BabyGirlMay251963.

The screen blurred, words and faces melting like snow on a spring day. A familiar rock settled in the pit of her stomach. The burden she'd carried for so long. Decisions taken from her that were irreversible. It was too late. She couldn't do this. She should tell Bethany to take the post down.

"No, Gram. Not yet," Bethany insisted. "It might take a little while to get around the world. Look, it's been shared 427 times."

"The world? You think my daughter might be in another

country?" She hadn't thought of that. What if she did find her, but she was in France, or Japan, or some third world country? What would she do then? She didn't have the money to chase all over the world looking for her.

"The world's a pretty small place now, with internet access almost anywhere," Bethany assured her. "And lots of people travel to other countries for work. It's not like in the olden days, Gram."

Mary Alice suppressed a smirk. The olden days indeed. "Okay, I'll give the world another ten days. But if no results by then, I'm done. I can't take some of the awful things people say on there."

"Well, what about the good stuff? Like the girl who wants you for a Grandma. Or the dozens of comments from other mothers looking for their kids. Lots of people are rooting for you you don't even know."

Seventeen

2017

Mary Alice patted her hair, looking in the rear-view mirror before exiting the car and heading out of the city parking garage, into the street. It had been years since she had been in downtown Youngstown. It seemed the gentrification had not been too successful. The once-bustling streets were eerily quiet. A few businessmen and women hurried by with briefcases heading toward the Court House, apparently the only true activity in the area. Most of the department stores were gone. A homeless man with a crumpled cardboard sign stretched his legs across the sidewalk, and Mary Alice had to step off the curb to avoid stepping on him.

If it weren't for her concern about the lack of funds in the checking account, she would have canceled this meeting with Steve Willoughby. But as unpleasant as it was to admit she knew so little of her own finances, it had to be done. Surely there was a good explanation. Charlie was nothing if not responsible and decisive.

Mary Alice found the red brick building on West Boardman Street. Beside the glass door was a brass plate engraved with the number twenty-five. This was the place.

The door creaked as she entered, and she found herself in a narrow, dark lobby. According to the directory on the wall, Steven Willoughby, C.P.A was in Suite 412.

When the elevator doors shuddered open, she considered taking the stairs. The interior of the small cab smelled of urine and fried food. But four floors? Her old legs would never make it. She stepped in and prayed it was at least fast. Of course, her prayers went unanswered. It was the slowest ride in history, and the clanging in the shaft made her question the safety of it. Would the cab come crashing down before she got off?

Mary Alice sighed in relief when the elevator dinged. The doors opened and she stepped onto the faded carpet of the 4th floor hallway. Mr. Willoughby's name appeared on a scratched brass nameplate under the numbers 412. She knocked. No answer. She tried the door. Surely there was a receptionist on the other side.

There wasn't. The room, maybe ten-by-ten, had the same faded carpet as the hallway. The striped green and blue wallpaper had seen better days. A small metal desk was in the middle of the room, piled high with folders. But no secretary.

"Hello?" Mary Alice called out. "Mr. Willoughby?"

A rustling came from the open doorway leading into the next room. "Yes, yes, Mrs. Goodson. Come in."

She followed the sound of his voice into the next room, which looked identical to the first except for the window behind the desk. It looked out at the next building across the alley.

Steve Willoughby leaned across his messy desk and offered his hand. "How do you do, Mrs. Goodson? I hope your Thanksgiving was nice. The holidays certainly are a busy time."

"Yes, thank you." She released his sweaty palm and took a seat in a straight back chair in front of his desk. She wished he'd get to it. A moldy smell tickled at her nose and she wiped at it with a tissue from her handbag.

"Mrs. Goodson . . ."

"Mary Alice," she corrected. "I think we can dispense with the formality."

"Certainly, Mary Alice." He shuffled some papers on this desk and tucked them into a folder. It said Charles Goodson on the tab. "Since Mr. Good . . . Charlie's passing, I have been going through his accounts to settle up matters and transfer any balances to you."

Good. Accounts, plural. There was money someplace else. Of course there was. "I see," she said. "As you may have noticed, I left all financial matters to my husband. But I guess I'll have to learn to handle it now, won't I?"

Steve Willoughby tugged at the tie around his neck. "You see, Mrs. . . Mary Alice. There is the problem. I am afraid his business had not been doing well the last few years, with him semi-retired and all. It's too bad he never brought on a partner."

Charlie had hoped his son would be interested. But woodworking was a far cry from concert pianist. Mary Alice couldn't even visualize those delicate fingers with splinters and abrasions from the sander the way Charlie's always had been. It wasn't meant to be. Mary Alice offered a polite smile. "Of course, the business will close now. At least we own the building outright."

"And at the end, his business profits barely covered the operating costs. My guess is he was tapping into personal funds by then too."

The checking account. That was why it was so low. How could he have kept a secret like that from her all those years? And why?

"Charlie, how could you?"

"Well," Willoughby cleared his throat. "You do have a little time to think about it. The next quarterly payment is due at the end of the month. Perhaps the best solution is to sell the building. The market is not great, but whatever you get will be better than continuing to pay taxes on an empty building. Or perhaps we can find a tenant."

"He has left me penniless. I can't believe this."

Mr. Willoughby pulled a few papers from the folder. "As for the business, we can dissolve it and sell all the equipment. And the building . . . I have a commercial real estate agent who could list it for you."

Mary Alice stood on wobbly legs. This couldn't be happening. "No. Don't do anything. I have to think this through. My house and the building are my only assets. How much are the taxes on the building? I can't rush into selling it."

"I understand. The taxes are $7,885.00 a year, or $1,972 a quarter. And of course, there are the utilities on the building as well." Willoughby stood and extended his hand across the desk. "Please, again, accept my apologies. I did not mean to surprise or upset you. Can I expect an answer from you before the end of the month?"

Mary Alice nodded numbly, shook his hand, and left. She didn't even notice the clanging of the elevator going down, the worn carpet, or the homeless man still in the same spot on the sidewalk.

She sat in the car practicing her breathing exercises; inhale, one two three, hold, one, two three, exhale, one, two, three. It always amazed her how well it worked. The fog slowly cleared around her brain. Okay. So, Charlie had kept a secret . . . a big secret from her. Of course, it was to spare her the worry. She shook her head. So . . . the money. Truth. It was almost gone. Maybe she would have to sell the shop. What would she do with it anyway?

She put the car in drive and headed for Chalmers Street. She should at least look at it again before she decides. She hadn't been there since Charlie's death.

She saw the shingle with Goodson Cabinetry swinging from the wrought-iron bar as she turned the corner and pulled up to the curb. Thankfully, nobody was parked near the shop, so she didn't have to practice her parallel parking skills. A lump kept her from swallowing. She cleared her throat. *Keep it together girl.*

Exiting the car, she fumbled with the keys on her ring. The big brass key was easy to find, even if it was barely used. She rarely needed to go there without Charlie. But practical Charlie always made sure she had a key 'just in case.'

The door creaked as it opened. Charlie would have fixed it right away . . . if he were here. She flipped the switch on the wall and fluorescent lighting above the clear drop ceiling panels lit the room. Her eyes scanned the room, taking in each display area: rich dark cabinets, *walnut*, with intricate recessed panels and white quartz countertops, honey-colored cabinets, *hickory*, in simple shaker style with speckled granite counters, white-painted cabinets, *maple*, with country filigree crown molding and butcher block counters. These were Charlie's other babies, and this shop was his pride and joy.

Why did Charlie have to leave? She wiped at the tears flowing freely with the back of her hand.

"I'm here, Mar. I'll always be here with you."

It didn't feel like he was there. The room felt cold and impersonal without him. It was his larger-than-life personality that warmed this place, not the ancient furnace banging and hissing from the back room. She followed the sound to the door at the rear of the showroom, passed through the door into the workshop, where the true magic began. It was a carpenter's dream. The scent of wood assaulted her before she could make it down the three steps to the concrete floor of the shop.

Pine sawdust tickled her nose. She sat on the steps to catch her breath. His memory was everywhere. Power equipment had been cleaned and oiled to perfection every evening; the floors swept clean before flipping the lights off each night. Now everything had a thin film of dust on it. A long workbench, *oak*, lined the entire length of one wall. Every hand tool was perfectly aligned on a pegboard wall above it. A partially finished cabinet, *maple*, sat waiting for skilled hands to bring it to life.

The opposite wall held divided sections with large panels of wood. Mary Alice stood on wobbly legs and walked the length of the room. She ran her fingers over the wood. There were the soft woods, like pine and cedar, their scent sweet and tangy, their texture grainy and raw. Medium density woods like hickory, chestnut, cherry, and alder. The back of the room held the hardwoods — oak, walnut and birch with their almost invisible grains. Each had a distinct smell and passing by each one conjured up memories upon memories, of another job he worked so hard on, of the pride he took in his work.

The workshop had been the children's favorite playroom. They played in the fresh sawdust, coming home with it sticking to their clothes, lingering in their hair. They smelled of the tangy evergreen of pine, the vinegary tartness of oak, and sweet scent of cherry or maple. They built toy race cars and doll

118

houses beside their father, securely encased in safety glasses. They were Charlie's favorite little proteges.

It was a shame none of them had wanted to continue in their father's footsteps. What would she do with the shop now that he was gone? Should she sell it? Hire a crew to continue his work? It was one subject the family had only briefly discussed.

"What am I supposed to do with this place, Charlie? It feels like a part of me . . . a part of you. It kills me to let it go."

You'll figure it out. Trust yourself.

Eighteen

2017

Mary Alice sat at the kitchen table with a cup of cold, forgotten tea. Her mind wandered back to the shop. His business floundering. How could Charlie have kept a secret like that from her? And why? They had never had secrets, at least none she was aware of. Were there others? Three times over the last two days she had reached for the phone to call Gladys or Sophia and three times, she placed the phone back in the cradle without calling. Could she even admit to her best friends maybe her perfect 'eleven' wasn't so perfect after all? Not that what he did wasn't noble, but keeping secrets?

It only made her more curious about this missing daughter. She was the beneficiary of a college education and then some from a man who, for the first time in Mary Alice's life, felt like a stranger too. She abandoned her chilled tea and wandered into the den.

She sat in Charlie's chair. His scent was almost gone, or was it her tamped down anger at him blocking it? She reached toward the button on the computer tower and waited for it to boot up. Boot up. Wouldn't Bethy be proud of my computer lingo?

Once the screen flashed to life, she clicked on the book-mark of the CH Reunion Page like Bethany had taught her. She read through the pages and pages of mothers and sons and daughters trying to connect. Some had heartfelt reunion posts.

Another tore her heart out when she read one reunion resulted in a bad experience of resentment and hatred. It could happen to her too. She had to prepare herself. Then, she noticed the PM symbol. She had a private message. Her stomach did a somersault. She said a silent prayer. Please let whoever it is at least be kind. She dared not wish for anything more. She clicked the mouse and the message opened.

> My name is Hope Pendleton. My birth certificate says I was born on May 25,1963 at St. Elizabeth Hospital. Parents are listed as undisclosed. I would like to find out if you could be my mother. I have my DNA on file with the DDC. We could see if I am a match. Please contact me by PM on my Facebook page, same as my name.

This could be it. Click on her page. After the disappointment with Constance Green, Mary Alice feared getting her hopes up. She mopped her forehead with a clean hanky. Her finger hovered over the mouse. She closed her eyes and her finger clicked down.

Mary Alice opened one eye, then the other. The profile photo was grainy. She could make out nothing distinguishable. It could be her, or not. She looked plain, like most middle-aged women. The hair was light, but that could be from a bottle. Mary Alice clicked on the profile page. It said she lived in Youngstown, not across the world. She works at the Mahoning County library, the main branch on Wick Avenue.

Mary Alice could drive right over there and see her. It was less than a half hour away. *Oh, what am I thinking? What would I say?*

She'd dreamed of this moment for fifty years. In her mind, it had all transitioned smoothly. There were no awkward moments, no hesitation. They flew into each other's arms and lived happily ever after. But this was not a fairy tale. It could go so terribly wrong.

Brutus lumbered into the den and flopped down beside her. She looked down and patted his huge head. "Should I reply, Brutus? What should I say?"

He looked up at her with big sorrowful eyes. Apparently,

he didn't have any answers.

Mary Alice squared her shoulder. "I'm going in. Wish me luck." She pecked with one finger and typed out her reply.

> *I think the DNA match is a good idea. I recently submitted my DNA to the DDC database. A little about me. I was sixteen and unwed when I gave birth in 1963. I was forced to give up my baby. I didn't want to.*

She waited. No response. Bethany had shown her where to look if Hope was online. She wasn't. It could take days for her to respond — if she did at all. Mary Alice would wait. What other choice did she have? She stared at the picture of Hope Pendleton. Was there any resemblance?

"Charlie's nose?"

Brutus let out a soft 'woof.'

She didn't look like any of the other kids, but Mary Alice could see how Bethany might look like her when she got older. If only it was a better picture.

She scrolled through Hope's page. Hope! What a lovely name. Someone must have really loved her. Could she dare believe this was her? She was single. Loved classical music. Really? Like Evan? Did she play? Did she have Evan's talent? Ah, there were more pictures. Some with friends, laughing and toasting with wine glasses. Clearer pictures. Was it her imagination or were those Charlie's eyes? It was true — this could be her daughter. "Hope." She mouthed the word over and over again. "Hope. Hope. Hope." The very word bubbled up within her. An old black and white photo of a man and a woman. Surely they were Hope's adopted parents. The ones who raised her, loved her, protected her. A twinge of jealousy spurred in Mary Alice's belly. That wasn't fair. They didn't take Hope away, they received her, like a gift. A gift of Hope not rightly theirs.

She may have actually found her. No point in telling the family yet, getting them all excited over nothing. It was too late for her. She was already beyond excited. After all these years. Could this be happening? Was this girl — no, woman — named Hope really her little girl?

Mary Alice kept the Facebook page open on the PC,

checking back every few minutes for a response from Hope Pendleton. The screen went blank. Her heart stopped. Mary Alice jiggled the mouse and the screen sprang back to life. She exhaled. She busied herself making a cup of soup and a sandwich and went through three cups of tea. Nothing. Was she hesitating in answering Mary Alice's post because she was nervous too? Did it mean she hadn't been happy with her adoptive parents? She said she worked at the library. Of course, she couldn't be checking her Facebook page when she was at work.

By the time the cuckoo clock had struck seven, Mary Alice had convinced herself this was not a match, then she convinced herself it was, then it wasn't again.

At 7:23 p.m., a message popped up on the screen. Mary Alice's heart skipped a beat.

> *I did a DNA test four years ago but never received any matches. I can send a request for a match to the DDC but I'd need your ID number. Mine is 6783011. I'm glad you have already filed your DNA. I'm sorry they took your baby away from you. I had a good childhood as an only child. If I am your daughter, do I have any siblings?*

A good childhood? Thank God. If this is her daughter, at least this one nightmare can be banished forever. An only child? How different life would have been for her with two sisters and a brother. Mary Alice's finger slipped on the keys and she had to delete and type over again.

> My ID number is 6782093. I will also send in a request for them to compare mine to yours. And yes to siblings: a sister, 49, and a set of twins, a boy and girl, 46.

She only waited a minute before Hope responded.

> *Oh wow, great. I've always wanted siblings. And their father?*

A familiar pain stabbed at her heart.

> My husband died last year. He would have also been your father.

> *I'm sorry. May I see a photo? What is your full name?*

Mary Alice was afraid that would come up.

> I've received some degrading comments. I'm not

> ready to subject myself to much publicity yet. This is very new to me. And I'm nervous. May we keep talking for a while first or wait until the matching results come back?
>
> *Of course. I understand. Tell me something about you.*

The cursor continued to blink. Her life hadn't been exciting. She'd worked for her husband, whom she'd adored. She'd raised three children. She was happy except for this one hole in her heart. Well, two holes now - one for her daughter and one for Charlie. Could she, should she, say that much?

> I answered the phones for my husband's business when I wasn't busy raising the children.
>
> *What kind of business?*
>
> Charlie was a cabinet maker. He loved wood.
>
> *Charlie? That would be my father's name? I love wood too. I dabble in wood sculpture.*

That couldn't be coincidence, could it? She loved wood like Charlie? And music like Evan? Hope must believe it too. She called Charlie, 'my father.' Tears blurred Mary Alice's eyes and she had to wipe them away before she could type. Her finger trembled on the keyboard and she had to backspace and retype several times to get an intelligible sentence.

> I see from your page you like classical music? Any particular kind?
>
> *Piano. Why, do you play?*
>
> No, I have a tin ear. But my son plays piano for the Youngstown Symphony.
>
> *Oh my. He lives in Youngstown? Perhaps I saw him at one of the concerts. I play a little, but only for my own enjoyment. Are you also still in Youngstown?*
>
> Yes, I am.
>
> *Wow. I'm sorry. I have to go for now. I have an 8:30 appointment. Can we talk again soon?*
>
> Yes, I'd like that.
>
> *Mary Alice, I hope you are my mother.*

My mother.

Those two simple words leapt out at Mary Alice like a neon sign on a Vegas billboard. She rolled her chair away from the desk; hands shaking. Could she, dare she believe this was her daughter? Her pulse quickened, and before she let doubt seize her, Mary Alice rolled back toward the screen, placed her fingers over the keyboard and typed:

So do I.

Mary Alice emailed the DDC that night with permission to compare her DNA with Hope Pendleton, then she sent Hope a PM asking if they could exchange email addresses. It was an easier way to communicate online. It took less than a day for a reply, and Mary Alice was pecking at the keyboard as soon as she saw Hope's message.

> *To: H.Pendleton@vmail.net*
> *From: Charles0173@yell.net*
> *Subject line: Re: Finding my daughter.*
> *Hope,*
> *I'm nervous and excited thinking about the DNA test-*
> *ing. I emailed them permission. Waiting for results.*
> *Fingers crossed,*
> *Mary Alice*

A response came back almost immediately.

> *Email to Charles0173@yell.net00*
> *From: H.Pendleton@vmail.net*
> *Subject line: Finding my family*
> *Mary Alice,*
> *Yes, me too. I know this may seem presumptuous, but*
> *I have a really good feeling about this. Looking forward*
> *to hearing from you soon.*
> *Hope Catherine Pendleton*

Mary Alice reread the email until she could recite it by heart. Why hadn't she started this search sooner? Hope could have met her father . . . *if* he was her father. She had to stop jumping ahead and getting her hopes up. Too late. A familiar stab lanced her heart.

"Oh Charlie. Wouldn't it be wonderful?"
Yes, Mar. It would be.

Joanne Simon Tailele

Nineteen

2017

Mary Alice watched the postman for the delivery every day. Why was she so nervous? She already knew the results, didn't she? It had been four days since she had sent the request. Today, right there in the mailbox, a manila envelope waited for her. The return address was discreetly labeled as DDC with a P.O. Box return address. Her heart thumped against her breastbone as she fingered the envelope.

Mary Alice rushed back to the house and threw the door open before hurrying to the kitchen. She sat down at her usual seat and clutched the manila in front of her like something holy.

The envelope was unassuming, a bar code running across the bottom left with the numbers 6782093 beside it. It was thin, couldn't be more than two or three pages. She ran her finger along the flap, slipping her nail under the loose edge. Deep breaths. In and out. What if she was wrong? What if after being so sure, the results turned out to be negative? What then? She couldn't bear to think of those possibilities. The flap gave way easily as she ran her index finger under it.

The word popped out from the page among all the legal mumbo-jumbo catching in her throat. MATCH. Of course it was a match. Even though she'd always believed it in her heart, holding the results in her trembling hand was overwhelming. "The cross reference of DNA results between Specimens #6782093 and #6783011 indicates a 99.9% positive match."

126

I knew it Mar. I am so happy for you. You did it.

Mary Alice ran her fingers over the words, "positive match." She burst into tears. Tears of joy, of relief? A wet circle spread on the page, right over the word MATCH. She grabbed a napkin to blot it away, but it smeared the ink on the page. The smeared word did not change the fact. They'd found her.

She wiped the tears from her eyes. Had Hope received her results too? Was she also crying into her tea, or coffee? She didn't even know if Hope liked tea or coffee? There was so much she didn't know. She couldn't wait to find out. It was time to make it happen. She rose from the kitchen table, the results still gripped tightly in her hand as she headed to Charlie's office. *"She's ours Charlie. She is really ours."*

She paused long enough to breathe into his chair. His scent was almost gone.

"Oh Charlie. Don't leave me now. When we are so close to having our daughter."

I'm here. Mar. I'll always be here.

She leaned down, turned on the computer tower, and waited for it to boot up. When it sprung to life, she clicked on the internet button and waited for it to load.

Usually, the home page popped right up, but it was still working on it. Her knee started bouncing and she steepled her fingers, leaning close to the blank page.

Then it loaded up. The screen sprung to life, but the page said it had no internet connection. Mary Alice swallowed and followed the directions. She refreshed the page. Nothing. She closed the internet and brought it back up. Nothing. She rebooted. Nothing. Everything Bethany had told her to do if she had any problems. She kept hitting refresh, but every time she did, she got the same message. No internet connection.

"No!" This could not be happening right now. The world around her blurred, like she was swimming underwater.

She should call somebody. Yes, the internet company — it was a technology issue. Once she called them, the internet would work and she could tell her daughter — *her daughter* — Mary Alice was her mother, had always been her mother.

Mary Alice shuffled through the mail in Charlie's paper

tray. She couldn't remember the name of the internet company, so she started opening everything. Electricity. Gas. Telephone. Insurance. She started flinging them as she went, her stomach flipping over and over until she was nauseous.

And then she found it. Comcast. That was it. Mary Alice clutched the paper in her hand and moved as fast as she could to the kitchen. She grabbed the phone on the counter and it almost slipped from her fingers, but she caught it just in time. Mary Alice dialed the number at the top of the overdue bill and pressed the phone so tightly to her ear it hurt. One ring, two, three, four.

Pick up, pick up, pick up.

"Hello and thank you for calling Comcast." A woman's automated voice answered, "Our normal business hours are between eight a.m. and five p.m., Monday through Friday. Please call again during normal business hours, and thank you for choosing—"

Mary Alice slammed the phone down. She stared at it, for how long, she didn't know.

She called Bethany, but it went to voicemail. She wanted to call Ellie or Evan, maybe they could fix the computer, but she didn't want them knowing what she was up to, not until she met Hope in person. This was supposed to be her moment, but how could she have her moment if she couldn't even talk to her daughter and tell her the results?

Mary Alice found the computer user manual in the file cabinet in a folder marked "computer" in Charlie's scribbled handwriting. She called the number on the back. Same thing—she had to call back on Monday.

She sat at the kitchen table with the phone lifted to her ear. Gladys and Sophia couldn't do anything about the computer, but Mary Alice was huddled in the chair with the phone to her ear, barely holding it together, and she needed them.

"Hey, Mary Alice," Gladys said. Her voice sounded distant; she was driving.

"The results were positive," Mary Alice blurted, "And I tried to email her and tell her, but the internet isn't working." Her lip quivered, "I've been trying all morning, and the internet company isn't in, and I . . . I want to see her." She tried to hold it in, but she'd never been good at that, and so the tears and the sobs burst from her like a broken dam.

"I'm coming over right now, Mary Alice. Please don't cry, we can fix this. I'll call Sophia and we'll both be there, okay? We will figure this out and you will see her soon. Mary Alice?"

She couldn't get any words out past the sobs.

"Mary Alice? Fix yourself some tea and wait for us. I promise, this isn't the end of the world."

"Mmhm," Mary Alice pressed her palm to her eyes as if it would stop anything.

"All right, see you in twenty." Gladys hung up.

Mary Alice buried her face into her hands and gave into the empty space in her chest. She wanted to see Hope, she wanted to see her baby and hold her again. And even if the internet could be fixed within the hour, it didn't take back the decades of wondering if her baby was okay, wishing her baby would try to find her, praying the hole in her heart would one day disappear. She wanted to see her, just once, please God, she needed her baby back.

Twenty

2017

Sophia and Gladys sat with Mary Alice at her kitchen table. The tea was brewing in the pot, and when Sophia opened the cookie tin, the scent of cinnamon from the snickerdoodles filled the air.

Gladys patted her hand, "It's only until Monday. It's not the end of the world. Hope will understand."

Maybe it wasn't the end of the world, but Mary Alice couldn't stop thinking about it. She was *so* close—she could almost smell the baby-sweet scent of her daughter's hair, could almost hear the chattering in the hospital hallway. Could almost feel the weight of the baby in her arms.

Gladys could have lent Mary Alice her laptop but it was getting repaired. Sophia's desktop was caput after Desmond accidentally downloaded a virus from an email. If she used Bethany's computer, Ellie might see what Mary Alice was doing, and there was no way Mary Alice was ready to share Hope. She'd been waiting almost her whole life for this moment. It was hers, and hers alone. Even if Charlie was alive, this would still be her moment.

She fell in love in that hospital. She'd never felt so complete, so right; it was like God had touched her the moment her baby was laid in her arms. Paradise. And when they ripped her baby away, something inside of her died. She loved her children more than anything, she loved her late husband, but this moment was private. Sacred.

"Monday seems so far away." Mary Alice stared at her hands.

"I know it does, but you will get through it. You've made it this far, you can make it another day."

It didn't feel like it.

The three of them went silent. It was a comfortable lull in conversation. After fifty-plus years of being together, they didn't need to talk in order to understand and take comfort in one another.

Monday. Until then, Mary Alice had to keep her chin up, she had to remember her search was over. One day, that's it.

Twenty-One

2017

The weekend had come and gone, slow as a snail. She hadn't stopped thinking about the results, about telling Hope. It was agonizing to wait, so every time she thought of the results, she would write. But it was Monday now, and it was all she could think about.

Mary Alice glanced at the clock again. 7:59 a.m.

She sat at her kitchen table with the internet bill and a pen in front of her. As soon as the hour hand inched to eight, she picked up her phone and dialed the number on the bill.

"Thank you for calling Comcast. If you are requesting new internet service, press one. If you are requesting new telephone service, press two. If you are a Comcast customer and calling for technical service, press three. If you need to pay your bill, press four."

"My goodness." Mary Alice pressed four.

"Thank you for calling Comcast. Anthony speaking. May I have your name and account number please?"

Mary Alice scanned through the bill in her hand. "My name is Mary Alice Goodson. The bill is in my husband's name, Charles Goodson. Where do I find my account number on the bill?"

"I can help you with that, Mrs. Goodson. Look in the upper right-hand corner of the bill."

"Oh yes. The number is 8573467. I'm calling because I'm

having a problem with my internet. It's probably got something to do with this internet bill, so I'd like to pay it, please."

"Sure thing ma'am, I'll get you set right up. Please hold while I pull up your account."

He went quiet for a few seconds. "Here it is. Can you verify your address?"

"My address is 681 Sexton Street, Struthers, Ohio. My husband has passed. Is that a problem since it is in his name?"

"No, not a problem. Your accountant called and we made note of that, and I'm very sorry for your loss."

"Thank you."

"Can you verify the last four digits of your social?"

She rattled off the numbers.

"Thank you, Ms. Goodson. It looks like your account is in suspension due to several unpaid bills.'"

Mary Alice's stomach lurched. "Several? How many unpaid bills? I wasn't notified of this." She stared at the stack of unopened mail through the open study door.

"Five months."

She gasped. "How much do I owe?" She held her breath.

"Five hundred, plus overdue fees."

Mary Alice sagged in her seat. She doubted there was even that much in the checking account. And even if there was, she still needed to eat. What was she going to do? She fought the tears stinging her eyes. "What is the minimum you would need to reconnect it?"

"$575.23, ma'am. We can take a credit card payment or echeck over the phone."

"Um, I'll have to get back to you. Sorry," she mumbled and hung up the phone. She flipped open the credit card bill. Also past due. Also maxed out.

How was she going to tell Hope they were a match? Did she know already but had no way to reach her? Had she tried to email her? Leave a PM on the Reunion page? She could be thinking Mary Alice decided she didn't want to meet her. She'll think I'm a terrible person. She probably thought it was a good thing she never met her good-for-nothing mother. Mary Alice had to do something. She could go to Ellie's and use her computer. But she wanted to do this by herself.

The library. She could go to the library and tell Hope in person. Maybe she hadn't read the email from the DDC yet. It would be okay. Don't panic. But she had to do it now, before Hope tried to contact her and couldn't. But what if Hope rejected her? It didn't sound like she was like that, but who knew? She couldn't be like Gladys. She couldn't be afraid to stand up, be brave. Gladys almost lost her life because she wasn't brave. *I must do better. Take the chance of rejection. If I don't, I could lose her all over again.*

Mary Alice marched herself into the bedroom and freshened up. Then she grabbed her car keys and handbag and headed out the door. "Hope, here I come, ready or not."

Twenty-Two

2017

Mary Alice set out with a mission to go to the Mahoning County library. Despite her palms slipping on the steering wheel and the trickle of perspiration running down the back of her neck, she was determined. She was going to do it—introduce herself to her daughter. Then reality slammed into her like she'd been rear-ended.

What did she think she was doing? She couldn't even think of a book she wanted to borrow if she needed a cover. She pulled into the parking lot of the library, threw the car in park, then hit the speed dial for Sophia's cell phone. She answered on the first ring.

"Hey, Mary Alice."

"Hello . . ." Mary Alice leaned on the steering wheel and stared at the building, "I'm at the library, I think I'm going to try and see her."

There was a very long pause on Sophia's end. When she spoke again, it was on an exhale. "Have you thought this through?"

"Not at all. I need to see her. Since I can't email her with the results, I'm going to tell her in person. I'll call you as soon as I come out. If you don't hear from me, I had a heart attack. Call 9-1-1."

"Not funny. You're not going to have a heart attack and you're never a bother. Practice your breathing."

Mary Alice dropped the phone in her bag, flipped the mirror down on the visor and stared at her reflection. She finger-combed her graying hair. Why didn't she ever have a comb when she needed one? She applied a fresh coat of coral lipstick and smeared a dab on either cheek, smoothing color across her wrinkled face. She was so pale.

She looked down at her polyester black slacks and yellow knit top with matching cardigan sweater. She looked like a frumpy old woman. Maybe she should go home and change or go to the store and get a comb. Mary Alice grabbed the keys in the ignition and almost cranked it, but stopped.

She'd been dreaming of this for decades. She missed her baby, grieved for her, wished for nothing more than to see her. Now she had the proof this was her daughter. She had to tell her. She couldn't stop now; she was almost there. Was she really doing this? Her heart pounded bass drums in her ears. She stepped out on wobbly legs. She prayed she wouldn't faint. How would that look?

She doesn't know who I am. I can go in and browse through the books. I'd have a chance to look at her first. Then I'll introduce myself. "Hello, I'm your mother." Oh goodness. Following Sophia's advice, she held onto the hood of the car and inhaled deeply for a count of five, held it for five, and exhaled slowly for five, but it only made her feel even more light-headed.

"*Okay, Charlie. I'm going in.*"

You've got this Mar.

The white brick building had a stately appearance: two-story, dentil molding around the roofline, curved walkway over perfectly manicured lawn, the American and state of Ohio flags flying high, the metal fasteners clanging against the metal poles in the wind. Young people clad in jeans and carrying backpacks scurried in and out. With the proximity to Youngstown State University, it was probably busy most of the time. The lack of cars in the lot painted a deceiving picture. Good. She could blend in with the crowd.

At your age, not hardly.

"*You're not helping, Charlie.*"

Her bones creaked as she climbed the stone steps. Inside,

the austere building was filled with books. She looked up to the mezzanine on the second floor. Impressive. She ran her hand down the long, light-colored tables, *birch*, as she passed. She inhaled the sweet leather and glue of the musty old books. the murmur of hushed voices was like a soothing lullaby. The internet could never replace this.

A few students glanced up, but then quickly returned to their studies. She looked around for the help desk. Would Hope be sitting there?

The pounding in her ears seemed louder. An older gentleman was checking out books for students behind a counter. Maybe it was Hope's day off.

She wandered up and down the aisles, running her fingers over spines, not really seeing any of them. She wiped her sweaty palm on her pant leg. This was insane. What was she thinking?

A soft voice came from behind her. "May I help you find something?"

Mary Alice spun around.

"Oh!" Amber eyes— Charlie's eyes, stared back at her. Her knees went weak and she gripped the bookshelf to keep from collapsing. Mary Alice's mouth went dry. Her tongue stuck to the roof of her mouth.

For fifty-four years, she'd waited for this moment.

She pressed her back tighter into the bookshelf and pushed her other hand against her thigh to keep from throwing her arms around Hope.

"Ma'am? Are you alright?"

Mary Alice knew she was staring. She looked away, trying to find her voice. "Um, no . . . I mean yes, I'm fine. I'm just browsing." Then her eyes went back to Hope's face. Her baby girl's face.

Hope smiled, even white teeth gleaming behind thin lips. "Fine. Let me know if you need any help." Her soft voice was like velvet.

Mary Alice watched Hope turn and walk down the next aisle. She pretended to peruse more aisles but kept her gaze on her daughter, who carried herself with the same poise

137

Charlie had. The way she moved, leaning intently in to listen to someone asking her a question, so much like Bethany. The resemblance was uncanny.

Mary Alice pulled a book from a shelf and sat at the nearest table before her knees gave out. She didn't know how long she sat there, pretending to read, watching her daughter's every move.

"Our daughter. It's really her."

Go ahead. Introduce yourself. Tell her who you are.

"Okay, okay. Give me a minute."

Students came and went, replaced with other young bodies. Twice, Hope looked over at her and smiled. A lump stuck in Mary Alice's throat. When she could no longer pretend to read, she exited the building. In the sanctuary of her car, the reality of it overtook her. A sob escaped her lips. She had chickened out. Not told her. Why? What was she afraid of? Tears flowed freely down her face, rivers washing down her neck, pooling in the hollow of her collarbone.

When she gained control of herself, she called Sophia back, breathless. "She's here."

"Wow. Did you talk to her?"

"Not really. I was dumbstruck when she approached me, I could barely get out a sentence, but she was so nice about it. She looks like Charlie, and a little like Bethany. She looks happy, I think."

"You can do this Mary Alice. Don't chicken out now. You've waited your whole life. Now, go back in there and tell her who you are."

"Not at her work. This was a bad idea. We need to do this privately."

"So, here is an idea. Go back in and use the library computer. You can send her an email like you would have from home. Tell her about the match and schedule someplace to meet."

She could do that, she had to since she didn't exactly have internet right now. She had to be brave. She wouldn't be a chicken. She was here. In the flesh. And so was her daughter.

"Okay." She muttered, "Okay, I can do this. Thanks,

Sophia. I'm going back in."

"Go get her, tiger."

Mary Alice huffed and hung up the phone, dropping it in her purse. She gripped the steering wheel with both hands and stared out the window at the library. *What if*— she thumped the steering wheel. *What if nothing.* This was her daughter.

She exited the car and climbed the steps to the library again. This time she did not see Hope. Perhaps she was on another floor, or in the back. Mary Alice made a beeline to the row of computers. Instructions were mounted above them.

Tap any key to bring the screen up.

Enter your library number.

Click on the Chrome button to access the internet.

Mary Alice sat in front of a computer and followed the instructions. But how did she get to the email? The blinking cursor was of no help. A young man with a ponytail sat down next to her. He glanced at her and smiled.

"Excuse me," Mary Alice said. "How do I get to my email? It comes up automatically on my computer at home."

"Go to your server." He said kindly.

"What?" She felt her cheeks warm. "I don't know what you mean."

"Who do you have your email service with? Yahoo, Gmail, Yell?"

Mary Alice recognized one. "Yell. My email has yell.com on the end."

"Good. Type in Yell.com into the browser, then enter your email and password."

"Thank you so much."

The young man smiled and turned back to his computer. Mary Alice watched his fingers fly across the keyboard. She turned back to hers and one-finger typed in her yell information. Her email popped up. No emails from Hope. She must not have received the results yet.

Mary Alice typed in Hope's email address.

To: H.Pendleton@vmail.net

From: Charles0173@yell.net

Subject line: Re: Match

> *Hope,*
> *I received the results from the DDC. We are a 99%
> match. I can't tell you how happy I am. I'd like to meet
> you as soon as possible. I feel like I've waited forever.
> How about tomorrow, at the Starbucks close to the
> library where you work? Would 9 a.m. work for you?
> My internet service is down, so please text me at 216-
> 555-3979 either way.*
> *So excited.*
> *Mary Alice (your mother)*

She stared at the screen. Your mother. Too much? *No, I
am her mother. I can say that.* She looked around the room again
for a glimpse of Hope. When she did not see her, she hit the
send key, logged out, and left the building.

Hope texted a few hours later agreeing to the meeting.
Tomorrow was it. Mary Alice would actually meet her daughter for the first time in fifty-four years, four months and sixteen
days. She pulled the journal from her nightstand drawer. The
pain of having her baby ripped from her arms still echoed in
the hollow of her chest sometimes. Today, when she was so
close to having her back, it was one of those days. Mary Alice
picked up her journal and began to write.

Twenty-Three

1963

"Should I call Mrs. Longsworth?" I asked, gripping tightly to Sophia's hand. ""When is the right time? I don't want to go to the hospital all by myself. Can you ask if you can go with me?" A brief fizzle of hope filled me, but it died as fast as it came. Nobody got to go with the girls when they left for St. Elizabeth. Mrs. Longsworth said she'd never had a girl deliver at the house and she had no intention of it happening.

"How far apart are your pains?" Sophia asked.

I stopped and sucked in my breath. "I don't know. I wasn't timing them." Something I'd remembered to do with both Gladys and Sophia. Why didn't I think to time them? It hurt so much. When Gladys went into labor, she screamed. When Sophia started contracting, she cried. I knew it wouldn't be easy, but I didn't realize how much it would hurt. Like my entire body was imploding. Would the baby even come out, or would my body give up?

"I'll time them for you," said Sophia.

I pulled some dainty note paper from my nightstand and handed it to her.

"Ugh." Sophia scrubbed at her face, "Why didn't you wake me? Tell me each time a pain starts and how long it lasts. If she asks, I'll tell Mrs. Longsworth you are sleeping through lunch."

I smiled as the next pain subsided.

141

By dinner time, my pains were a steady fifteen minutes apart and staying silent was getting harder and harder. I knew better than to try to eat anything, even if I could have — which I couldn't. I bit down on a washcloth to keep from crying out and squeezed Sophia's hands until she pulled away. My bed was sopping wet from sweat but my water still hadn't broken. Any calm resolve I had vanished like smoke. "Sophia, I'm afraid. I can't do this. Don't let them take me. I'll stay here, I'll have my baby right here."

"I can't deliver your baby," Sophia said, her voice rising anxiously. "It's time. I'm calling Mrs. Longsworth."

"No," I begged, but a new pain ripped through me and I groaned.

Before Sophia could go for help, the bedroom door flew open and Mrs. Longsworth was on the other side. "What is going on here?"

I wiped my face with the washcloth and didn't answer.

Mrs. Longsworth harrumphed and stepped toward my bed. "Why didn't you girls call me?"

"I wasn't ready to go yet," I said.

"Has your water broken?" Mrs. Longsworth lifted the blanket.

"I don't think so." I fell back against the pillow as another pain subsided.

Mrs. Longsworth reached for her walkie-talkie. "Franklin, we need an ambulance here. There may not be time for a cab."

"Yes Ma'am."

"Promise me you'll still be here when I come back." I pleaded with Sophia.

"I can't. I'm supposed to leave with Gladys' social worker. She's taking me to that half-way house tomorrow, remember? But if I'm not here, we'll stay in touch. I promise."

I made the V sign with the cross to Sophia. Some of the other girls gathered around the doorway to watch me in my misery. It was a blur. One minute, I was looking up at Sophia and the next, a medic. I felt straps go across my chest but I didn't protest. Faces went out of focus as they wheeled me down the hall, down the stairs, and out into the driveway.

The new girl, Natalie waved. "We'll be rooting for you."

I tried to push myself to my elbows, but the strap held me down. A warm spring breeze brushed my face and I noticed the distinct smell of hyacinths. They slid me into the ambulance, and I looked out the window as best as I could. The gate closed. I read the sign, burning it into my brain so I wouldn't forget: "The Florence Crittenton Home for Unwed Mothers" Would I really be coming back? Some of the girls, like Joanie, never returned.

The short ride to the hospital was a haze of blood pressure cuffs and hands pressing into my stomach and under my skirt. They wheeled me into a sterile room with white walls, white sheets. Stainless steel instruments sat on a stainless steel tray.

A pasty-skinned nurse in starch white from head to toe with a pointed cap was waiting for me. "Can you undress yourself?" She asked, not too friendly. "You're from the Crittenton Home, right?"

The room was freezing, which took my mind off the pains long enough to be coherent. "Yes, I think so, and yes. Is someone going to call my Mom or my boyfriend, Charlie?"

I couldn't have this baby alone. I was afraid. Where was my Mom?

Not answering me, the nurse pointed to a straight-backed chair. "Remove all your clothes and set them over there." She opened a closet and snatched a gown, tossing it at me. She didn't offer to leave the room. "Put this on, open in the back."

I turned my back to the nurse. I hadn't been naked in front of anyone in daylight since I was ten years old, not even Charlie. I took my top and bra off, folded them, tucking the bra under my shirt and trying to cover my breasts with my arm. The next pain ripped through me and I grabbed the table for support. "Aahh." I felt the nurse behind me, tugging my maternity pants down to my ankles, along with my panties.

She patted the exam table. "Up you go."

"I . . . I don't think I can. Wait, wait a minute." I clung to the edge of the table, no longer concerned about my nudity.

"We're going to need some help in here," the nurse hollered into the hall.

A young man appeared, clothed in the same stark white. He didn't look older than twenty and I blushed at my nakedness as the pain subsided. The nurse held one of my arms and the man took my other arm. On the count of three, they lifted me onto the hard, plastic-covered table. The thin white paper liner crinkled under me.

"Are you a nurse too?" I asked the young man, anything to take my mind off my nakedness.

"Orderly," he muttered, not looking me in the eye, red creeping up his neck and onto his cheeks. He looked away as he opened the thin gown and slipped it over my body.

"That will be all, Jonathan."

The boy was gone as quickly as he came. The nurse snapped a cold, folded sheet open and laid it over me.

My teeth clattered with the cold. "C, c, c, can I have a blanket?"

The nurse glared at me like I'd asked for a million dollars. "You girls are all alike. You spread your legs for any Tom, Dick or Harry but when it's time to pay the piper, you all cry for your mamas and want special privileges."

I opened my mouth to protest when another pain tore my insides out. "Aahhh."

The nurse forced my feet into metal stirrups and strapped my arms to the side of the table.

"Aahhh. Pl-pl-please help me." Somebody, I didn't care who. "Mama!"

"You got into this all by yourself, and your mama ain't gonna help you now. Now lay still, I'm gotta shave you and give you an enema."

I felt cold water washing between my legs and a razor blade scraping against my skin. Then I was told to push up on the stirrups, so the nurse could put a cold metal bed pan beneath my bottom. Another pain gripped me as the nurse inserted the enema tube, but at least warm water filled my insides.

"Relax," the nurse snapped. "I can't get the tube all the way in."

How was I supposed to relax with my insides being torn out?

A brown-skinned doctor with green scrubs appeared as my bowels let loose. Oh, goodness. I pulled against the straps holding down my arms. I wanted to hide my face in embarrassment.

"Mary Alice?" The man's voice was soft and gentle. "I am Doctor Patel. I am going to deliver your baby." He patted my knee, still raised in the stirrup, and pulled the sheet up that had slipped down. "How are you doing?"

His soft voice and kind words brought tears to my eyes. Like a savior, I knew he would take care of me. No one else had said a kind word to me since I'd left the home.

"I'm cold." and anxious and afraid.

"Nurse Stillman, why haven't you given Mary Alice a heated blanket? It is standard procedure for ALL patients. You know that."

Nurse Stillman glared at me as she stood behind him, then retreated and returned with a blanket. She draped it over me with efficiency, but no tenderness.

Ah, finally. The warmth from the blanket was like manna from heaven.

"Mary Alice," said Dr. Patel. "I'm going to take a look under here." He pointed to the blanket. "Let's find out how much longer this process is going to take." His calm and gentle voice eased a bit of my anxiety. Maybe it would all be okay if he only stayed there beside me.

The cushion on the stool let out a whoosh of air as he took a seat between my legs and raised the sheet and blanket. I nodded and closed my eyes. His fingers probed inside me and his hand pressed down on my belly.

"Hmm, I'm afraid you still have a way to go. You are only six centimeters. And your amniotic sac is still intact. It's holding up your delivery. We will do an amniotomy to move things along."

I had no idea what he was talking about, he could have been talking Swahili. Nurse Grumpy taped an IV to my hand. It pumped something into my veins that made me groggy, and

145

Joanne Simon Tailele

the pain lessened slightly. Between pains I could almost relax. I felt the warm gush as my water broke.

"That will get things going," said Dr. Patel. He patted my knee and left the room.

I wanted to cry out for him not to go, but the pains started coming harder and closer together. Nurse Stillman came in and out of the room, but there was no more sign of Dr. Patel. I watched the big black hand on the round clock over the doorway.

Ten o'clock.

Eleven o'clock.

Twelve o'clock. With no window in the room, I drifted in and out of awareness. A new set of nurses appeared, and then Nurse Stillman was back. Seven o'clock. Nine o'clock. I had been there for fourteen hours.

""Don't you think you should call the doctor?" Surely something was wrong. Why was it taking so long? I couldn't take it anymore.

"Be glad you're here, Missy," the nurse hissed. "I'd leave you to drop in the street if you were my daughter. When are you girls going to learn?"

What had I ever done to merit this wicked woman looking after me? "Charlie. Please Charlie, come save me."

After another hour of alternating between cringing in pain and gasping in exhaustion, Dr. Patel finally appeared. His head swiveled around, and he glared at the nurse. She backed away and gave a slight shrug behind his back. He examined me and growled, "Nurse Stillman, why didn't you call me? You have been warned before about your treatment of the Crittenton girls. This girl has been suffering needlessly. It is unacceptable and you can expect a report in your file and a visit from the administrator."

He turned his head back to me and his scowl melted away for another small, gentle smile. "Mary Alice, we are going to give you a saddle block now."

He lifted my legs out of the stirrups. They were numb from being in one position for so long, and from whatever drugs were making me groggy. "Swing your legs over the sides now.

Yes, like that. Now, sit still. I'm going to insert a small needle in your back. And you'll feel much better in a few minutes."

Pure euphoria washed over me as the anesthetic settled in. The pains were still there, but they were tolerable. Things happened quickly. Nurse Stillman and the orderly moved me to a hospital cart. The fluorescent lights from the ceiling whizzed by as I was wheeled down a long hallway and into a huge operating room with bright floodlights and stainless steel everywhere. A masked man said he was going to put me to sleep, and to breathe deeply. Count backwards, Ninety-nine, ninety-eight, ninety-seven.

No, no, I did not want to be put to sleep. They would take my baby. I fought against the wooziness enveloping me. Then it all went dark.

When I woke up, I was in a room with eight or ten beds separated by green curtains pulled from tracks near the ceiling.

"Well, good morning. You are in the recovery room. How are we feeling?" A round woman pressed ice chips to my lips.

We? "Umm, is it over? Did I have the baby?"

"Yes, Sweetums, it's over."

I tried to sit up.

"Whoa there, Cowgirl. Take it easy. You had a spinal. No moving for twenty-four hours."

Nausea washed over me. "I . . . I think I'm going to be . . ." Bile spewed from my mouth, down my chin and into the creases of my neck.

"Uh oh, Lamb Chop. That's the ether. Don't you worry. I'll get you all cleaned up."

I closed my eyes then opened them again when my head started to spin. "My baby? Do I get to see him?"

She checked the chart clipped to the end of my bed. She shook her head, a sadness to her big brown eyes. "Umm, I don't think I'm supposed to say anything."

Tears sprang to my eyes. I pleaded. "Please, please, is he okay?"

She leaned in close and whispered in my ear. "Not he. You had a little girl. And she is fine."

A girl. I had a baby girl. Mine and Charlie's little girl. *"Charlie, you have a daughter. Can you hear me? Please come for us. We need you."* I smiled at the kind nurse but her face blurred and I couldn't keep my eyes open.

When I awoke, I was in a regular hospital room. My bed was raised and both sides had metal bars, making it impossible for me to get up. I needed to pee. There was an empty bed next to me. Nurses and aides scooted past the open door. "Excuse me? Can somebody help me? Hello?"

"May I help you?" Another new face attached to a nurses' uniform stepped into the doorway.

"Umm, I need to use the bathroom."

The young woman shook her head. "Oh no, you can't get up for at least twenty-four hours. I'll get you a bedpan." She disappeared behind a heavy wood door. *Oak.*

The woman reappeared with a stainless steel bedpan. "Can you lift your bum?"

I maneuvered clumsily onto the cold pan, now thankful for the metal handrails to grip onto. But now I couldn't go. I shrugged sheepishly at the nurse.

"Shy bladder. I'll step outside for a minute. See this red button? Press it when you're done, and I'll come and remove the pan." She smiled pleasantly and left.

The minute she was gone, my bladder let loose and I sighed in relief.

"Can I see my baby?" I asked when the nurse returned.

"You're from the Crittenton Home?"

"Yes," I nodded.

The nurse frowned. "I'm sorry. Your baby is scheduled for a closed adoption."

My throat closed in a choke hold. I couldn't breathe. "But, but, I never agreed to an adoption." My heart pounded wildly in my chest. I couldn't utter another word but I shook my head. No, no, I would not give up my daughter.

The nurse tsked and gave me a sad smile, turned and left without a response. I was alone. A cacophony of squeaky wheels, rubber-soled shoes on tile, and crying babies filled the hallway. Hope filled my lungs. They had to let me feed my baby. All the babies were given to the mothers to feed. I straightened my covers, waiting for my precious little baby to arrive. Nurses whizzed by my open doorway, pushing bassinets with both arms. Doors closed in each of the rooms. But no bassinet appeared in my room. The hall was suddenly quiet. No, no, no. They couldn't keep her from me. The searing pain in my chest rivaled my labor pains.

Somewhere in that hospital, my daughter was crying for me. Who was going to feed her, love her? I could almost see her in my mind, that tiny bundle in a pink blanket, her eyes pinched shut while she wailed for me. I had to get to her. I pushed the red call button beside my bed. I pushed it again and again. I shook the metal side rails. If I could get them down, I'd go find her myself. I screamed at the top of my lungs, "I WANT TO SEE MY BABY!" No one answered.

My head fell back against the pillow. Tears streamed down my face. My arms physically ached to hold my child, as if they had been severed from her. An hour later, the procession repeated in reverse as the babies were wheeled back to the nursery. This time quieter, satiated with full tummies, wrapped in the love of their mommies.

The agonizing procession repeated every four hours. Each time I prayed, this time they would bring my daughter. Each time, I sat ready to hold her in my arms. And each time, the bassinets passed by without stopping in my room.

On the third day, a nurse bound my breasts to stop the milk. The pain was excruciating, but I couldn't decipher it from the internal ache in my chest. They allowed me to get up to walk the halls now, and slowly I made my way down the corridors, walls painted a soft green, adorned with smiling photos of mothers and babies, some with fathers and grandparents. I never felt so alone. I gazed in the open doorways at the other women, rooms adorned in pink and blue balloons, every flat space overflowing with flowers, cards, and teddy bears.

My bottom was still sore, and I grasped the metal handrails on the wall as I made my way down the hall. No one paid any attention to me. No one asked if I needed help or wanted a chair. I pushed forward to the sign pointing to the hallway to the left—Nursery. I made the turn at the corner and stopped to catch my breath. Would I see my daughter? Would I recognize her? I made my way to the window, next to fathers and grandparents cooing and waving to the bundles in the plexiglass bassinets. A father held up a blue card with his last name, and a nurse lifted an infant toward the window. She pulled the blue cap off the tiny head to show a shock of full dark hair. Grandparents slapped the father on the back. He beamed with tears of joy and handed out cigars to everyone. He even offered one to me. I shook my head. A few other mothers in new robes and slippers smiled happily on the arms of their husbands. Each wore a pink or blue plastic ID bracelet matching the tiny bracelets around the infants' ankles.

That should have been me.

I inched closer to the window. A nurse made a sign for a card with her hand, then tapped her wrist, indicating I should show my ID bracelet. I raised my hand, but my bracelet was white. The nurse gave a sad smile, turned away from the window, and busied herself with the other infants. I searched each bassinet. I searched for a pink card with the last name of Cranston. Or a white one to match my ID bracelet. There was none. Was my daughter in another room? Had they taken her away? Panic gripped me. I tapped on the window. When the nurse ignored me, I banged a little harder. Some of the babies stirred and started to cry.

The nurse frowned at me and waved a finger. But I only pounded harder. Where was my baby? I needed to see my daughter. The nurse came through a side door, accompanied by a huge man in scrubs. "You can't be doing that. You are waking all the babies." She wasn't mean, but her words slapped me in the face.

"My daughter," I said weakly. "I want to see my daughter."

The nurse lifted my white wristband and read it. "Oh," she said, as if that was an explanation. "Your baby is not here. She's been taken to the pediatric ward."

My knees gave out. "No, no, no," my voice getting softer with each word. I slid to the floor. The male orderly lifted me off the floor and deposited me into a wheelchair.

"Take her back to 303A, Freddie."

Every day for the next four days someone from the adoption agency came by with the papers for me to sign. Every day I turned them away without a signature.

"You need to think of the welfare of the child," a woman with a terse British accent said, pushing the papers across the rolling tray, waving a pen in my face.

"No, never. I told you. I want my baby. My boyfriend wants the baby. We're going to get married. Why won't you believe me?" I burst into tears. "I want my baby!" I wailed at the top of my lungs. Security came and told me to calm down. I'd calm down when these people left me alone and I had my baby safely in my arms.

I didn't have a phone in my room, but there was a pay phone down the hall. One of the other patients lent me a dime to try to call Charlie's house. When Mrs. Goodson picked up and recognized my voice, she hung up without saying a word. I didn't even have a chance to tell her she had a granddaughter.

On the fifth day, my parents arrived to take me home. They approached my bed cautiously, as if I had a disease they could catch.

"Mary Alice, we are told you still have not signed the papers."

No hello. No 'How are you?' No 'We missed you.' I crossed my arms across my bound chest. "I'm not giving up my baby. I told them. You can't make me."

My father cleared his throat. "Mary Alice, be reasonable. You can't take care of a baby. You're only sixteen. I had hoped four months to think about it would have put some sense into you."

Who was this man who was so cold? What had happened to my Daddy who had bounced me on his knee, played catch in the backyard, called me his little Alice-in-Wonderland?

My father paced in front of me. "The adoption agency will pay your hospital bill in full, as well as your room and board at the Crittenton Home. Do you have any idea how much money that is?"

I had no idea. I had never thought about who was paying for my stay at the home or at the hospital. Perhaps I did have some things to learn. "I don't want to give up my baby. I haven't even seen her."

My mother took my hand. "Darling, think about what is best for the baby."

Why was someone always saying that to me? *I* was what was best for the baby, me and Charlie.

"How can you be so selfish?" my mother continued. "This is a living human being, not a baby doll you can set on a shelf when you tire of her."

Oh my gosh. How old did they think she was? Ten? "I won't tire of her. I'm her *mother*."

My father pulled the papers from the envelope and slapped them on the dinner tray. "Enough of this nonsense Mary Alice. You will sign these papers and we will take you home and it will all be over."

Tears streamed down my face and I crossed my arms over my bound, aching breasts. "No."

Father's voice boomed. "If you don't sign these papers, you are on your own. We will not bring a bastard into our house. YOU will have to support it on your own. YOU will have to pay the bill from the Crittenton Home—$500.00. And YOU will have to pay the hospital for your stay, your delivery charges, for room and board for you and your bastard child. $200.00 a day—or a total of $1000. Do you have one thousand, five hundred dollars, Mary Alice?"

Of course I didn't. I shook my head. I had $37.50 in the piggy bank in my bedroom back home.

It was over. The truth settled over me like a storm cloud. I had no way to take care of my baby, especially if Charlie was really gone. I didn't have a job, or a place to stay or any money. How could I ever explain to Charlie how I let them take our baby? Would he hate me forever? I rocked back and forth, arms wrapped around my middle. Vomit churned in my throat. Was I going to vomit? I could beg. I could wail. I knew it would do no good. A moan escaped my lips. I stared at my mother, eyes pleading for help. She was a mother. Surely, she would empathize.

Mother's eyes averted and she stared down at the papers on the dinner tray. "If you sign the papers I'll tell them you can see your daughter once, to say goodbye." The papers were shoved closer. Someone placed a pen in my hand. The words blurred through my tears. The heading said, "Voluntary Surrender of Infant." There was nothing voluntary about any of this. Ice filled my veins. I didn't bother to read the five pages of small print. No one explained its contents or offered any legal advice. With a shaky hand, I scribbled my name on the last page, above the word MOTHER.

I was dressed and ready to leave. I sat in a small, upholstered chair. A nurse brought the small bundle in and placed her in my arms.

"I'll give you a few minutes alone with her." She closed the door.

The baby felt so warm. She was so tiny. Big round blue eyes stared up at me. They would be Charlie's amber eyes when they changed. I was sure of it. I gently lifted the pink cap from my daughter's head and ran my hand over the soft peach fuzz of blond hair. I watched as the baby's forehead pulsed with her tiny heartbeat.

"Hello, my sweet." I laid her on my lap and unwrapped her, kissing each perfect finger and tiny little toe. I marveled at the tiny cupid lips, the wrinkles inside her thighs. I memorized every soft curve, every tiny wrinkle. I unbuttoned my blouse and nestled her against my chest, feeling skin to skin, heartbeat to heartbeat. I inhaled her scent, Johnson's baby powder. It was almost too much and I cradled her in my arm. A bubble of milk formed on her cupid lips. Who's milk? Was it formula or did someone else already nurse her? I kissed her little ear and whispered into it. "I would have named you Charlene, after your daddy." I choked on the words, but I had to say it. "I am so sorry. Please know I don't want this. I love you. I will always love you. Your daddy is Charlie Goodson. Remember that. He loves you too. Please forgive me. I'm sorry. I'm so sorry." Huge wet droplets fell on the little head. I kissed the salt away.

Too soon, the nurse came back into the room. "It's time," she said, lifting the baby from my arms. "I'm sorry." And she was gone.

I sat alone in the room, suddenly cold to the bone. I examined my arms resting on my lap—empty arms. My body trembled. Everything went blank. I have no idea how long I sat there before my parents appeared in the doorway.

"All right." Father swiped his hands together as if washing away unpleasant crumbs. "Let's get you home and life back to normal."

I got up, slowly. As I walked past him and sat in the waiting wheelchair, I gave him a hateful stare. Under my breath, I whispered. "May God forgive you . . . because I never will."

Twenty-Four

2017

Today was the day. Nine a.m. *Today*. This was it.

By five a.m., Mary Alice was sitting in the kitchen exchanging the tea for strong black coffee. She didn't even like coffee. She finished off the pound cake. She needed to find something decent to wear that didn't make her look a hundred years old. Coffee cup in hand, she headed into her room and her closet. What do you wear to meet your daughter for the first time? The coffee did not sit well. Her stomach lurched. Maybe she was going to be sick. Maybe she'd die of a heart attack.

Mar, stop. She's our flesh and blood, she'll understand. You've got this. Now, take a long soak in the tub and practice your breathing. And wear that pretty little paisley dress I like so much.

Mary Alice stared at the closet door for a long time before she opened it. she was looking for pieces of Charlie. She could almost see the twinkle in his eyes as he met his daughter for the first time. This was something they should be doing together. She pulled the small wooden box from the top shelf in the closet. *Cedar*, his favorite wood. It smelled like him. He had made it for her after he'd moved the wood shop from the garage to the downtown location on Chalmers Street.

Mary Alice climbed onto the bed and flipped open the small box. She inhaled the rich cedar lining. The box was meant to hold her handkerchiefs, but she preferred to keep her most precious possessions in it. Charlie's letters. She had the ones that had made it through the pilfering by her mother and the few sent to the FC home, but it wasn't until her parents' passing that she found the ribbon-tied bundle of letters from the USS Kitty Hawk. Charlie had sent those letters from the ship while he'd been offshore in Vietnam, after she'd already given up their baby.

Mary Alice often pulled out those letters and read them. They were so familiar now; she knew every word by heart. She reached for one of her favorites and gently pulled the thin stationary from the envelope.

> *September 19, 1963*
> *My darling Mar,*
> *I have no idea if these letters are getting through to you. I miss you every day. In the quiet of the evening, when the planes have returned, (or not), and things quiet down, I think about our little girl, our little Charlene. I hope she is loved and in the arms of someone singing her to sleep every night. I know this must tear your heart out, but I can't get her out of my head. When I get home, we'll find her. I promise.*
> *With all my love forever,*
> *Charlie*

She looked at the clock. Now she really did have to get moving. No time now for a long leisurely soak. Leaving the open letter on the bed, she took a quick shower and pulled Charlie's favorite, the blue paisley dress with a v neckline, from the closet and slipped it on. Why couldn't he be here for this day?

Her eyes filled with tears. She fingered the photo from her wedding day, tucking it inside her purse along with some other photos of the family. "You're coming with me, Charlie."

At eight-twenty, Mary Alice strapped the seat belt across her lap and checked her coral lipstick in the rear-view mirror. A twenty-five minute drive from the house to the Starbucks, she practiced her breathing and maneuvered through the traffic. Her hands slipped on the steering wheel, palms sweating. She wiped them on her dress. *I can do this. I can do this.*

A handful of cars were already in the parking lot when she arrived. Mary Alice could see through the large plate glass windows. No sign of Hope. Should she go in and wait or stay in the car until she saw her arrive?

A tan Nissan Rouge pulled in three spaces over from her white Hyundai Sonata. The woman glanced over the two empty spaces between them at her and gave a quick nod. It was Hope. She checked her hair in the rear-view mirror and ran her hand through her locks. She looked nervous, too.

Mary Alice looked away so as not to be caught staring, but she heard the car door open and slam shut. Hope, dressed in khakis and a persimmon cowl-neck sweater, crossed in front of her on the sidewalk and made her way into the coffee shop. Her blond hair showed off a professional new cut in an inverted bob that swished across her jaw, new since she'd seen her at the library. She had Charlie's confident walk, rising on the balls of her feet with each step. Almost a bounce.

Mary Alice touched a hand to her own hair. She should have canceled until she could get to the salon. From her vantage point, Mary Alice could see Hope standing in line, accepting a large paper cup, finding a seat by the window.

Mary Alice wiped her hands on her dress again. Hope would be able to see her exiting the car from her seat by the window. Mary Alice would have to walk directly in front of her to get to the door. She should have gone in first. Been the one already seated. Too late now.

Mary Alice swallowed the bile in the back of her throat. *Don't puke. Don't faint. Just walk.* Her knees felt like jelly as she stepped out of the car and she had to pause by the door until she got her land legs. She caught Hope watching her from the window as she made it to the door. Deep breaths, Deep breaths. The bell rang on the door as she pushed it open, startling her.

Bypassing the order counter, she headed straight toward Hope. *Eye contact. Give her eye contact.* She tried to smile but it felt forced. Ice ran through her veins.

Hope spoke first, not rising from her seat or offering her hand. "Mary Alice?" A look of recognition crossed her face. Mary Alice nodded, frozen in place. Hope's voice was stronger

157

than she expected, but she'd only heard it once as a whisper in the library.

"May I sit?" Mary Alice's voice sounded strange to her ears. Higher pitched. Desperate.

"Of course, I'm sorry." Hope's voice softened, and she gestured to the seat across from her. "Do you want some coffee? I can get it. Regular, decaf, espresso?"

Mary Alice gulped and slid into the bench across from her. "No, nothing, thank you." This was surreal. Sitting across from her, not touching, making small talk.

Hope's brows furrowed together. Her amber eyes seemed to take her in, scanning the top of her head, her eyes, nose, lips, the wrinkled hollow below her neck, down her chest to where her body was hidden under the table. Mary Alice froze under the scrutiny.

"Um, don't I know you?" She searched Mary Alice's face.

Mary Alice gave a nod, or so she thought. *Say something, stupid. She doesn't remember from where*. She squeaked, "Yes, from the library. I can explain."

Hope's eyes bore into Mary Alice. She picked at the paper wrapper around the cup with short clear-polished nails. Silence. Was it disapproval or curiosity?

"Okay." Mary Alice inhaled deeply. "I received the results from the DDC. I was so excited to tell you, but when I tried to use my computer. It didn't work. I thought I would go to the library to tell you in person, but . . ."

"Then why didn't you say something?" Hope said, unsmiling. This was not good.

"I don't know. I wanted to, but then I panicked. I didn't know how you would react. So I emailed you instead from the library computer."

Mary Alice released the breath she didn't realize she'd been holding. The table started wobbling. Mary Alice jumped and glanced under the surface. Hope's knee was bouncing against the wooden leg, and her fingers were working at her cuticles.

Mary Alice felt her insides twist into knots.

Hope's throat bobbed and her lips flattened into a straight line. She opened her mouth to speak, but a broken sound spilled out and she cleared her throat, looking down at the table. It started moving faster. Mary Alice didn't breathe, her shoulders tightened until her muscles thrummed with a warm ache.

"So, were you . . . making sure of me first or something?"

"Well, no, I wanted to talk to you." Mary Alice folded her hands tightly in her lap and squeezed her hands together. "Badly . . .. but then I got scared and decided it wasn't good to ambush you like that at work."

Hope shook her head. "But that is why you came, right?"

Mary Alice knew she was stumbling over her words, "Yes . . . but—"

Hope took a deep breath and nodded, still staring at the table. "I've been waiting for you for a long time, it feels like." Her voice was quiet. Mary Alice had to lean in to hear her clearly. "I've been waiting for you, thinking there was somebody out there who missed me or . . . and it . . . it always felt like I was missing something, and then I thought you were the thing I was missing. If I had found you first. If I knew where you were . . ." She looked up. Her bottom lip twitched. She started again. "If I knew where you were, I wouldn't have hesitated. I wouldn't care if you were at work, because I've wanted to see you for so long. I wouldn't have let the chance run by me. Life is short, and you could have been gone the next day. You waited, though. You hesitated." Hope let out a long, heavy breath and straightened her shoulders. She reached toward her purse and slung it over her shoulders before shooting to her feet. "Maybe this is a mistake. My friends warned me against this. They said it was too late to start a relationship. Maybe they're right. I'm not a passing curiosity or a chance for you to feel better for giving me up. I'm a person, and I can't start something with you if you based this on whether or not you thought the reward was worth the risk of talking to me. You let your nerves get in the way of meeting me—that shows me how important I am to you."

"Wait, wait, please," Mary Alice begged. The words

159

spilled from her mouth like a waterfall. If she could only make her understand before it was too late. She couldn't lose her now, "My full name is Mary Alice Goodson and I live in Struthers. I know how bad this looks. I didn't mean to mislead you. I should have introduced myself in the library. I was being overly cautious and foolish. But the DNA test did not lie. I am your mother."

Time stood still. All sound blurred into a low hum. She had said it. I am your mother. How long had she waited to say those words? She couldn't lose her now, not after all this time. She reached out and took Hope's hand.

"Please. Let me show you. I have pictures of your father, your brother and sisters. Don't you want to see them?" Mary Alice held her breath, not taking her eyes off Hope.

Hope's eyes glistened with unshed tears and she sank back into her seat. An awkward silence hovered between them. The sights and sounds of the coffee shop came back into focus. An elderly couple at the next table was staring. Had they overheard the whole conversation? Mary Alice didn't care. A waitress came over with refills.

"So, do I?" Hope asked softly.

"What?"

"Look like your other children, or your husband? I don't look like you."

Mary Alice exhaled. "Yes, you do. You look a lot like my Charlie, your father." She emphasized the last word. "You have his eyes and nose." She reached for her handbag and produced two photos, the one from the silver frame on her nightstand taken on their wedding day. Charlie was wearing his Navy dress blues. The other was a more recent snapshot taken six months before he died. She laid them on the table.

Mary Alice's cell phone rang from inside her open handbag on the bench seat beside her. She glanced down beside her. Charlene's face showed on the screen of her phone. *Not now.* Mary Alice hadn't heard from her in three weeks. Now she calls?

Hope looked up from the photos. "Do you need to get that?" Her eyes went right back to the photos, not waiting for an answer, her face moving closer and closer to them.

"No," Mary Alice said quietly. "It can wait." She punched the ignore button and silenced the ringer.

Hope was running her finger over Charlie's face. "My God. He does look like me, or me like him."

"Yes. I knew it the minute I saw you." Mary Alice choked, no longer able to hold back the deluge of tears pouring down her face, running over her collarbone, pooling between her breasts. She reached out to touch her daughter's soft blond head, bent over the photos.

Hope didn't pull away but looked up and cupped her hand over Mary Alice's. "So, it's true. You are my mother." Her voice was almost reverent.

"Yes. I am."

Mary Alice scrambled to pull more photos from her purse with her free hand, her heart pounding in her chest. "And this is your sister, Charlene, and twin brother and sister, Evan and Ellie."

Hope stared at each photo, lightly touching a finger to the edge of each one.

Mary Alice didn't know who made the first move, but soon they were standing, arms wrapped around each other. Hope's body fit perfectly to hers, although Hope was taller, thinner. She pressed Mary Alice to her breast, kissing the top of her head like a child.

The room came back into focus. Through one eye, Mary Alice could see the elderly couple smiling up at them. Others were staring but she didn't care. She had her daughter back.

When the tears finally abated, they sat back down, both throwing questions so fast, they stopped and laughed.

"You first," Mary Alice said. "Tell me all about your life. Well, the short version. What did your parents tell you about being adopted?"

"My parents were older when they decided to adopt after many years of unsuccessfully trying to have a baby. I was their last chance, or Hope, thus my name." She shrugged a slender shoulder. "They told me I was adopted since before I can even remember. For years I thought all children were chosen, their words, instead of born naturally. They said they took one look at me and knew God meant for them to have me. I know it must sound strange, but I never asked about my birth parents until my adoptive parents were dying a few years ago. I suppose it was because I had such a happy childhood. I had no burning desire for anything different. Mom was diagnosed with liver cancer three years ago."

Hope's gaze dropped to the photos still on the table and swallowed hard.

Mary Alice wanted to hold her, squeeze away the pain from her. She felt the phone vibrate in her bag against her hip.

"She made it another eighteen months and died October 3, 2015. Dad had COPD from being a long-time smoker. We thought he'd go first, but he lived another six months after we buried Mom and died April 15, 2016. When they were sick, they thought I should know more about you. They explained you were very young and unmarried, and you'd been living at the Florence Crittenton Home for Unwed Mothers. That and my birth date and hospital was all they knew. I tried contacting the home about four years ago, but they told me all the records were destroyed. Ohio Adoption Agency opened a case on me, but I saw your Facebook post before they got back to me."

"I'm so sorry about your parents. So close together. I'm glad you had a good childhood. And you've been here, a few miles away from me all along. And now? I know you work at the library and your Facebook page said you were single. What else? What do you do for fun?"

She shrugged. "I guess I've never met Mr. Right. I've always loved books and I'm kind of an introvert, so becoming a librarian was a no-brainer. I love my work. My other passion is sculpting. Wood is my medium of choice. There is something special about taking an element that was alive and shaping it into a new form. In a way, I feel like I am breathing life back into it. I have a few pieces at a boutique art gallery on Wick Avenue near the university."

Mary Alice sucked in her breath. A wood sculptor. She had Charlie's talent and love for wood. "Charlie, do you hear that?" A warmth spread through her body. He heard.

"What about you? Your family?" Hope laughed out loud. "My family?"

Mary Alice examined their hands, clutched together. That was where the similarities were. They both had long, narrow fingers. Piano fingers, Charlie called them. Like Evan's. Their hands looked identical, except for a few extra wrinkles and age spots on Mary Alice's.

"My son—your brother," Mary Alice tapped the photo on the table. "Evan lives in Struthers with his partner, Ricky. Evan is a concert pianist. We are so proud of him. His twin sister, Elinor, or Ellie as we call her, lives in Struthers with her husband, Greg, and beautiful daughter, Bethany." Mary Alice tapped the recent family photo of the Proctor family. "Our other daughter, Charlene, is single and lives in Columbus, teaching theology at The Ohio State University." Her finger rested on a photo of Charlene taken when she gave a speech at the university.

"Your biological father was the most wonderful man in the world. I called him my eleven, because on a scale of one to ten, he blew the top off the scale. We were childhood sweethearts." She watched Hope soaking in every word. "He wanted you from the very beginning, but we were both only sixteen when I got pregnant with you."

Mary Alice gulped down a fresh round of tears. "Charlie, your father—you would have loved him. His passion was his family first, his infatuation with wood second. He passed away on August twentieth last year. A massive stroke."

Hope squeezed her hand tighter. "I'm sorry I didn't get to meet him. He sounds wonderful."

Mary Alice nodded. "I was the receptionist for his cabinet business, but I was mainly a housewife. I devoted my life to my family. I love to bake, as you can tell." She laughed and swept her hand across her round middle. "And I almost always have fresh baked goods for whoever drops in."

Hope gave a slight smile. A silence passed between them, but not uncomfortably so. They had no words, and yet so many things to say.

Mary Alice stroked her daughter's cheek. "I can't believe

you are really here, after all these years. I found you." The words caught in her throat.

Hope inhaled, placing her hand over Mary Alice's on her cheek. A fresh stream of tears leaked from her eyes. "Can you believe it? Does this feel surreal to you too? I don't even have words to express how I feel."

Hope's amber eyes sparkled. "Can I meet my brother and sisters? I've never had a sibling before. Imagine, two sisters and a brother?"

"And a teenage niece. You've inherited a huge crew. But I haven't told them I found you yet."

"Why not?" Hope tilted her head, her eyes burrowing into Mary Alice. She had Charlie's eyes, alright, but they were more intent, searching, curious. If only Char wouldn't be such a stubborn woman, the two of them might get along. Char had the same intense stare.

"Well, maybe this is silly, and it's definitely selfish, but I didn't want to share you yet. This is our moment. I've been dreaming of this day for a very, very long time, and I want to enjoy meeting you without my gaggle poking me with a million questions. When they ask if they can meet you, I want to be able to say 'of course, why don't we meet right now?'"

Hope nodded and lowered her eyes as they softened into something almost shy. "I understand. I was afraid the test wasn't going to be a match. I was terrified to get the results. And then, I thought, what if it is a match? Well, I don't know what I thought: scary and exciting, going into the unknown, anticipating the surprise and not knowing if it's going to come."

She shrugged with a bashful little grin, "I'm a little bit of a horror nerd, I guess. Shirley Jackson is my favorite author, and I always go to Halloween haunted houses in October, a silly thing I still do with my friends."

Not another one. Charlene is obsessed with horror flicks, which totally goes against her holier-than-thou persona. See, they already had one thing in common.

"There's actually this amazing house I went to with these gorgeous walnut columns—teak wood throughout. It's for sale right now, and I'm seriously considering putting an offer down."

For a split second, Mary Alice considered whether there was something Hope might want besides a family. Sophia's daughter flashed through her mind. She quickly brushed it away.

"Well, I hope you get your house." Hope wasn't going to ask for money. She was being paranoid. "Though, fair warning, I am terrified of ghosts." Mary Alice remembered a particular Halloween when Charlie popped out in a sheet and said 'boo!'

"Frankly, nothing will ever come close to petrifying me the way that DNA test did. The wait was almost unbearable." Mary Alice laughed and placed her hand on Hope's again. "But, yes, of course you will get to meet the family. Give me time to tell them, and I'll let you know as soon as they do."

"Okay, I'm very anxious." Hope said, a grin spreading ear to ear, her eyes sparkling. She looked at the slim, silver watch on her wrist. "I wish I could stay all day, but I have to be at the library by noon."

"I understand. Can you believe we've been talking for almost three hours? And I feel like we have only begun." Mary Alice got to her feet. She hated to leave too. Hated to let Hope out of her sight.

"We'll talk again real soon." They each hesitated for a minute, awkward on how to close this reunion. Then simultaneously, they reached out and embraced. Mary Alice planted a kiss on her temple.

They walked out arm-in-arm to Mary Alice's car. Hope gave her one more hug before heading to her own car. Mary Alice couldn't wipe the smile off her face as she unlocked the car. "We did it Charlie. Did you see her? Isn't she wonderful?"

I saw Mar. She is beautiful.

Mary Alice clicked the seat belt and started the engine. Her handbag vibrated again. She reached in and picked up the phone. Nine missed calls from Charlene. No messages. She dropped it back into her bag. She'd call her when she got home.

Twenty-Five

2017

Char's Lexus gleamed in Mary Alice's driveway. She pulled up behind her daughter's car and took a breath. Should she have interrupted her time with Hope to answer her? Was she choosing one over the other?

The driver side door popped open and Char's long legs slid from her Lexus. Mary Alice watched her shoot to her feet and stomp up the walk, a scowl on her face. She was clearly upset.

Mary Alice should have answered her messages as soon as she got in the car at the Starbucks. She'd been so preoccupied she forgot. "Char, is everything okay?"

"Where have you been? I've called you over and over." She shook her cell phone in the air above her head.

"I'm sorry." Mary Alice hadn't even looked at the missed messages yet. She'd had other things, another daughter on her mind. "Come in."

Char's hair, normally perfectly styled, looked like it hadn't seen a comb in days. No make-up. Baggy sweats. Trembling hands. Mary Alice had seen this look before. It spelled trouble. "Do you want some tea?"

Char nodded and Mary Alice led them into the house through the kitchen door. "I can't reach my sponsor. I guess I needed someplace to go . . . someone to talk to . . . so I don't go . . ." Her voice trailed off.

Mary Alice breathed a quick thank you to the Lord. At least she hadn't gone off the wagon yet. Or to a bar. One day at a time, wasn't that the AA motto or something? "Of course, dear. You know you're always welcome here. This is your safe haven. Has something happened?"

"Yes . . . no." Char followed Mary Alice into the kitchen and sat down at the table. Her lips were pursed, and her hands fluttered between fingering the tablecloth and clasping and unclasping her hands.

"You've done so well lately. I thought your faith was helping." She was an absolute zealot about it most days. Mary Alice's mind flashed back to her other daughter whom she just left. One that looked poised and secure in her life. What a contrast. Mary Alice set the hot cup of tea in front of Char, who twirled the spoon in her cup, staring at the milk swirling into the tawny liquid.

"It did, it does. But sometimes the urge is still so strong, even praying doesn't seem to help."

Mary Alice sipped her tea and waited. She should ask Char where she'd been and why she disappeared, but there was always a risk of arousing her temper. She didn't want Char flying off the handle and disappearing again. She had to be careful.

Char didn't immediately answer. Instead, she dropped a sugar cube into the tea and kept stirring it. If Char wanted to talk, then Mary Alice would listen. And if she wanted to be silent, that was okay too. Mary Alice set the cookie tin on the table and set out two small plates.

Charlene dropped a second cube into her teacup. "Do

you remember when I started drinking?"

How could she forget? Char had been a sophomore at Youngstown University. Things were going so well; she'd been accepted into Phi Sigma Sigma. It was the only sorority she rushed. Char had never been an A student, but her grades were okay until they suddenly started to slip. First, a call from the dean that she would be dropped if her grades didn't come up. Then the calls from Char started coming late at night. Her voice, loud and belligerent, vowels slurred together, rants about how Mary Alice and Charlie loved the twins more than her. She said horrible things when she was drunk.

"Yes, I remember." Mary Alice knew something must have happened for her to start drinking heavily but she never knew the reason why. What made this sudden change in her daughter? True, she'd always been strong-willed, much more outspoken than the twins, but she was never as snappy and mean as she'd become. She'd had a perfect childhood. Nothing pointed to what brought on the sudden change. Charlie had tried to get her to tell them. He'd begged her to go for help. Mary Alice had tried to reinforce the love they had for her. But nothing they did helped.

"I never told you what happened, why I started drinking."

Mary Alice nibbled on a peanut butter cookie. "No, you didn't. Papa and I figured you'd tell us when you were ready."

A tear escaped from one of Char's big round blue eyes. She wiped it away with the back of her hand. "I . . .I . . . he . . . something happened to me at school."

Mary Alice's heart pounded loudly in her chest. "Uh, huh."

"There was a party." Char slurped at her tea. "Things got kind of out of hand. I was drinking. Everyone contributed something to the punch bowl. Truthfully, it was awful. I don't know if it was the punch or if someone slipped something in my drink, but the next thing I remembered, I was upstairs, in a bed, bruised and naked."

Mary Alice's mouth dropped open. "You were raped?"

Char sank lower in the chair, nodding ever so slightly. "I

didn't even know it. But he made no bones about giving me all the gory details later. He even bragged about it."

"Oh, sweetie. I'm so sorry. Why didn't you go to the police, or come to us?"

"I couldn't stand myself. I felt so dirty. The only thing that helped was to forget about it. And the only way I knew how to do that was to drink."

Mary Alice's heart broke for her daughter. "You could have come to us."

Char shook her head. "No, I already felt like a failure. Ellie and Evan were always so perfect."

"They were never perfect, and you were never a failure. That's always been in your head, but it's not reality, Charlene. But you found yourself, didn't you - when you found God? And look at you now. You're a success story if I ever saw one."

"After I hit rock bottom."

"That's usually the way it works, sweetie." Mary Alice slipped her hand atop Char's and twined their fingers together. "But what has brought on this new temptation? Why the change now?"

Charlene pushed her cup to the center of the table and dropped her head onto her crossed arms. "Bethany's news—and your news." Her voice was muffled in her arms, but Mary Alice still heard. "Bethany's pregnancy has brought up more than old memories for you. They've put me into a tailspin I can't seem to get out of.

"And something else. The Lord may have forgiven me, but I still can't forgive myself." Minutes ticked by without speaking. Char's voice dropped to a whisper. "I had an abortion."

An abortion? A sound escaped Mary Alice's lips. A squeak, a hiccup, she wasn't sure. So that's why Bethany's pregnancy bothered Char so much, and more importantly, her decision to keep the baby. She slid into the chair next to Charlene, one arm still on her daughter's shoulders. "The situation was very different."

Char lifted her head but stared into space, avoiding Mary Alice's eyes. "It kills me Bethany's a better person than me. That you're a better person than me. Everyone is a better person than me. I'm a fake, and a hypocrite. I felt righteous when I heard you gave away your child. Not as bad as what I did, but at least you weren't perfect." She dropped her head back on her arms. "And I know I was overreacting and should have come to Thanksgiving dinner. I got drunk instead. I wanted to apologize, but I needed my sponsor and . . .I need a drink."

The tea kettle whistled. Mary Alice stood and set a fresh pot of tea in front of Charlene. "I am far from perfect and, no, you do not need a drink. You only need to believe you are loved, and not judged. Be a little easier on yourself, Charlene. You did what you felt you had to at the time."

Mary Alice let Charlene cry inconsolably. She'd always suspected something like the rape, but she'd never imagined an abortion. She had told herself she was being overly pessimistic. She had to quit reading all those articles in the Women's Day magazine about college date rapes. But she had changed so dramatically and so quickly, something traumatic had to have happened. But an abortion? Hearing the truth was hard. All these years, Char had walked around with this secret burden on her shoulders, afraid to share it, even with her mother. More secrets. Like Hope.

They had tried to reach out to her. Charlie brought her home from school and made her spend the summer at home. He contributed it to stress. Lots of college kids had trouble adjusting to life away from home. They hoped a few months at the house would do the trick. But Char never opened up and Mary Alice was convinced it was more than stress. Did she not feel loved enough to confide in them? Did they fail her? Should they have forced the issue?

"Why don't you go up and wash your face? You can stay all day and overnight if you want. I'm here for you until the urge to drink passes. Do you want to pray? I'll pray with you."

"Thanks Mom." She placed her palm on top of Mary Alice's hand and smiled. One of those small, sweet smiles Mary Alice hadn't seen on her since she was very young. "I'll go wash my face."

Char stood and looked down at Mary Alice, like she

was about to say something. Instead, she pursed her lips into another little smile, leaned down, and kissed the top of Mary Alice's head.

A warmth rolled through Mary Alice, so new from Char and yet so distantly familiar she didn't know how to react at first. She was still trying to understand as Char left the room. What had transpired here? Had that been a breakthrough? Should she be happy Char had finally revealed the truth? Should she be more upset by the rape or the abortion? It had been so long ago, but they both had altered her life forever.

A loud crash came from upstairs, and Mary Alice shot to her feet. "Charlene?" She walked to the stairs at a brisk clip, "Sweetie, are you okay up there?"

"Aaahhh" Charlene stormed down the stairs, a white piece of paper gripped in her hands. She made it to the bottom step and rounded the banister, holding the paper high. "Her name was Charlene?" Char screamed. "You named your first child Charlene? What does that make me? Her replacement?"

"No, no," Mary Alice tried to explain, realizing she had left Charlie's open letter on the bed. "We knew she'd get a different name when she was adopted. That was just . . .the name we used when I was pregnant. We didn't know what her name was, really."

Charlene stormed toward the kitchen and Mary Alice hurried behind her. Charlene slapped the letter on the kitchen table. "Papa called her Charlene. Not me. Is that why I was always 'Char' to him? Because he already had a Charlene? I thought it was a pet name because he loved me. Now I see why I've always felt like I didn't belong in this family. I was her substitute. It was her you wanted all along, not me. My whole life is a lie." She grabbed the letter from the table, ripped it in half and tossed it in the air.

Mary Alice gasped as she watched the pieces flutter to the floor. Frozen in place, she couldn't say a word as Charlene stormed out.

Twenty-Six

2017

Mary Alice had to talk to Char. It had been three days. A text or even a phone call would not do. She wasn't answering anyway. She'd been trying every hour since Wednesday when she found the letter. School was out for the winter break. Christmas was only a week away. She hoped Char would be home at her condo in Columbus and not out on a binge.

It was a two-hour drive in good weather. As the snow picked up and visibility diminished, Mary Alice started having second thoughts. She tried to think of pretty, snow-covered Christmas cards. She turned on the radio to listen to Christmas carols. But this snow wasn't pretty. It was wet, heavy and gray and clogged her windshield wipers. The roads were coated in black ice, cars on either side of the road already wedged in ditches. Even though it was only late afternoon, it was as if the sun had turned off its light. If only she could make it safely there, she'd wait it out before trying to head back home.

Thankfully, she arrived at Char's condo in one piece. But as she steered the car into her parking lot, she hit a patch of ice and almost rammed into somebody's red Corvette. Missing the car by inches, she sat and exhaled, trying to calm her nerves. Should she have called first? Even if it was only a text Char would not answer? Well, too late now. She was here, and clearly not going anywhere for a while.

She opened the car door and swung one leg out. The

wind grabbed the heavy door and slammed it back onto her leg. She screamed in pain. She tried to pull her leg free, but the door was too heavy. The wind battered her face and stung at her eyes, pounding against her relentlessly as she clutched at her knee and kept trying to pull. White-hot pain lanced up her ankle and icy wetness leaked into her clothes, making her shiver. Her fingers were going numb.

Somebody, please come out. Please help me.

No one in their right mind would be out in weather like this. The parking lot was empty of people. Most of the students would have gone home for the holidays. No one to see or help her. She felt like a fool now for even attempting to go out. The pain made her woozy. She tried reaching for her purse, which held her phone, but her bag had twisted behind her with the strap still on her shoulder, tangled in the seat belt.

Freezing wind and snow whipped through the open door. Tears froze on her cheeks. Finally, she untangled the seat belt and wrestled the purse to her side so she could reach inside. She felt around for the phone. Why did she have so much crap in there? Her stiff fingers traced everything: her wallet, a hairbrush, a notepad, prescription bottle, keys, lipstick, pens. No phone. Then she saw it on the floorboard under the steering wheel, next to her right foot. It must have slipped out of her purse when she slammed on the brake.

"Help! Help!" she screamed, as much from frustration as from pain, even as she knew her voice would never carry over the sound of the wind and the traffic from the nearby highway. She tried again to push the door off her leg. The wind pushed back. She tried to reach under the steering wheel. Even in her best physical condition, she'd never been a contortionist. She tried kicking the phone with her right foot. It moved an inch or two but slid under the seat so now she couldn't see it at all. Pain and anger bubbled up inside her. She pounded on the steering wheel and the horn honked. The horn! Why hadn't she thought of that before? She laid on the horn, the blaring sound adding to an additional increase in her blood pressure.

The manila envelope from the lab had slipped to the floor of the passenger seat. She couldn't reach it either. She glared at it, as if it was the cause of all of this. Was it, in a way? Would Char have been this upset over the letter from Charlie if she, Mary Alice, hadn't started this whole venture to find her daughter?

Sh, Calm down Mar. You can do it. Get your leg free. Watch the trees.

"Trees? Whatever are you talking about Charlie? How can that help?"

Mary Alice let off the horn and concentrated on the trees, *pine*, how they swayed eerily with the wind. The green thistles bowed, their tips crystalized in snow bent almost to the ground, then straightened before the next gust came. There was a distinct rhythm to it. She had to time it right – push between the gusts of wind. She waited until the trees stilled then shoved her shoulder against the door with all her might. It opened just wide enough to pull her leg back through the door before the wind slammed it against the car again.

She dropped her head back against the headrest. Her leg throbbed, and her face felt stiff from the cold, but at least she was completely enclosed in the car. She still couldn't reach her phone. She leaned on the horn again. She'd have to sit there until someone found her, or spring came, whichever came first. Winters in northern Ohio were hell. Why hadn't they moved to Florida like her brother Tommy and so many of their friends? What a day this had been, and it wasn't even over yet.

She turned the engine back on and cranked up the heat. At least she had plenty of gas and wouldn't freeze to death. *Breathe. You're okay.* Was her leg broken? It could be. It throbbed beneath her pant leg and she smelled metal or iron. Blood. She had to think positive. Char would see her and come out for her. Soon, she hoped. The warmth of the heater soothed her. She closed her eyes.

Bam, bam, bam! Pounding on the door scared the living daylights out of her. "Mom, what are you doing in there?" Char was standing beside the car, hair salted with snow, her arms wrapped around her middle, shivering against the cold, dressed only in jeans and a T-shirt. She pulled on the door and held it against the wind.

"I hurt my leg," Mary Alice began. "I don't know if I can walk."

"What? When? Wait right there. Let me get help." She closed the door gently and sprinted up the steps of the condo building.

Soon, Char returned with some guy Mary Alice had never met. Was he a boyfriend of Char's? At this point, who cared? They lifted her out, each supporting her under an arm, practically carrying her up the steps and into the condo. They deposited her on the soft cream leather sofa and helped her out of her coat. The room was warm and inviting to her frozen extremities, but she didn't miss the array of empty beer bottles and a filled ashtray on the coffee table.

Mary Alice reached for her pant leg and lifted it to her knee, exposing a nasty gash. Blood was beginning to clot, and her leg was streaked with dark red and purple bruising around her shin. "I caught it in the door, trying to get out. I blew the horn. I guess you didn't hear. The wind . . ."

"Um," Mister savior-in-a-t-shirt said. "Should I call an ambulance?"

Char knelt beside her. "Oh God. That doesn't look good. Do you think it's broken?"

The man vanished into another room and reappeared with a small bowl of water and bandages. "First, we need to clean up this cut, and get you bandaged up," he said. "You probably should have x-rays, but I think it will wait until the weather lets up. Stay put and don't walk on it." Char took the bandages from him and efficiently cleaned her wound and wrapped it in soft gauze.

A whiff of stale beer emanated from Char. "Thank you." Mary Alice looked from Char to the man. "I don't know what I would have done if you hadn't found me."

Char frowned and stood, picking up the empty bottles and ashtray. "I was coming out to get the mail. I was so surprised to see your car. Why didn't you call first?" Her concern seemed to have morphed back to hostility.

"Well, thank God for the mail," said the strange man who reached out a hand toward Mary Alice. "I'm Robert Hastings. I live across the hall."

Ah, so not a boyfriend. "Well, thank you Mr. Hastings for helping to rescue me."

"Robert, or Rob." He smiled back and glanced at Char. Was that some sort of intimate non-verbal communication? He did have a nice smile, and gorgeous thick jet-black hair.

"I still think we need to get you to an emergency room, but it looks like you won't bleed to death until it lets up. Charlene did a good job patching you up."

Charlene physically flinched at the sound of her name.

"I wasn't thinking. I needed to talk to you. About . . ." Mary Alice looked at Char and then to Robert. "The weather didn't look bad when I left the house. And then I dropped my phone and couldn't reach it."

Robert seemed to get the clue she had something personal to talk about and backed toward the door. "Well, if you need anything, or help getting to the ER, I am right across the hall."

"Thanks Rob," said Char before he closed the door behind him. She looked over at Mary Alice. "I don't have anything to say to you, Mom. It's good to finally know my place. It explains a lot."

Mary Alice sighed. "Oh, Char. You know better. You haven't answered any of my voicemails or my texts. We haven't talked since...." She let the sentence dangle in mid-air, not wanting to state the obvious — since Char found the letter from Charlie.

"I've been busy," Charlene said, her voice as cold as Ohio winters. She turned her focus back to straightening the magazines on the coffee table.

Mary Alice waited in silence, her fingers twisting the straps of her purse. Char couldn't ignore her forever. She'd wait until Char had no choice but listen. It felt like a stand-off. When Mary Alice didn't respond, Charlene snapped her head back, eyes piercing Mary Alice's heart.

"What? Did you expect me to be drunk in a ditch somewhere? Well, I'm not. I didn't fall off the wagon. I found my sponsor." The empty beer bottles were not so convincing.

She brushed her hand in the air, like a dismissal. "You don't need to worry about me. I'm fine. Go find the real Charlene. Maybe she needs you."

The comment punched Mary Alice in the gut. "Char."

Bloodshot amber eyes stared dry-eyed back at her. "Is there something else I can help you with? I have class in a half hour."

"That's not true now is it, Char? It's winter break. Can't we talk?"

"Why, Mom? What good would it do? You can't change history." The edge slipped a little from her voice. "I've prayed about this. I'm good now. I'm sorry you had to drive all the way down here . . . and I'm sorry about your leg. I'll take you to the ER if you want."

The way she crossed her arms over her chest, eyes turned away avoiding contact, the slight tremor to her hands, the iciness of her voice, all showed she was anything but good.

"It's still snowing. We can go to the ER later. Please. I'm not leaving until you hear me out."

Good for you, Mar. Don't give in. Stand up to her.

"Thanks, Charlie."

Charlene's shoulders drooped, and she attempted a smile that didn't quite make it to her eyes. "Want some coffee, or tea? Can you walk?"

"I think so." Mary Alice let out a sigh of relief. If only she would take the news about Hope as easily. She followed Charlene slowly into the tiny kitchen.

"Okay, Mom. I'm listening." Char folded her fingers into a church and steeple, her index fingers tapping against her lips.

It reminded Mary Alice of the nursery rhyme that went with the hand motion. Here is the church, here is the steeple. Open the doors and see all the people. "Do you remember that from when you were little?" It reminded her of the sweet little Charlene of her childhood. When she sat on Charlie's lap and made up outlandish stories. When she sat on the kitchen counter covered in flour helping bake cookies. Before life turned her bitter and judgmental.

"Remember what?" Char dropped her hands.

Mary Alice mimicked the hand motion and repeated the rhyme. "You were doing that, you know." Her heart warmed with the memories.

"I was?" A genuine smile crept across Char's lips and she made her little church, wiggling her fingers to see all the people. "Yes, I remember. Papa taught us."

Mary Alice watched Char's shoulders relax. A crack in Charlene's armor? "I was worried about you. You had to know I'd come looking for you."

"It's a two-hour drive, Mom. It's not like I'm going to drop in for coffee every day."

"True, but you missed Thanksgiving. And then last week . . ." She reached across the white shabby-chic painted wooden table, *oak,* and took Char's hands in hers. "I didn't mean to upset you. And neither did Papa when he wrote that letter. We didn't name you Charlene to replace her. That was never a thought in our heads. It was my idea. I wanted to name you after your father. The baby . . . your sister was gone. She was nameless. You have to believe me."

Mary Alice watched her daughter's face redden and bite down on her lower lip, a familiar sign she was upset. Char stared at the table.

Char didn't answer but pulled her hand from Mary Alice's and gripped the coffee mug so tightly her knuckles turned white. Was she going to throw it? She loosened the stranglehold on the mug and twirled her spoon through the liquid. Her knee bounced, shaking the table. Hope did that too when she was nervous.

Before Mary Alice could continue, she noticed Char's head was bowed, both hands now under the table. She was praying. Mary Alice waited. What had she prayed for? For Hope Pendleton not to exist?

She had to tell her. Regardless of how she would take it, she had a right to know. No time like the present. "I found her." Mary Alice said softly when Char looked up.

Char's spoon stopped mid-air. "Who?"

Okay, if that was the way she wanted to play this. "Your older sister."

178

"I don't have an older sister. That's strictly biology. And I'm not interested in hearing any more about it."

How could she say that? Mary Alice's heart pounded in her chest. This wasn't a child from some scandalous affair. This was her full-blooded sister, Charlie's daughter, as real and legitimate as Char, or Ellie and Evan.

"I think that's going to be a bit impossible. I've met her. We did DNA testing. You can't pretend she doesn't exist. Your brother and sister want to meet her. Don't you? Aren't you even a little bit curious?"

Char held up a hand. "Stop. No," she shouted. She lowered her voice, cold as the ice forming on the windowpane. "I do not, and I'd appreciate it if you would respect my wishes. Leave me out of your little reunion with your bastard child. It was wrong then and it's wrong now. If you want her, you can't have me. There isn't room for two Charlenes in my world and there shouldn't be in yours."

A bastard? God, no. She was nothing like that. She was Charlie's and hers. Their marital status had nothing to do with it. And there weren't two Charlenes. There was only Hope and Charlene. Both their beautiful daughters. "But . . ."

"No. End of subject."

Mary Alice didn't want to fight with her daughter. If she was honest with herself, there had been times she had questioned if finding Hope was the right thing, but that was before she found her. How could she not want to connect with her now? She couldn't pretend she'd never found Hope and she certainly couldn't give up Charlene.

"Help Charlie. What do I do now?"

Be strong, Mar. Don't give in.

A numbness settled over Mary Alice. She felt the same helplessness as when her father whisked her away to the Florence Crittenton Home. No choice, no voice in what happened with her own baby. She couldn't let it happen again. She was stronger now. She had a voice. She would not, could not, let anyone take her child away again.

They finished their coffee in silence, or more accurately, Char did. Mary Alice couldn't swallow anything with that lump in her throat.

"I really do have appointments I must keep," Charlene said, standing and moving the mugs to the sink. "It was nice of you to check on me, Mother," her voice as icy as the roads. She looked out the small window over the sink. "The snow has stopped. Let me get you to the ER."

Mother? She was going there? The only time the kids called her Mother was when she was angry or condescending. If Mary Alice thought she could drive to the ER herself, she would have refused the offer. Instead, she bit her lip and nodded.

"I wouldn't have sprung this on you so sudden, but I wanted to invite her for Christmas, so you could all meet at one time."

Char's face clouded into a dark scowl. "Then it will be without me. You have to choose Mother. Either her or me."

Mary Alice's mouth dropped open. No, she couldn't. There had to be a way. She would not even dignify that with an answer.

"Well," Char said. She crossed her arms and tapped her foot. "Who do you choose?"

Mary Alice felt the hairs stand on the back of her neck. Now she was angry. How dare Char pose such a question to her? Of course she was concerned about Char's feelings. That was being a parent. But by refusing to choose between daughters, she was opting for a life with Hope in it instead of the guilt she'd carried so long after giving her up. "I choose both of you Charlene. You can't ask me to pick one over the other."

Charlene chewed on her lower lip. "I see. It seems like you already have. Let me make this perfectly clear. I will not have anything to do with her. I will not be in the same room with her. I will not attend any family function she is at. Is that clear enough for you?"

Mary Alice bristled, her hackles up now. If she wanted a fight, well, she was in for one. "Charlene Sophia Goodson. I will not allow you to speak to me like that. I am your mother, as you choose to address me, and neither you, or your brother and sister have any say in who I accept into this family. I was only offering an opportunity for you to know your sister, not asking your permission."

"Do you want a ride to the ER or not? This conversation is over."

Mary Alice nodded, the anger already abating. She'd never spoken like that to anyone, least of all one of her own children. Her skin prickled like a thousand ants crawling over her. She needed her daughter, all of her daughters, and her son. Had she gone too far? She hadn't realized she was crying until the tears dropped on her folded hands.

It was getting dark by the time they left for the hospital. After another hour wait in the emergency room, the X-rays showed a hairline fracture of the tibia. They splinted it and wrapped fresh bandages around the gash. Mary Alice was given crutches and told to stay off the leg for a few weeks.

"Take me back to my car please. I need to get home." They had barely spoken a word since the argument.

"It's late, Mother. You can stay in my spare room . . . or I can get you a hotel room."

If spending the night in the same place with her mother was that much of a strain, she'd drive home. At least she could still drive since it was her left leg and she had an automatic transmission. "No, thank you," said Mary Alice. "I think I'd prefer to go home."

Twenty-Seven

2017

Mary Alice made it to her house, her leg throbbing the whole drive there. She had held off on the pain meds until she got home, not wanting to drive under the influence. She hobbled into the house and collapsed in the double recliner close to the door.

After resting for a bit, she used her crutches to make it to the kitchen and fill a glass of water, took her pain meds, then made her way to the front hall. She glared at the steep staircase. No way was she going to climb them. She hobbled back to the recliner.

She was almost asleep when the landline rang. It was clear across the room. She didn't have the energy to go for it. The answering machine kicked on: "Mom, where are you? I've tried to reach you, but you aren't picking up on either this line or your cell. If I don't hear from you soon, I'm calling out the regiment to find you. Love you. Call me."

Evan. He would call out a full-blown manhunt if she did not call him back. Her handbag sat on the floor beside her chair where she dropped it when she came in. She reached for it and dug down for the cell phone. She tried to turn it on. The battery was dead. Ugh. Sometimes she really hated technology. Maneuvering back out of the recliner with pain meds swimming in her head was a herculean feat. But she made it and used her crutches to reach the landline.

Evan picked up on the first ring. "Mom. Where have you been? The weather is terrible out there."

"I'm fine, son. I just got home from Char's."

"Char's? What were you doing all the way in Columbus? It couldn't have waited until I could take you?"

"No, it couldn't wait." She hesitated. Should she tell him about the leg or the conversation about Hope? She really wanted to get some sleep and let the meds kick in all the way. "Listen Evan. I am really beat. Is it okay if I talk to you tomorrow?"

Evan didn't sound too enthusiastic, but he agreed. "Okay, Mom. As long as you are safe. I'll come by tomorrow. I'll tell Ellie to come too. Get some rest. And no more galivanting around in this weather."

"Okay." She could barely keep her eyes open. "Love you, son. See you tomorrow." Oh boy, was he going to have a fit when he saw the leg and crutches tomorrow, but right now, Mary Alice simply did not care. She fell asleep in the recliner and did not wake until the morning sun was shining in her eyes.

Mary Alice had barely had time to wash up in the half bath on the first floor before Evan was letting himself in the garage door the following day. She had hoped to have had a chance for a cup of tea in silence before all hell broke loose. No such luck.

"Mom?" Evan called from the kitchen. "It's me and Ricky. Are you decent? We brought bagels."

She was in the bathroom, of course she wasn't decent. And she was still in yesterday's clothes. She called through the closed door, "Almost. Give me one moment and I'll be right out."

Mary Alice tried to press the wrinkles out of her blouse with her hands. No such luck. She grabbed her crutches, took a breath, and hobbled out of the bathroom. She'd barely made it into the kitchen before Evan and Ricky gave one look at her and rushed to her side, practically carrying her to her seat at the table.

"Oh my God. Why didn't you tell me you were hurt last night? I would have come right away. What happened to you?"

She waved them both away. "I'm fine. I had a little mishap with the car door."

"Why were you even outside? You know how cold it can get, Mom. You could fall, or trip, or this!" Evan gestured wildly at her leg.

"And not telling anybody." Evan shook his head, "Mom, you can't do that. It isn't fair to us. You'd want us to call you if we were hurt, wouldn't you? And how did a car door do this? What do you mean 'a mishap?' I knew that thing was getting too old. You're getting a new car, Mom. You can't keep driving that old thing around."

"It wasn't the car's fault." Mary Alice said sternly, almost snappy. She wouldn't be buying another car, that was Charlie's car. She'd keep it even if it literally fell apart. "The wind closed the door on me, my purse got snagged around my shoulder, and I didn't have enough leverage to get the door off my leg. It was an accident. I had to see Char, so not driving wasn't an option."

"Okay, fine, so it wasn't the car's fault, but what I don't get, is why you felt you had to drive all the way to see Char in a snowstorm."

Her eyes fell on the torn halves of Charlie's letter she had retrieved from the floor and left on the counter. Both of them followed her gaze.

"She found an old letter from your father. She got very upset. I had to go talk to her," Mary Alice said quietly.

Evan walked toward the counter and reached for the torn letter. "May I?"

Mary Alice nodded. Evan placed the torn halves together, his eyes darting all over the page. Ricky hovered behind him, reading over his shoulder. They exchanged glances and moved away from the counter quietly, in unison, sliding into the chairs at the table.

"I take it she didn't handle that well," said Ricky.

That was an understatement. Mary Alice shook her head. Then, another car pulled into the driveway, rolling tires crunching loudly under the snow.

Evan leaned toward the window and peeked through

the blinds. A little huff of relief followed a tiny frown. "It's Ellie." He turned his head and looked at Mary Alice, "Does Char know about the leg?"

"She drove me to the hospital," Mary Alice said. When Evan's face turned stormy, she clamped her mouth shut. Oh, dear.

"She knew and she let you drive home?! That . . . ugh! She's such a —"

"Evan." Mary Alice hadn't used such a thundering tone with him since . . . had she ever? "I chose to drive home and your sister respected that. I was fine, and I wanted to drive home myself. She may be stubborn as a mule, but so am I."

She jabbed the table with her finger and Evan's eyes widened. That felt good. Maybe she wasn't being completely honest, and nobody had ever accused her of being stubborn before, but maybe she should be. Evan opened his mouth to say something, but the kitchen door popped open and Ellie hustled into the kitchen, making a loud 'brr' noise.

"Remind me why we didn't move to Florida." She closed the door behind her and shook out her snow-freckled hair.

"Because you hate sweating more than snow, dear." Mary Alice quipped. Ellie looked at her strangely, then her eyes drifted to her leg.

"Mom!"

Well, at least they were all together. This is good. I can tell them all together about finding Hope. "Put the tea pot on and set out the plates. I guess we are having an impromptu family meeting."

"What? What's going on? What happened to your leg?"

"She slammed it in a car door when she drove to Char's yesterday."

"But —"

Mary Alice didn't want to get into this with Ellie too. It didn't even matter. What mattered was the wonderful news. "If you will all stop fussing over me, I have some news I'd like to share with you, like I did Char."

"Why? What's wrong?" Ellie asked.

"Nothing's wrong. Actually, everything's right, more

185

than right. It's wonderful." Mary Alice grinned through the pain of her leg.

Evan raised his eyebrows and gave Ricky a do-you-believe-this look before folding his arms and eyeing Mary Alice. "Wonderful enough to overshadow a fracture?"

"Yes, actually." She took a deep breath. "I found her." Mary Alice could feel the smile on her face cracking through the drowsiness of her medication.

"Her?" Evan asked, his blue eyes wide with astonishment. "As in my long-lost sister? When? How?"

Ellie's mouth dropped open to form a perfect O.

Mary Alice's head bobbed up and down and tears pooled in her eyes. She didn't even get to answer the initial question before a barrage of rapid-fire questions assaulted her, swimming through her fuzzy thoughts and piling up until it became overwhelming. Mary Alice held up her hands in surrender and the room settled into a strange, tense quiet.

"I got the results from the DNA test. And there was a match. I have the DNA right here. And best of all, I met her."

Evan leapt from his chair at the table and wrapped her in a bear hug. "Oh Mom, that's wonderful. Where? When? Do we get to meet her?"

Ricky followed suit on the other side. Ellie hung back, always the cautious and practical one.

"You can thank Bethany for all this. She is really the one who did it. With social media. And Book Face."

"Facebook," all three said in unison with a laugh.

"Yes, yes." Mary Alice waved her hand. "Anyway, Bethany found the Crittenton Home on Facebook. She made a page and a post for me, and after a couple of duds, she found me. We agreed to compare our DNA and, well, it was a match. I met her at the coffee shop last Wednesday. Her name is Hope."

"Ah, Mom. Almost a week ago? Why didn't you tell us?" said Ellie. "This is so exciting. What is she like?"

"Well, I was dying to. But then Char . . .. Anyway, she has your father's eyes. She does woodwork like him too," she glanced at her son and gave him a grin, "and she has Evan's talent on the piano."

186

Ellie's face lit up. "We could all meet her at Christmas. Wouldn't that be a wonderful gift for all of us? Of course, Christmas dinner has to be at my house this year. With that bum leg, I'm definitely not having you host it."

Mary Alice thought about Char's ultimatum. She wasn't ready to tell her other children about that yet. "I don't know. We'll see. But the holidays have always been here. I don't want that to change."

"Things change, Mom. You know that."

Yes. Another holiday without Charlie.

"We will discuss this more later, Mom. Right now you need to get plenty of rest." said Ellie.

Mary Alice hated the idea of the holidays anywhere but in her house. And she hated the idea of not having Charlie to celebrate with her, and now maybe Charlene too, maybe Hope. It didn't do her any good to dwell on it right now. She'd figure it out when she was alone with her thoughts. She could talk about Christmas planning, though. "I was going to invite Sophia's family and Gladys for Christmas. I can't expect you to feed them too."

Ellie shook her head. "Nonsense. They can come to my house as easily as yours. End of subject." Ellie held out her hand and gave Mary Alice a flat, stern look. She used to look at Bethany like that when the girl wasn't listening, but Mary Alice hadn't ever been on the receiving end of it. Maybe the discussion could wait, or maybe she could let Ellie have Christmas at her house. She didn't know. Her head was too foggy and sluggish for thinking too much or arguing.

Mary Alice took her daughter's hand and Ellie helped her to her feet. Evan handed off the crutches leaning against the table and Mary Alice was led out of the kitchen. Before she knew it, she was staring at her recliner. Ellie lowered her into the chair and Evan seemed to appear from nowhere with an afghan in his hands. He tucked her in and warmth settled around her like a cocoon.

Ellie pulled the reclining lever and the footrest popped up, forcing Mary Alice to relax into the cradle of the seat.

"I am excited about you finding her, you know. I was

too concerned about you to let it sink in very much." Ellie said.

Mary Alice could almost see the wheels turning in her head. She reached for Ellie's hand. "I told Char. She didn't take it well. She wouldn't talk to me to me since she found Papa's letter."

Ellie looked at her, a question burning in her eyes. Evan left and came back with the halved paper in his hands. He handed the letter wordlessly to his sister and she unfurled it, reading silently. She sighed moments later. "Oh, Char." Ellie shook her head and dropped the letter away from her face to look at Mary Alice. "I can see why she was upset. We'll get through to her. Now, seriously, enough talking. Take a nap. I'll bring over some chicken soup later. We will let ourselves out." She kissed her mother on the forehead and slipped out of the room, Evan trailing behind her after he kissed Mary Alice as well.

A few minutes later, Mary Alice heard their cars pull away and smiled. She was so lucky to have these wonderful children and this amazing life. As she began to drift to sleep, hazy and warm, she thought that maybe it would all work out after all.

Twenty-Eight

2017

Mary Alice slipped into her trench coat, grabbed the keys from the rack by the kitchen door and hobbled to the car. She'd obeyed the doctor's order for almost three days, which meant that she'd been completely stuck in her house. The kids and Bethany came to visit often, which was a nice distraction, but the thing that kept her spirits up was Hope.

They'd been texting so much that Mary Alice had gotten quite good at using both of her thumbs to type. That was when Hope was at work, though. Whenever she got off work, she called Mary Alice and they would talk. About anything. Everything. There was so much to learn about this woman, decades stolen away from both of them. Sometimes, when she got off the phone with her daughter, she would lay awake and imagine raising her.

She wanted more than anything to see her again, but she was afraid. Hope kept asking about meeting the family, but Mary Alice had managed to keep up the lie that she had a terrible case of the cold. Hope accepted the excuse. Mary Alice was no spring chicken, so it was possible to have a cold for that long. She knew because it actually happened to her two years ago.

Christmas was getting uncomfortably close and she still hadn't managed to get ahold of Char. If only Mary Alice could reason with her, just one last shot, then maybe she could salvage this and have all of her children for the holiday. She would keep trying, even if she had to wait until the last minute.

Mary Alice limped out of her house and into the cold, biting air. She glared at the car door that had chomped on her leg like a sausage, as if this whole thing was its fault. Not this time. She marched to it as best as she could and grabbed the door handle, holding it firmly as she pulled it open. She didn't let go of the door until both legs were securely inside. Driving with only one good leg was awkward but thanks to automatic transmissions, not impossible. At least the roads were clear and there was no snow in the forecast. Despite Ellie's offer to drive her, she was busy with Bethany, who was in the throes of the second trimester.

She wasn't about to miss her monthly luncheon with the girls.

Mary Alice was first to arrive at Scarcella's Italian Restaurant on Market Street in Youngstown. The lack of updates to the place gave it character and a comforting warm feeling, remembering many Saturday nights from her childhood, and later dinners with Charlie and the kids. The same plastic, red-checkered tablecloths, red plastic seat cushions on metal frames. A bottle of merlot with three glasses circled a candle wedged into a wine bottle and a small bud vase with plastic flowers. And the aroma - ahh, the tomato and basil and garlic wrapped around Mary Alice's senses like a warm blanket. The food was to die for. And the fresh baked bread was famous for its crunchy crust with the perfect amount of chewiness and the incredibly soft and delightful insides.

The first Scarcella's cut their teeth on the American dream in 1957. Since then the faces had changed, grown up, moved on, but they were always replaced with other Scarcella family members.

Sophia blew through the door, a large satchel slung over her shoulder, long-slender legs in capris, her now snow-white hair pulled neatly into a bun at the nape of her neck. She planted a kiss on Mary Alice's cheek. She stared at the crutches. "How you doing, Hop-along?" Both Sophia and Gladys had been filled in on the accident by phone so thankfully Mary

Alice didn't have to go through it all again.

"Dandy. A bit unhandy, but I'll survive." She checked her watch then poured wine into the three glasses. "I wonder what's keeping Gladys. She's never late."

Sophia swirled the red liquid in the glass and breathed in the heavenly scent. "Hmm, luscious," and placed it back on the table. "She sent me a text that she was still unpacking from her trip. She'll be here."

She was still working full time. Nothing either of them could say would make her slow down. As if on cue, Gladys walked through the door.

"You're late." Mary Alice said, not waiting for pleasantries. They were way past that. Gladys dropped her squat body into the remaining chair at the table with a heavy sigh. "I spent the last twenty-four hours standing in one spot passing bricks like a conveyor belt to build that school. I'm getting too old for this. So, give me a break if I'm a little slow today." She ran her hand over her close crop of still dark curls and waved her hand. "Enough about me. We want to hear all about Hope."

The server, a new young girl with shiny black hair and florescent yellow bands on her teeth offered them menus. She introduced herself as Angelina. She had to be at least a fifth generation Scarcella. They waved the menus away, already knowing them by heart. The normal, spaghetti and meatballs for Mary Alice, chicken parmesan for Sophia and homemade cavatelli for Gladys.

Gladys scooped salad from the family-style salad bowl that arrived and placed it on her clear glass plate. Sophia bit into the warm Italian bread.

"It was wonderful, and terrifying," Mary Alice said. She relayed every detail of the meeting with Hope. "She's so beautiful. I can hardly stand it. She looks so much like Charlie. I told the family that I found her. Of course, Evan was ecstatic, Ellie, a bit cautious and Char — good grief, that didn't go well at all. Can you believe those different personalities came from these same loins?"

Sophia and Gladys nodded, their mouths full.

Mary Alice sipped her wine in silence, remembering the

ingnni!

differences in her children. Evan had always been the happy child, content to play by himself, Ellie, the "why" child, so curious and fascinated with life. And Char came out kicking and screaming, demanding attention from her first breath, and only increasing in fervor after the twins were born.

"Charlie had the talent to balance them all," Mary Alice said, sighing. "He'd cuddle Evan in one arm with a book, pausing every few minutes to answer questions from Ellie, all the while praising Char for her ballerina twirls or somersaults or whatever other distraction she could think of for his attention."

"He was a good man and a great father," Sophia said. "He'd be a hard act for any man to follow. Even my Desmond doesn't have Charlie's patience. Never changed a diaper in his life and his idea of fatherhood is showing up for the boys' baseball games."

"Oh stop," Gladys said. "Desmond is a great guy and you're lucky to have him." She waved a breadstick in Sophia's face. "And you know it." She turned to Mary Alice. "When do you plan to introduce Hope to the family?"

Mary Alice set down her fork. "Therein lies the problem. Char gave me an ultimatum. I told her I wanted to have Hope for Christmas to meet everyone. She said, and I quote, 'there is not room for your bastard child and me in your life. You must choose.'"

Gladys froze with her fork mid-air. "She really said that? Called her a bastard?"

Sophia about choked on the wine she sipped.

Mary Alice nodded and tried to tamp down the lump in her throat. "How could she say that? Hope is her full-blooded sister. Not some product of a sordid affair."

Even as she said the words, she knew the answer. Jealousy. That had always been the big one for Char, the one thing that she couldn't let go of, even when she was so dedicated to her faith. She had nothing to be jealous of though. Nobody had tried to make her a replacement, it was only a name that Mary Alice and Charlie loved. When they couldn't give it to their firstborn, they gave it to Char. The name meant something to them, and they wanted to give it to their child, that was all.

Gladys and Sophia were probably thinking the same thing judging by their knowing expressions. At least they were kind enough not to say what Mary Alice already knew.

"What are you going to do?" asked Gladys.

"I don't know. I know Hope is expecting me to invite her to Christmas dinner—but I don't think I can do that to Char. She already missed Thanksgiving. Don't I have to put her first?"

She'd sworn to herself that she wouldn't choose between them. She'd held firm with Char, but the closer it got to Christmas, the more backed into a corner she felt.

Neither friend spoke for a few minutes. Totally unlike Sophia, who had an instant opinion about everything.

"That is so unfair to put you in that position," said Gladys.

Mary Alice couldn't agree more. She was tired of everyone telling her what to do and how to think. It felt like it had been going on her whole life. She wanted to take a stand, put her foot down as the head of the household now and insist that everyone, including Hope and Char, were expected around the dinner table this Christmas. She had waited long enough to have her whole family together. Charlie wouldn't be there, of course, but she wouldn't think about that. She was already having to face the thought of missing one of her girls, she didn't want to think about him on top of it right now.

Sophia reached for another breadstick. That woman could eat even if her house was on fire around her. "Do you really think Char won't come if you invited Hope?"

Mary Alice felt her resolve slipping. "I do. You know how stubborn she can be."

"Maybe," said Sophia, "and I'm not trying to tell you what to do, but . . . maybe . . . Char needs a little more time. You have sprung this on all of them pretty fast. They have gone from not even knowing they had a sister, to the chance to meet her in only a couple weeks. That is a lot for anyone to take in. And with Char . . . well . . . after the letter thing, I can kind of see her hesitation."

Gladys looked at her incredulously. "Sophia, she is not hesitating. She called Hope a bastard. Did you forget that already?"

"No, but I still think time will heal some of these wounds. We all have had experience with that."

Mary Alice twirled the stem of her wine glass. "I can't lose Char over this. She has been my daughter forever."

"So has Hope," said Sophia.

"Yes, but I did not know her until recently. I've learned to live without her. Maybe I could again."

"Not on your life," chimed in Gladys. "Now that she is here, you can't undo that. Nor do you want to. Maybe she would understand if you told her that the family needed a little more time to get used to the idea. You could promise it would happen, just not for Christmas."

Mary Alice looked at Sophia. "Is that what you think too? Do you think I'd lose her if I made her wait on Char? And what if Char never comes around?"

Sophia held up three fingers. "One - yes, I think you should ask her to wait. Two - No, I don't think you will lose her, and Three - I think Char will come around, but if she doesn't, that doesn't mean you still can't have a relationship with Hope."

It wouldn't be the right one, though. It would be like walking on eggshells to see her. But maybe Gladys is right. Hope is more reasonable than Char; most people were. If she asked Hope to adapt to what amounted to scheduling family functions around Char's non-attendance, she would be more likely to say yes than Char allowing Mary Alice to have her way.Have her way, like Mary Alice was a kid and Char was the parent. It was infuriating, but more than that, it hurt. What else was there to do at this point?

"Okay. I am trusting the two of you. I know you wouldn't steer me wrong. I hope you are right. I'll tell Hope she'll get to meet the family later, after Christmas." Mary Alice sighed and sagged into her seat. "Oh! I almost forgot. Christmas is at Ellie's this year, and you two better be coming."

"Wouldn't dream of missing it." Sophia said.

"Good." Mary Alice smiled ruefully. "If neither of my girls come and you two leave me to mope on my own, I'll never forget it."

Twenty-Nine

2017

"Hello, Hope? It's Mary Alice." Christmas was only a few days away and Mary Alice had to tell Hope that she couldn't meet the family. She'd been dreading this conversation all week, trying to put it off, but she knew she couldn't put it off any longer. Even though she had never officially invited her, Mary Alice was sure Hope was expecting an invitation. Dread filled her stomach and made her feel almost like she was out of her body, a surreal unfocus to the room.

Hope laughed over the line. She sounded so happy and optimistic, it made Mary Alice cringe. "I told you, caller ID is a thing. I knew it was you before I picked up."

Right, she knew that. She needed to snap out of it and do it. Mary Alice tried to say it, get it out there, but her words froze on her lips and left a strange silence over the line. Hope took a breath and charged ahead of the lull in conversation.

The silence on the line was palpable.

"So . . . anyway, how was your day so far?"

"Can we meet for coffee?" Mary Alice blurted. Her heart was hammering against her chest.

"Sure," Hope said, her voice quiet and cautious. "I'm free today. Same place, Starbucks on Belmont? Does eleven work for you?"

"Perfect." Things were far from perfect.

"Is everything okay?" Hope's voice sounded so small.

Afraid. She couldn't do this to her girl. No, but she had to. It was only for Christmas, she would understand.

"Yes." Mary Alice choked out. "I'll see you then."

Two hours later, Mary Alice was sitting in her car in the parking lot of Starbucks. Hope was sitting in the same booth by the window where they'd first met. It was like déjà vu. She stared at her daughter as she sipped from a white coffee cup, a book open in front of her. There was a second cup on the table, probably for Mary Alice.

Her eyes traced the slope of Hope's nose, the fullness of her cheeks, the strands of blonde falling around her face.

She would understand. She had to. There was no way around this. Mary Alice couldn't lose Char, and that's exactly what would happen if she let Hope come for Christmas. It would be a nail in the coffin.

Mary Alice took deep, calming breaths, opened the car door, and hobbled on one crutch into the coffee shop.

As Mary Alice limped closer to the table, she could make out the tea bag hanging from the cup. Hope had remembered she wasn't much of a coffee drinker. It wasn't fair that she was so thoughtful. That made this so much harder. Returning her kindness with making her wait to meet her own family.

Hope suddenly looked up from her book and her eyes widened into big amber saucers when she saw the cast and crutch. "What happened?" She jumped up from the booth, awkwardly taking Mary Alice's elbow and helping her to her seat.

Mary Alice grimaced. "I had a small run in with a car door. But it's not serious. Hairline fracture to the tibia. I went to Char's to tell her about you in person." She didn't need to know about the other issue, the letter, or the name calling. Better to get everything out now. "She didn't take it too well. Char has . . . issues."

Mary Alice settled down in the hard shop seat and folded her hands on her lap. "Thank you for the tea," she said without actually touching it. Hope pushed her book away and tilted her head a little. Mary Alice didn't know how to get her voice past the lump in her throat.

Hope leaned on the table and took a small inhale, dodging past Mary Alice's silence like an obstacle. "I'm sorry she was upset. And your leg—I feel responsible since you were delivering news about me." She genuinely seemed concerned.

"Don't be silly. You had nothing to do with the car door or the wind. I was foolish to be out in weather like that. You know how quickly it can change around here. And I told Evan and Ellie about you the next day. They were over-the-moon excited."

Hope nodded, sipping at her coffee before setting it down. She scanned Mary Alice's face without smiling. "But not Char."

Char's words flashed through Mary Alice's head. Bastard child. You have to choose. She gulped. "No, not Char. About that. I'm afraid Charlene is not completely on board with this yet. She's put me in kind of a pickle. I wanted you to meet the family at Christmas, but Char has threatened not to come if you are there."

"Oh." The disappointment was palpable in Hope's voice. Her face fell entirely. The light went out of her eyes and she dropped her gaze to her cup, aimlessly swirling her spoon through the dark liquid. Mary Alice's heart ached. Her stomach felt queasy, like she was going to be sick. This wasn't supposed to be so difficult, it was supposed to be a simple explanation and then understanding.

"I'd like to give her a little more time," Mary Alice continued. "Charlene has some personal things she needs to work through before she can accept this. I'm sure she'll come around. It really has nothing to do with you." Of course, that wasn't entirely true.

Hope's eyes were glassy when she looked up. She didn't answer.

Mary Alice cupped Hope's hands in hers. "This is going to happen. I promise. But in the meantime, we still have each other. And we can continue to see each other. That's huge, don't you think?"

Hope nodded wordlessly. She did not look convinced. Mary Alice wasn't convinced, either.

"I know it's not fair." Mary Alice said. "But, it isn't forever. I don't want to lose her over this."

"Me." Hope said suddenly, her voice quiet and hoarse. "You don't want to lose her over me."

Mary Alice gaped at her for a moment. There was a good answer for this, but she didn't know what it was.

Hope's eyes shifted from sadness to a fiery anger. Clearly a defensive posture. She stood up swiftly, her chair scooting back. "How long is that going to last? Another half a century? I don't have that much time."

Mary Alice stood too, her hand instinctively reaching for Hope.

Hope shied away from the touch and slung her purse over her shoulder. "I'm not going to wait on her, Mary Alice, or you. I've waited long enough already."

Hope had been calling her mom for the past two weeks. It had been awkward for her, Mary Alice could tell, but the word rolled off her tongue so easily after the first few tries. Now it was a cold, hard 'Mary Alice.'

She turned to walk away, but then she stopped and spun on her heel, her face pinching into something that looked like a blank mask. Like Char. "You shouldn't have caved in. You should have told her to deal with it instead of letting her decide whether you could see your own daughter or not. I bet you weren't even sick last week, were you?"

Mary Alice looked down.

Hope huffed out a humorless laugh. "I'm not surprised. You didn't fight very hard for me the first time, so why should you now?"

Mary Alice looked up sharply, her voice welling up in her. It wasn't the same, Hope knew that. She had to know.

"Have a wonderful Christmas, Mary Alice." Hope turned around again and walked at a clip, breezing through the coffee shop like wind.

"Wait," Mary Alice called when Hope was halfway to the door. She hadn't been expecting Hope to be so hurt, she expected her to understand, but she was hurt and she didn't understand. How could something so simple go so wrong?

Hope didn't stop. She stomped through the shop, and by the time Mary Alice had reached the door, she was already backing out in her car.

She shouldn't have brought up Christmas in the first place. She should have tried harder with Char, or maybe even set her own ultimatum. Hope was right, she didn't fight hard at all. Again. And now, she might lose her eldest because of that. Again.

Thirty

Christmas, 2017

Mary Alice's heart was heavy as she packed the last tin of Christmas cookies to be taken to Ellie's for Christmas dinner. She paused to look around her own home. Ellie and Bethany had helped her to hang a wreath on the door and scatter a few holiday knick-knacks around, but she had opted not to have a tree. Instead, she'd hauled down the ancient box of heirloom decorations that always hung on the tree. This year they would hang on the tree at the Proctor house. Greg had purchased a huge tree, balsam fir and had strung the lights. Mary Alice reminded herself to be thankful for Ellie's hospitality and Greg's help, despite the fact that they should be in her home, not Ellie's, and Charlie should be putting up the Christmas tree, not Greg. Charlie would have chosen a different tree, a douglas fir. Why didn't Greg remember that? Wrong tree. Wrong house. Wrong man on the ladder.

She loaded the car and made the five-minute drive to Ellie's. Greg and Ellie came out and helped her unload the car full of pies and cookies. Mary Alice carefully handed her the box of ornaments.

Ellie's eyes got wide. "Mom, are these—."

"Yes, but they are only a loan. Next year, they will be back on my tree, where they belong."

Ellie gave her a hug. "Yes, Mom."

The scent inside the house was heavenly. Bethany was

helping trim the tree with shiny new bulbs and ornaments. But this wasn't the Christmas that she used to know. So many things were wrong with it, and all of it was because Charlie wasn't here. Having family around helped ease the pain of experiencing the holidays without him, but only for a little while. She would start getting comfortable, or laugh, and then she would remember the empty space in the room.

Ellie set the box of ornaments on the coffee table. "Here, Bethany. Put these on the tree. But be very careful with them." She smiled at Mary Alice and headed back into the kitchen.

Mary Alice watched as Bethany carefully unwrapped each individual ornament. It reminded her of doing the same thing dozens of times. Some were from as far back as her grandparents. She'd loved the holidays as a child. She used to help her mother with the ornaments and the baking. They made dozens and dozens of cookies, all carefully placed in festive tin cookie cans and passed out to friends and family. It was all a competition, although Mary Alice didn't recognize that until much later. Could Dad put up more lights than Mr. Wilson across the street? Could Mom give out more cookie tins than Aunt Esther? Who sang the carols louder in church on Christmas Eve? Who had the biggest turkey? It was all about image, and everything to do with why she couldn't keep her baby as an unwed mother.

After she got pregnant, she no longer fit into that Norman Rockwell painting. Sure, her mother still asked her to help hang ornaments and bake Christmas cookies after she came home from the FC, but the joy of it had lost its luster. Her fairytale world had been shattered and no amount of sprinkles or fancy ornaments could bring that back.

That was until she married Charlie and the kids started coming. Charlie didn't care about images or competition, but he put more in the collection plate and donated more of his time than anyone. Always anonymously. He wanted his family around him to do everything; decorate the tree, hang the stockings, sing loud and off-key at the top of his lungs. And because it was Charlie's favorite time of the year, it had become Mary Alice's again too. Both sets of parents were invited to every holiday meal, as well as Paul and Tommy. The secret past they all

201

shared was buried for all time, or so they thought. Charlene, Evan, and Ellie were blessed with two sets of grandparents and two uncles who loved and adored them. Although Mary Alice and Charlie couldn't say they ever truly forgave them, they buried the hatchet for the benefit of their other children. Now only Uncle Tommy was left, and he lived 1,200 miles away in south Florida.

Mary Alice roused herself from her memories. "How's school going, Bethany?" She promised herself not to think of Hope while she was around her family. Or Char. It brought everybody down and it didn't solve anything.

Bethany's face lit up. "Gram, the FC's so awesome. I'm ahead in my classes, which I never was at Struthers High. I'll be able to go back to public school after the baby, if I want. But I might stay at FC until I graduate." She ran her hand over her belly. "Did you know the baby can hear things in the womb, like my voice and conversations? Estelle said it's important to use soft, soothing voices. A baby could get distressed if the mother was arguing. I'm not going to fight with Mom and Dad anymore. I want my baby to hear nothing but happy words. Estelle says he can hear music too, so I'm playing music and putting the earbuds on my stomach."

It still amazed Mary Alice that the Home had made such a remarkable turn in its philosophy since she'd been a resident there. She wasn't sure the baby could really hear through the earbuds, but she didn't say as much. The important thing was Bethany and the baby were healthy and happy. "That's wonderful, Bethy. Have you decided if you want to know if it's a boy or a girl yet?"

She'd been so indecisive about that the whole time. Bethany always loved surprises. Greg smiled from his perch on the ladder above the tree. It was good to see the father-daughter relationship healing. Greg was a good man and Ellie and Bethany were lucky to have him. He had only needed time to accept the fact that his baby was going to be a mother. He certainly was handling it better than her father had.

A half century earlier, things were very different. Although by all appearances, everything had gone back to normal after Mary Alice came home with empty arms, things were never the same. They went through the motions, said the right things, made cookies, went to church, sang songs, but the subject of Mary Alice's vacation was never mentioned. Even after she and Charlie were married, and the other children came along, it was understood that it was taboo to ever be spoken about again. Seeing the differences and the parallels between herself and Bethany left a pang in her heart.

"Yeah, I caved. I'll get the sonogram right after Christmas," Bethany said, pulling Mary Alice from her memories. "I've got an appointment for Thursday, January 4th. I'll be twenty-two weeks. The doctor said that before that she couldn't be positive because it was in a weird position. I know it's a boy. I feel it. I told Mom to buy blue baby clothes to put under the Christmas tree."

"You might want to stick with green or yellow until you know for sure."

"Well, even if I'm wrong," Bethany smiled, "Girls can wear blue. I'm totally not wrong, though. I think I felt him kick the other day, although it felt more like a tickle, or butterflies in my stomach." Bethany took Mary Alice's hand and laid it on her small baby bump. She was barely showing. Ah, the joys of new motherhood. The miracle never ceased to amaze.

Mary Alice swallowed a lump the size of a turkey leg when she viewed the seating arrangement around the table. A chair on one end, four on each side. The chair on the far end was conspicuously missing. Charlie's spot. Everything felt wrong. Charlie missing. Hope missing. Maybe Char, too. She had called several times and left voice messages and texts that Hope would not be coming, so hopefully she would, but she'd gotten no response.

She never should have agreed to Ellie hosting Christmas. They should be around their table, in their home, with Charlie in the kitchen sampling everything. "Get out of the way," she should be saying. "You're going to burn your fingers sticking it in the gravy like that." But there was no Charlie to shoo out of her kitchen, no Papa to beat the girls in a game of chess, no #11 to tickle the back of her neck with a kiss when her hands were too occupied for her to wriggle away. How was she ever going to get through another holiday without him? Or the next, or the next?

Hope should be coming to meet her family for the first time. But she wasn't coming and now, it looked like Char wasn't coming either. She lowered herself into one of the dining room chairs, careful not to bump her leg. If ever she needed Charlie, it was now.

Ellie stuck her head through the archway between the kitchen and dining room. "Mom? Are you all right?"

Mary Alice brushed away the telltale tear that had escaped and nodded. "I'll be fine."

Ellie sat beside her taking both her hands in hers. "I miss him too. I was hoping it would be a little easier for you here, less memories, and a lot less work."

"I don't want to lose the memories." Mary Alice's voice cracked. Memories were all she had. Would there ever be new memories? With all her children? With Hope?

The doorbell rang, interrupting her thoughts. From her view at the dining room table, Mary Alice watched Greg open the door to Sophia, Desmond and their boys, Clark and Philip. Sophia was loaded down with apple crumb cake, green bean casserole and a tin of Snickerdoodles.

"Merry Christmas," Ellie called from the dining room. She gave Mary Alice an apologetic smile before getting up and striding toward the front door. She walked up beside her husband. "Let me help you with those." She took the goodies from Sophia's hands, passing one to Bethany. "Set it in the kitchen for now." She leaned in to Sophia. "Mom's in the dining room. She's having kind of a rough day."

"I can see you, you know. And hear you. Don't talk about me behind my back," Mary Alice echoed from her place at the dining room. "At least not in my earshot."

Sophia laughed out loud at her friend and made the short walk down the hall to the dining room, where she joined Mary Alice at the table. "Behave yourself old woman. Ellie's gone to all this trouble for you."

"I never asked her to. I wanted to be in our own home

today."

Mar. Let Ellie do this for you. It's okay. I'm here.
"Oh, Charlie."

Evan and Ricky arrived next with Gladys pulling in the drive right behind them. Gladys headed straight to the kitchen to give Ellie a hand but was quickly ushered out as a 'guest.' Sophia and Gladys took the napkins Mary Alice had folded and placed them around the tables.

"Looks like everyone is here." Gladys said.

"Not Char, and not Hope. I've texted and called Char. No answer. We haven't spoken since last week." Mary Alice wiped a water spot from a crystal goblet near her. "And I told Hope not to come. What kind of family are we, knowing she has no family other than us, yet leaving her alone on a holiday like this? I feel terrible."

"I'm sure she understands. Once Char comes around, it will all work out."

"And if she doesn't? Hope said she is done waiting. I've lost her waiting for Char."

"I doubt that. She was hurt. She'll come around. What about Ellie?" Sophia asked. "Has she talked to Char?"

Mary Alice shrugged. "Briefly, from what I understand. She set a place for her." She eyed the place settings again and her glance settled on the empty space at the end of the table.

Sophia's gaze followed hers. "He's here, if only in his spirit."

"I know, that's what he said."

Sophia and Gladys exchanged knowing smiles. They knew all about Mary Alice's conversations with her dearly departed.

"Don't look at me like that. I know you think I'm crazy. But I need to keep talking to him. And he answers me, if only in my mind."

Ellie came into the dining room, frowning. She looked at the clock above the buffet. 3:15. Dinner was scheduled for 3:00. "Dinner is ready. I can hold things off for a few more minutes, but ..."

Mary Alice waved a hand in the air. "Don't ruin your

wonderful meal because of your sister. If it's ready, call every-one to the table."

Ellie hesitated in the doorway. "I hate to do that. She does have to travel the farthest. Maybe she's stuck in traffic on I-71. I'll give her ten more minutes."

At 3:30, she asked Bethany to help move everything to the table. Greg would have the honor of carving this year. It was fitting. He was the head of this household, and Charlie was gone. Everyone gathered around the table. Ellie had added a card table at the end for Bethany, Clark and Philip. "Who's going to say the blessing without Aunt Char?" Bethany asked.

"I'll do it," Greg said. He offered a blessing to all, and blessings for the food. It was thirty seconds compared to Char's five-minute blessings. "Amen" said everyone in unison. They each picked up the dish in front of them, filled their plate and handed it to the person to their left. For a while, accolades on the delicious food filled the conversation. Mary Alice listened to the conversations, adding little. They were all avoiding the elephants in the room, the absence of Char, the discovery of Hope. Her eyes settled on the empty chair across from her and then the empty space at the end of the table. She pushed her plate away and hurried from the room.

In the kitchen, she let the tears flow, gulping down the sobs as best she could. Sophia joined her after a few minutes as Mary Alice knew she would. She had to stop doing this, ruin-ing everyone else's good mood.

"Ah, Mar, don't do this," Sophia said. "Char could still show up. Let me try and call her."

Mary Alice laid her hand over Sophia's. "Don't. She knows we're expecting her. She wants me to choose between her and Hope. I did what she wanted, I didn't invite her to Christmas. But after this, I need to tell her — because Hope is not here today, it does not mean I can give up my child — again."

"You won't. No one can force you to ever make those kinds of decisions again. If Charlene cuts out her family, it's her choice to make, not yours." Sophia gestured with her chin toward the doorway to the dining room. "The rest of your chil-dren and grandchildren out there want to meet their lost sister.

Don't you owe them that?"

Mary Alice mopped at her eyes with a tissue. "I want to. So badly. But it doesn't seem right to introduce them without Charlene. These last few months have been such a roller coaster. First Charlie's death, then Bethany's news. Now finding Hope and not being able to introduce her to the family. Am I doing the right thing? What if I lose Char trying to stand up for Hope?"

"You've got to believe it will all work out."

Gladys came into the kitchen and after a few words of encouragement from her best friends, the three of them rejoined the family in the dining room for the rest of the meal. The meal went on, Char's chair sitting vacant as a reminder what the stakes were. Everyone knew about Hope now and eventually they prodded Mary Alice for details. At least Mary Alice could talk about her freely without Char in the room, and it felt good to tell them about her.

Mary Alice relayed some of the conversation she'd had with her daughter. "Hope says that she has a collection of her wood sculptures at a small local gallery. I didn't ask her which one, but how many galleries can there be that have wood sculptures? I'd love to see her work."

Evan's eyes brightened. "Oh yes, me too. I'm sure we can find it."

"I'll check the internet right after dinner." Bethany chirped.

"I'd like to go too," Ellie said. "Wouldn't Papa be proud of someone inheriting his talent? God knows none of us can do that."

"I tried to whittle a totem pole when I was in Cub Scouts," Evan said, laughing. "It looked more like a snake with six eyes."

"Well, it'll be hard to go see them if the place is closed. It is Christmas. But maybe we can look through the window." He glanced at his watch. "Which means that we better be at the homeless shelter by seven."

Mary Alice frowned. Char usually had them out of the door an hour early. She was the one that had suggested they go to the shelter when she was little. Now, it was a family tradition, and Char was vehement that they weren't ever late. It was easy to forget how thoughtful she could be, sometimes. Char had been volunteering there on the last weekend of each month since she got out of college. Maybe she'd still been going all this time that she refused to talk to Mary Alice.

"Ugh," said Greg patting his stomach. "I am so full I can hardly move. Maybe I—"

"Don't even say it Greg Proctor," Ellie scolded. "We are ALL going to do our part, like we always do."

Bethany's face lit up, holding her phone close to her face as she announced. "I found it!" She held her phone out so the table could see the small picture on her screen. It was a building. "There's only, like, five art galleries in Youngstown, this one is the only one with wood sculptures. It's on Wick Avenue. Isn't that close to the homeless shelter we are going to? Can we go peek in the windows?"

Mary Alice hesitated for a moment, before pulling her purse from the back of her chair. She rummaged around in it and found her little notebook. She scratched the address on a blank sheet and tucked it into her handbag. "Maybe. We'll see, after we go to the shelter."

Maybe Char would even be there already, undeterred from her duty to her community, even if she knew Mary Alice would come.

The thought filled her with hope.

Everyone was busy dishing out food for the long line of people. Mary Alice looked over at her family. How lucky she was to have them, and all that food they just finished eating. What they were serving was nice, but it didn't have the personal touch that home-cooked food made with love did.

Mary Alice took a break and headed in the back to check her phone to see if Char or Hope had called. There was a voicemail. Char hadn't been at the shelter when they got there, and the manager said that he hadn't seen her in weeks. It was deflating at best.

But she did have a voicemail, and that was something.

She hurriedly keyed in the prompt for her voicemail and pressed the phone tight to her ear, her belly filling with eager butterflies.

An unfamiliar voice echoed in her ear. "Mrs. Goodson. This is Sergeant Gleason. Everything is going to be okay. Your daughter . . ."

Mary Alice's head started to spin and she fumbled with the phone, almost dropping it. She started the message again.

"Mrs. Goodson. This is Sergeant Gleason. Everything is going to be okay. Your daughter, Charlene, has been in an accident. The Kentucky state police found Charlene's car in a ditch off I-75 near Lexington. She ran a stop sign and hit another car before careening into the ditch."

Mary Alice's mind raced ahead. Kentucky? What was she doing in Kentucky?

"She will be fine. No life-threatening injuries. She's in Lexington Memorial. They are keeping her overnight for observation. A warrant has been issued for her arrest. DWI. She'll need to appear in court for her arraignment before she can leave the state of Kentucky. The KSP, sorry, Kentucky State Police, notified us and asked us to contact you. You are listed as her emergency contact. We recommend that she seek legal counsel. This is her second DWI in two months and she was on restricted driving privileges to get back and forth to work only. Sorry to have to give you this news over the phone in a voicemail, and on Christmas Day. We tried your house but no one was home. Feel free to give me a call back at the station, 301-555-6677, if you need to speak to me."

Mary Alice found a dusty, straight back chair and sunk into it. Char, in an accident, in Kentucky. It didn't make any sense. She looked down at her phone, hit play, and listened to the message again.

How did this happen? A DWI? She was drunk? Char had said she was fine, that she'd been with her sponsor, had prayed. What happened to all that faith she'd spouted that had kept her on the straight and narrow? Was it all a lie? A ruse? Had she been drinking all this time? Or when did she start again? Mary Alice dropped her head into her hands. This was all her fault. If she hadn't divulged the secret about Hope's birth, and sought her out, Charlene wouldn't have started drinking again. Was it the letter from Charlie that sent her over the edge? Was that why she didn't respond to anyone's voicemails and only a few of Evan's texts? She wouldn't be lying in a hospital bed in Lexington, otherwise. Mary Alice had to take responsibility for this.

"Mom?" Ellie came in from the serving line out front. "Are you okay? You've been gone quite a . . . what's wrong Mom? You're white as a ghost."

"Char," Mary Alice mumbled. "The police . . . they left a voice message."

Ellie looked at the phone in Mary Alice's hand. "The police left you a message? About Char?" She took the phone out of Mary Alice's hand and listened to the message.

Mary Alice stood. "I've got to get to her. Lexington Memorial. I'll go right away. And I need to call my attorney."

She headed toward the door.

"Wait Mom. Calm down first. Stay right there. Sit back down. Let me get the family."

Yes, yes. Of course, Ellie was right. She needed to stay calm. Take those deep breaths. Gladys was always telling her to do that when she got anxious. Deep breath in, hold for five, deep breath out. One more time.

Everyone gathered around her, crowded in the small back room. They all seemed to be talking at once. Any more thoughts of feeding the homeless were gone. Evan calculated that it was a seven-hour drive to Lexington in good weather, which is not what they had. When were they ever going to catch a break on the weather? It felt like the planet was conspiring against Mary Alice's every move. Char could be discharged by the time they got there. Surely, there wouldn't be an arraignment on Christmas Day, would there? They'd have at least a day for Attorney Cline to get there and discuss the options, if there were any.

"Let's call the hospital first. See if we can talk to her," Evan said.

Mary Alice nodded, rubbing her temple. She was not

going to cry. She was not. Her son tapped his phone and pressed it to his ear. After a moment of tense silence, Evan spoke.

"Yes ma'am, Merry Christmas. I'm trying to get ahold of my sister, Charlene Goodson. Apparently, she's been in an accident, and an officer gave me this number to call."

He paused for a moment and nodded, "Yes, thank you."

"They're patching me through to Charlene's room," Evan said, tapping the speaker on the phone so everyone could hear.

"Hello?" A weak voice said, sounding nothing like the aggressive, confident Charlene Mary Alice knew.

"Char? Is that you? This is Evan."

Mary Alice leaned toward the phone. "And Mom. I'm here too, sweetheart. Are you okay?"

What sounded like a sob came through the receiver. Then a sniffle. "Yes, no. I don't know anymore."

Evan squeezed Mary Alice's hand. "What happened?"

Silence.

"Char? Are you there?" Mary Alice asked.

A muffled voice responded. Evan turned up the volume.

"I don't know. I was going . . . somewhere. I don't remember why. I guess I fell asleep at the wheel. I hit somebody. Oh God. I hit somebody. He's here too. I hurt him and I don't know what I've done to him, they won't tell me."

Mary Alice remembered what Sergeant Gleason had said about the DWI's. It didn't matter. All that mattered now was that Char was okay. Everything else could be fixed, as long as the other driver pulled through.

Mary Alice leaned closer to the phone. "I'm calling my attorney, Bill Cline. The police said you have to go to court."

"The police were there?" Charlene sounded alarmed. "At your place? Why?"

"They left me a voice message when I wasn't home. We were at the homeless shelter. I'm your emergency contact, remember?"

When Charlene didn't answer, Mary Alice said, "I'll have Mr. Cline call you. He'll know what is best. And I'm coming. Don't worry baby, it will all be okay."

"No," Charlene said, a flat monotone. "Don't come. I don't want you to. I don't need you."

The words cut through Mary Alice like a knife. She didn't mean that, did she? She was probably upset and embarrassed, after claiming to have it all together. Please don't let this have tipped her over the edge.

Mary Alice sat a little straighter. "Now you listen here, young lady. I am your mother. You don't have a say-so in this. I'm coming and that's final."

She had to get to Charlene. What if Charlene had died thinking she was somehow of less value than a girl Mary Alice had met twice? Hope wasn't really a part of this family, was she? Not yet. But Charlene was. Maybe Char had been right all along. Maybe she did have to choose, and it had to be Charlene.

Thirty-One

2017

After much grumbling from both Ellie and Evan, Mary Alice booked a flight to Lexington on the red-eye for that night. They both tried to talk her out of it, but she was not deterred. "I started this mess, and I'll clean it up," she said. She had to make this right between her and her daughter. Whatever it took, however long it took, didn't matter. She would make sure Charlene knew she was loved, had always been loved. Maybe then Char could chase away the demons that haunted her and had forced her toward the bottle. And maybe she'd open up her heart to Hope.

Mary Alice arrived at the hospital at seven a.m. on Tuesday, after paying a king's ransom for a cab ride from the airport. Charlene looked like hell. There was no other way to describe it. Her hair, normally perfectly coiffed, looked like it hadn't seen a brush in days. She was clean, thanks to the dutiful aides, but dark, ugly bruises graced both her cheeks and one eye was swollen almost completely shut. She had bandages on both arms and her left foot and ankle. Mary Alice felt the hot tears threatening to fall. No. Now was not a time for tears. It was time for strength.

"Help me, Charlie."

Mary Alice managed a smile. "Well, I must admit I've seen you look better." Her shot at levity missed by a mile and was met with disdain.

"I told you not to come. We don't have anything to say to each

213

other." Charlene turned her face to the window.

Mary Alice set her purse down on the metal lunch cart and crossed her arms over her chest. "I'd say we have quite a lot to say to each other. First of all, we need to make sure you are okay. What have the doctors said? And then I need to know the reason you were driving drunk in Kentucky."

"I never said . . ."

"The officers told me. You were drunk, Charlene. This has got to stop. You need help. And I'm sorry . . . for everything. I'm here to help, sweetheart."

Charlene peered through her black and blue eyes. "Have you heard how the other driver is? I didn't mean . . ."

"Of course, you didn't. You were upset. It's my fault. I'm sorry if I ever made you feel unloved. I'm dropping all efforts to unite with . . ." A lump the size of an apple lodged in her throat. She forced it down. She couldn't even say her name. "I'm done. I am here for you, Charlene Sophia Goodson. Are they discharging you today?"

Charlene looked down at her lap and shook her head. She tried to speak, but her voice cracked. She cleared her throat and tried again. "Tomorrow. I'm so tired and I've got to go to my arraignment in the morning."

"Well, you need to get some rest. I'll stay right here with you."

Charlene put up a half-hearted fight. "Mom, you can't stay here all day and night. There's no place for you to sleep."

Mary Alice clucked her tongue. God, she sounded like her mother. "You never mind about me. I'll be fine. I am not leaving you." If she had to sleep in a straight chair all night, she'd show Charlene she was there for her all the way.

A nurse came in and Mary Alice asked if it was okay for her to stay in Char's room.

"Of course, Mrs. Goodson," the nurse replied. "Charlene had quite a knock on her head. We've given her a sedative so she'll most likely sleep most of the day. We can wheel in a recliner for you, and a pillow and blanket."

"Thank you," Mary Alice said. "See?" She patted Char gently on her bruised cheek. "You close your eyes and rest. We'll get this all straightened out when Attorney Cline gets here."

Char's eyes closed. Mary Alice watched her sleep. How could she have slipped so far off the wagon? As far as Mary Alice knew, she hadn't had a drink in over five years. Her poor baby. No matter how old she was, she'd always be that precocious little girl with non-stop energy. She wiped a tear from her cheek and settled into the recliner, watching the gentle rise and fall of her daughter's breath.

A few hours passed and two lunch trays were brought in, but Char barely woke enough to eat more than a few bites before she went back to sleep. Mary Alice hoped the drugs would wear off before morning. She needed to be alert and attentive for the arraignment.

Hours dragged on. Mary Alice watched the hands on the big round clock on the wall across from Charlene. Thoughts of Hope fought their way in, even as Mary Alice was trying to concentrate on Charlene. Could she really give up on Hope? Had she made a promise she couldn't keep?

By the time the dinner trays were brought in, Char was a little more awake.

"Do you want to talk about it?" Mary Alice asked. She hated to push, but there were questions that needed answers. It took a few tries, but eventually she got a few answers. Why was she drinking?

She was depressed.

How long had this been going on?

A few weeks.

Was this all about finding Hope or was there something more going on?

A shrug of the shoulders.

Char's answers told her nothing more than she already knew. Maybe Bill Cline could get more answers from her. Her daughter fell asleep again and the sky turned from light to dark. Before Mary Alice turned in for the night, she made her way to the lobby to call Ellie and give her an update. Not much to report except Charlene was going to be okay, if only physically. Emotionally, that was another story.

Mary Alice settled into the recliner and pulled the blanket up around her. Why was it always so cold in hospitals?

"Charlie, I need to get through to her. She's not telling me everything. I can feel it. What do I do?"

Just love her Mar. She'll get better.

The sun peeked through the blinds and woke Mary Alice up. A nurse was standing over Charlene taking her vitals. "Good morning," the nurse said. "It looks like our girl is feeling much better today. And getting a discharge."

Why did nurses always do that? Talk in plural. 'Our girl' indeed.

"How do you feel?" Mary Alice asked her daughter.

"Better. Probably better than you trying to sleep in that chair all night."

Mary Alice tsked. Regardless of the kink in her neck and the ache in her back, she was fine. This wasn't a time to be concerned about herself. "Let's get you cleaned up and dressed for this arraignment, then get you home. Attorney Cline will meet us at the courthouse."

Charlene burst into unexpected tears and Mary Alice startled. When was the last time she had seen her daughter cry? Not even at Charlie's funeral.

"Sweetheart, what is it? You can talk to me." Mary Alice pleaded.

Char brushed the tears from her bruised cheek and shook her head. Mary Alice reached out for her and Char curled in on herself, avoiding the touch altogether. Charlene had never been one for physical affection. She liked words and presents.

Mary Alice opened her small carry-on bag and pulled out a new cashmere sweater and matching cream wool slacks. She had unwrapped them from the presents she had for Char under the tree. She laid them at the foot of the bed and extracted undergarments, black flats and trouser socks. At the moment, that's all Mary Alice could do to try and make her stop crying.

"Merry Christmas. Sorry I opened it for you."

Charlene stopped sobbing and stared back at her mother, speechless for once in her life. She reached a hand toward her mother, trembling a little. She hadn't done that since she was very little. Mary Alice took it in her hands and sat on the bed, gently kissing the knuckles. Fresh tears coursed down Char's face.

"Now stop that. If you start, I'll start. We can't go into court all puffy-eyed. Well, not both eyes, anyway."

Charlene touched her swollen red eye. Her lips spread into a small, watery smile. A rare, real one. Mary Alice didn't know what that smile meant, but her shoulders relaxed anyway.

"Okay, Mom."

Thirty-Two

2017

Bill Cline was waiting outside the courtroom in a long narrow hallway, the glass walls looking out at the downtown Lexington high rises and Phoenix Park. Any other time, Mary Alice would have taken the time to explore. Not today.

"Hello, Mary Alice," he said warmly.

She hadn't seen him since the reading of Charlie's will. "Hello Bill. Good to see you again. Thanks for coming."

He shook her hand and nodded at Charlene. "Charlene."

The smile he had for Mary Alice vanished. Was he unhappy about the trip to Lexington or disappointed in his late friend's daughter? Mary Alice needed him to be in Charlene's corner, not her judge and jury.

"Are you well enough for this?" he asked Charlene. "I can try to get a continuance."

"No," Charlene said. "Let's get this over with." She nodded toward the closed double doors. "What's going to happen in there?"

"This is not a trial, Charlene," he said. "It's an arraignment. I need you to be perfectly honest with me about what happened here. I can't help you if you are not totally transparent."

Charlene took a deep breath and hung her head. "I kind of lost my mind for a bit there. Everything felt so hopeless. That bottle of Johnny Walker felt like my only friend. I don't even remember getting behind the wheel."

"Okay," Cline said. "I'll do the best I can. There won't be anyone else in there but us, unless the other driver's attorney makes an appearance. I understand he was upgraded from critical to stable condition. That's good news for you."

Mary Alice squeezed Charlene's hand and peered into her downturned face. "Why would you feel the need to drink a whole bottle of whiskey? I'm here for you. So is your brother and sister. You are not alone, Charlene. You never have been."

Charlene shrugged, examining her shoes.

"The judge will read the charges and ask how you wish to plead." Cline said. "I recommend that you plead guilty. There is no point pretending you weren't drunk. Your blood alcohol level was twice over the legal limit."

Twice? My God. It was a wonder she didn't kill herself and the other driver. How was she even alert enough to get into the car? One glass of wine gave Mary Alice a headache. How many drinks did it take to be two times over the limit? Did she even want to know?

Charlene stared at the new black flats Mary Alice had brought.

"The prosecutor may provide the defense with lab reports of any blood or chemical tests that were performed after you were admitted to the hospital, and they may be used against you in the case. The judge will decide if there is enough evidence — probable cause it's called — against you to stand trial," Cline continued.

"A trial? You mean she could go to jail?" Mary Alice's pulse pounded against her temples. This couldn't be happening. Char didn't need to be in jail. She needed help.

"That's why I'm here." Cline said. "I'll do my best to see that does not happen."

Charlene rested her hand on Mary Alice's arm. "It's okay, Mom. I deserve it. I'll do whatever he says. I'll plead guilty. I am guilty."

Mary Alice stared at her. Who was this contrite girl? Certainly not her daughter.

The double doors opened, and the bailiff called Charlene's name. Mary Alice tucked her arm in her daughter's, and they walked, locked together and huddled close. Mary Alice was told to sit behind the half wall, *mahogany*, that separated the judge and defendant from the spectators.

After the charges were read and Charlene pled guilty, Attorney Cline addressed the judge, rocking slightly back and forth as he spoke, reminding Mary Alice of a tree, willow, in his light gray pinstriped suit. He praised Charlene's work as an upstanding professor of theology and expounded on her many virtues. He explained that Charlene had recently lost her father and was suffering from depression. He recommended a plea bargain in lieu of a trial: restitution to the other driver and out-patient care for her addiction and depression.

Mary Alice stared at the back of Charlene's bent head. Was Char really depressed from Charlie's death, or was Cline only using that to further his case?

The judge was a stocky man of about fifty with a Caesar ring of hair around his shiny balding head and bushy eyebrows pinching together in a unibrow. He pushed the bifocals up his long, straight nose with a chubby index finger.

Mary Alice held her breath.

"You are a very lucky woman, Ms. Goodson," the judge said. "You easily could have been killed or you could have taken the life of Mr. Murdoch, the other driver. Your blood alcohol was 0.16. And you were already driving on a restricted license. It was reckless and irresponsible for someone of your education and position in life. I would hope this is not the kind of behavior you would recommend to your students at Ohio State."

"No, your Honor."

Mary Alice had never heard her daughter sound so contrite.

"Given your exemplary history at the University, I am inclined to offer a summary judgement. You will not have to stand trial if you agree to the terms I am about to set forth. Is that understood, Ms. Goodson?"

Charlene nodded. "Yes, your Honor."

"Good." He took off his bifocals and laid them on the desk. "The defendant, Charlene Sophia Goodson, shall be remanded to an in-patient addiction rehabilitation center for not less than ninety days, pay a $2,000 fine, be held responsible for Mr. Murdoch's medical expenses, and relinquish her Ohio driver's license for two years. Upon the evaluation of the facility, said defendant may be required to extend her stay for not more than thirty additional days. Case is dismissed." The gavel came down with a crack.

Mary Alice jumped. The whole thing had taken less than ten minutes. They all made a hasty retreat from the courtroom.

"Can I take her home now?" Mary Alice asked Attorney Cline outside the courtroom. Charlene looked exhausted as she slumped onto a padded bench. The attorney shook his head. "You heard the judge. She's got to check herself into a rehab facility."

"Now?" Mary Alice said. "But she's hurt. She needs to go home first and mend. And it's Christmas. We'll find a place for her after."

"That wasn't the directive. She must go straight from here. The judge has ordered a thorough evaluation, which will determine whether she is on a 90 or 120 day in-patient program. From there, the court system will work closely with her AA sponsor or assign her a new one if they feel she wasn't provided the assistance she needed. She'll have another six months in out-patient therapy. And she'll be on probation for a year."

Charlene stood. "Wait. I can't be gone for three or four months. I have a full load of classes to teach."

Cline swayed on his lean frame. "I guess you should have thought of that before you went on a drinking binge between Youngstown and here. This isn't optional, Charlene. Unless you'd rather spend your time in jail?"

Mary Alice put her arm around her daughter's shoulders. "She'll go into rehab. Do we have a choice of where?"

"There is a facility in Cincinnati that works closely with the courts on both sides of the river. There can be no contact with the outside world for the first thirty days. After that, she can have weekly visitors." He held his arm out, gesturing down the hallway and looking at Charlene pointedly. She hesitated, only for a second, and then held her chin up before beginning to stride away, Cline turning to walk with her. Mary Alice's head was spinning. "Wait. Can't I go with her?" She wrapped her arms around Charlene and kissed her cheek.

"No, I'm sorry. I'll take her from here."

Mary Alice grasped her daughter's shoulders and turned her around. She pressed her face against Charlene's, nose to nose. "You're going to be okay, sweetie. I love you."

"Thanks Mom. For coming . . . for everything."

"It's time," Cline said.

Two police officers approached, and Charlene broke away with a soft, sad smile. The officers flanked Charlene and Mr. Cline. All Mary Alice could do was stare after them as they walked away, the clip of Charlene's flats on granite floors the only sound in the hall. Mary Alice sank onto the bench Charlene had been sitting on. Ninety to one hundred and twenty days. She counted it out on her fingers. March or April.

"Oh Charlie"

Thirty-Three

2017

By the time she made it back home from the airport, the exhaustion was formidable. Her body ached from the freezing plane ride, and the lack of sleep in the hospital recliner made her feel at least a hundred. Yes, Bethy, I truly am a dinosaur. If her body was wrecked, it was nothing compared to her state of mind. She had come so close to having it all. Her whole family. And it slipped right through her fingers like a ghost. How did she let this happen? Her hand went immediately to the phone. She'd call Sophia and Gladys. They would come to her rescue.

Then she stopped. She leaned on them like she used to lean on Charlie for everything. She must learn to stand on her own two feet, to take control. That's what got her in this situation in the first place. Always listening to other people.

A dull emptiness settled in Mary Alice's stomach and she sighed, staring down at the phone. Things were really over with Hope, and she would have to get through this somehow. On her own. She lived through losing Hope the first time. She lived through Charlie's death. She'd live through this too. The important thing now was Charlene. She had to come first. Put one foot in front of the other. Keep going. She remembered the Bible passage that had given her comfort so many times in the past. "This too shall pass." Yes, she'd get through this, one day at a time. Life could go back to normal, couldn't it?

It still felt like she'd lost both daughters.

She dropped onto the sofa, fully dressed. Pulling an afghan over her shoulders, she gave in to the exhaustion. In the distance, she heard the phone ringing. She was too spent to pick up. Too tired to have conversations with anybody.

It was dark by time she roused herself from the sofa. It felt like an act of God to make it to the powder room to splash water on her face. She picked up her phone on the way to the kitchen. While she waited for the kettle to boil, she checked voicemail. Three from Ellie, two each from Sophia and Gladys. Plus, a text message from Evan and one from Bethany.

"I'm fine. I'm fine," she muttered. "But I don't feel like talking to any of you." She sent them each a brief text message. Home. I am fine. Need rest. Talk soon.

After some tea and a few sugar cookies, she felt better. She placed her hand on the doorknob to the den. As she entered the room, her eyes went immediately to the screen on the desk. What good was that thing with no internet?

She unplugged the computer from the wall and watched the screen go black. She glared at the pile of bills.

"Isn't it about time you deal with this?" she grumbled. She sunk down into Charlie's chair. One by one, she opened each bill and logged the amount on a yellow legal pad, totaling it all up. The amount was mind boggling. She had been so irresponsible. Bills weren't going to automatically pay themselves.

And now she had to figure out how to pay them.

Asking for help was not in her DNA, but she didn't have any money and most of these were overdue. The last thing she needed was to live in a dark, cold, empty house in the middle of an Ohio winter.

She had to ask for help with this.

It took an hour of picking up the phone and putting it back down without dialing before she finally hit send on the call. Evan answered right away.

"Mom, so glad you called. I got the text that you were home, but I didn't want to disturb you if you were still sleeping. How is Char? What happened?"

Mary Alice sighed and tilted her head back, staring at the ceiling. "She got into the accident and the other man was hurt. We went to a hearing with Bill Cline." She paused to keep her voice even, "She'll be in rehab at least until March."

"Oh, Mom, I'm so sorry. I know how hard that is on you. Do you want me to come over?"

This was her open. She could confess her predicament, ask for help. She swallowed a lump of pride. "Yes, Evan. That would be good. I've got some other things I need to discuss with you too."

"What other things?"

Mary Alice stared at the pile of bills and the huge number at the bottom of the legal pad. "I'll explain when you get here."

Twenty minutes later, Evan was sitting in her kitchen eating leftover Christmas cookies and drinking eggnog. Mary Alice waited until he was finished before she asked him to follow her into Charlie's den.

The pile of bills and the legal pad were stacked on the desk, right in front of the computer like a centerpiece. She pointed at them and didn't look at Evan's face. "I'm afraid I've let things go since Papa died. Now I am in a bit of a pickle."

Evan sat in Charlie's chair and shuffled through them. "Mom, we can pay most of these online. I'll help you." He reached to turn on the computer.

She placed a hand over his. "I'm afraid they cut off my internet, too." She felt the heat rising to her cheeks.

"Okay," said Evan slowly. "Then we'll write them checks. I can go take them in person so they'll restore your service right away. Where is your checkbook?"

"Evan, there is no money in the checkbook. At least not enough to pay all these past due bills."

Don't make me ask out loud, Evan.

He looked up, clearly shocked. "Mom, how? Papa never said anything about money problems."

"I think he was ashamed that things had gotten this bad. The accountant said that his business had been going downhill for quite a few years. So I guess he was tapping into our personal account. And now it's all gone."

Evan leaned back in the chair and his ran delicate fingers through his hair. "I can hardly believe this."

225

They sat in silence a few minutes, four eyes staring at the pile of bills. Each second that ticked by made Mary Alice more and more aware that this was a bad idea. Evan shouldn't have to help her with this. Mary Alice was the elder here.

Suddenly Evan swept them all up. "Well, for now, I'll take care of these. I'll pay them from home today."

"Oh son, after I sell the shop —"

"You're going to sell the shop?"

"The building. The business will close. What other choice do I have? It is the only asset I have . . ." She waved a hand around the room. "Except this house."

"Mom, what about a life insurance policy? Did the accountant mention anything about that? This does not sound like Papa, that he would leave you with nothing."

Mary Alice shook her head. "No, he didn't mention one."

"Maybe it's here someplace. It's possible Mr. Willoughby didn't know everything." Evan rolled the chair back and started pulling out drawers, rifling through the files.

Mary Alice felt like it was an invasion of Charlie's personal space. Even she had never gone through his drawers and file cabinet. It was intrusive.

"Got it," shouted Evan as he pulled a folder from the back of the desk drawer. He shot up straight in the chair with a victorious grin. Mary Alice hovered over his shoulder as he flipped the folder open.

"Mom, this is a whole life insurance policy for $200,000. And another one for you. You won't get rich on this, but it should be enough for you to live on if you're careful."

Mary Alice's mouth dropped open. "$200,000? That's a lot of money."

"Not really." Evan clapped the folder shut and looked up at her. "Think about it. If you stretch it out until you're ninety, that's only $10,000 a year. But that and your social security should work. And it will draw a little interest over the years. Let me call the insurance man listed here and find out what we have to do. Most likely only provide the death certificate."

Mary Alice frowned at that. Didn't even like to think about it.

Evan whipped out his phone and tapped in the number before bringing it to his ear. Mary Alice backed away slowly and sank into the little chair on the side of the desk. Maybe if she'd thought with her head instead of her heart, she would have found that before the money got so out of hand. And all it took was Evan peeking into the drawer.

Privacy. How ridiculous. Her husband was dead, he left her a way to survive him, and she never even looked.

The focus in the room got fuzzy and Mary Alice slumped in her chair, numbness seeping into her. Half relief, half shame. She didn't know how long she sat like that. Evan snapped her out of it by pumping his fist in the air and hanging up on his call.

He turned to her with a little smile. "The policy is still in effect, and it's definitely for $200,000. With a death certificate, the funds could be in your account in a few weeks."

That was one boulder off her back, at least.

"I promise I'll pay back every cent of the money you're going to use for the bills. I won't let it happen again."

"I know, Mom." He leaned over and took her hands. "Don't worry about it right now. The bills are going to be paid and you won't have to worry about it again."

He leaned over and kissed her cheek.

"Thank you, honey." Mary Alice patted his hand. "I don't know what I'd do without you."

After Evan left, her mind went back to Charlie's shop. As much as it broke her heart to let it go, it still didn't make sense to keep it. If only one of the children had an interest in it.

She ran a hand along her mouth absently, lost in thought and still sitting in the little den chair. Somebody had to want it.

Slowly, the answer became clear. Hope.

She loved woodwork. She could turn the cabinet shop into a gallery and use the workshop below to build her creations. It would be perfect. Mary Alice closed her eyes and pictured it. The front room was the perfect size for a one-artist gallery. And the location could work. She could almost smell the sawdust, hear the whir of power tools. She saw Charlie

227

helping Ellie and Charlene build doll houses. She remembered the soap box derby car he built with Evan, even if Evan did very little of the work. Maybe Bethany's child could play in that same workshop someday. Wouldn't that be something.

The question was, how was she going to give it to Hope if Hope didn't want to talk to her again? How was Mary Alice going to give Hope anything and keep her promise to Char?

Thirty-Four

2018

Days had turned into nights, and the holidays were over as quickly as they came. January crept by at an agonizing pace. Each day felt like another stab in Mary Alice's heart. She wanted Charlie. She wanted Char. She wanted Hope. It felt like her arms were crying out to hold all of them.

Why did the days keeping passing, the sun still rise and set, the world go on when all three of them weren't there with her?

Mary Alice sipped at her tea, her elbows resting on the kitchen table. Thanks to Evan, everything was back up and running. The insurance money was on its way. She should feel relieved.

Her fingers itched to turn the computer back on and see if Hope had been online. Maybe she should message her. No, she wouldn't do that. Hope had her phone number. She could have called, but she didn't, which meant that she didn't want to.

Mary Alice understood why, it's just that . . . if she were Hope, she would have called. But Hope seemed to easily accept that it was over.

It wasn't easy for Mary Alice. She would have called. Or is it backwards? She should call. No. Hope didn't want to talk to her, and Mary Alice couldn't blame her for that.

Her phone rang and she startled. She stood and walked

to the kitchen counter, glancing down at her cell. Evan. She answered.

"Hi, sweetie."

"Hey, Mom," Evan's cheerful voice sang over the phone. "Ellie and I want to take you out to lunch for your birthday. Today instead of Saturday. We both have conflicts that day."

"Ah, honey. That's sweet. But I don't need anything. I'm too old for birthdays, anyway."

"Nonsense. Nobody is too old for birthdays. Besides, we need to get you out of that house. Have you even left at all since your trip to Kentucky?"

"I don't need to thanks to the blessing of online grocery ordering. I have everything I need right here."

"Nope. Not good enough. Put a pretty dress on. Ellie and I will be there to pick you up at noon. And while we're out, we can look at cribs for Bethany. You'd like that, wouldn't you?"

The anticipation of a new baby did have a way of lightening the mood. The sonogram had shown that Bethany was right. Mary Alice was going to have a great-grandson. And once Evan got something in his head, there was no arguing with him.

Mary Alice sighed. It had been so long since she had shopped for baby furniture. She did, admittedly, like it more than shopping for herself. "Okay. I'll be ready."

Ellie's car pulled in the drive at exactly noon. Mary Alice was glad they had given her enough time to talk herself into this outing. They were right about one thing. She couldn't hole up in the house forever.

Evan opened the passenger side door for her and planted a kiss on her cheek before he climbed into the back. Ellie smiled at her from behind the wheel.

Mary Alice rested her purse in her lap. "So, where is lunch?"

"There's a new Italian restaurant on Wick Avenue I thought we would try. I know you like Italian. And the Babies-R-Us is in that vicinity."

"We don't need anything fancy for me. Scarcella's is fine."

Ellie shook her head. "Not today, Mom. Today is special."

Mary Alice shook her head, but she couldn't stop the small smile from spreading. It would be nice to have something special. What was the harm in letting her kids treat her?

Ellie backed out of the driveway, and then they were off. Ellie sped down the side-streets and hummed to herself, one hand on the wheel and the other resting on the console. Mary Alice grabbed the handle above the door and took a deep breath, closing her eyes whenever Ellie jerked to a stop at a red light.

She should be used to her daughter's lead foot after three decades. At least Ellie got them to the city in half the time it would have taken Mary Alice.

Parking downtown was always a challenge, not so much because it was busy, but more because the regentrification efforts demolished the streets and made the center of town into a walking open-air mall. 'Poor planning if you ask me.'

They finally found a spot in a parking garage a few blocks from the restaurant and Mary Alice climbed from the car, letting Ohio's cool winter breeze fan over her face. The air was crisp, but the sun was shining, and for Youngstown in February, that was almost a miracle. Mary Alice pulled her scarf a little tighter around her neck and followed the twins out of the garage.

The walk was short, but it was nice. Her kids sandwiched her between them and talked a mile a minute to each other, to her, about nothing in particular. That's how they were. On their own, they were Evan and Ellie. Together, they were a blizzard of energy.

Lunch was lovely, Evan was right about the restaurant. The ambiance was warm and inviting, more upscale than Scarcella's, and the food was fabulous. They spoke briefly about how Char was doing. It was past her thirty days, which meant that she could have visitors. No one mentioned Hope. They each had a glass of merlot and the maître d' brought over a little cake with a candle in it after the meal. The servers joined in, and even other patrons sang along to Happy Birthday as Mary Alice blushed from head to toe.

After lunch, Evan steered them in the opposite direction from which they had came, saying something about the scenic route. Mary Alice had the feeling he had a destination in mind. The weather was starting to deteriorate, and she was ready to get to the car. Before she could say anything, a sign caught her attention up ahead. Rockford Art Gallery. She sucked in her breath and the cold air sent her into a coughing fit.

"Are you okay, Mom?" Ellie patted her on the back.

Mary Alice nodded but coughed again into a clean hankie. "Evan," she said when she caught her breath. "What's the meaning of this?"

"I thought you'd be pleased, Mom. We never got to see the gallery on Christmas Eve. And it was right around the corner from the restaurant."

Mary Alice shot him a knowing glare. "Or . . . was the restaurant was right around the corner from the gallery?"

Evan shrugged sheepishly. "Come on. Let's go take a look."

Mary Alice hesitated. What if Hope was there? Of course, Ellie and Evan were hoping for the affirmative—so they could meet their long-lost sister. She probably wouldn't even speak to Mary Alice. She might even ask her to leave. Evan rubbed his gloved hands together. "Here we go."

He opened the heavy wood door, *oak*, with frosted glass panels. Ellie waltzed right on in, but Mary Alice stood outside the threshold, trying to glance past the doorway and into the room beyond. She didn't see anybody. Just do it.

She moved into the gallery, one foot in front of the other. Evan brought up the rear. The door closed behind them with a thunk. Inside, the air was warm. The rich travertine floors were marbled black and grey, and they made the perfect back-drop for the soft grey walls. A young woman dressed smartly in black with large, black-framed glasses greeted them. She couldn't have been more than thirty.

"Welcome to the Rockford Gallery. Is this your first visit?"

"Yes," Evan answered. "You have some beautiful pieces here." He leaned in to look closer at the pastel-colored paintings on the walls, each illuminated with a spotlight hanging from the ceiling. Mary Alice knew Evan preferred bolder, more vibrant pieces.

"Please take your time and enjoy," the hostess said. "We have four rooms, each with different mediums, from watercolors such as these, to oils and pottery and wood sculpture."

At the mention of the wood sculpture, Mary Alice's heart skipped a beat. "Are any of the artists here?" she asked. Her voice sounded too loud to her own ears.

"No, I'm afraid not. But I do have an itinerary of when they will be. We have a small gala once a month where customers can meet the artists and make purchases." She handed Mary Alice a tri-fold brochure with a picture of the front of the gallery on the cover.

Mary Alice accepted the brochure and thanked her without looking at it. Was that relief or disappointment she felt?

"I was hoping she would be here," Ellie whispered. Mary Alice only nodded.

Slowly, the three made their way through the gallery until they came to the wood sculpture room. Mary Alice sucked in her breath and stared at the inside, her hand clutching at the threshold of the archway.

Intricate carvings of small woodland creatures stood on marble podiums. The first was a small chipmunk sitting on a log. The details were so exact, Mary Alice thought she saw its nose twitch. The room was only slightly smaller than the display room in Charlie's shop. Yes, the shop could work nicely for Hope . . . if she was interested.

Mary Alice released the wall she was anchoring herself to. She stepped into the wood room and inched closer to the chipmunk. Ellie moved to stand beside her.

"Mom, look," she said, motioning to the left with her chin.

She looked.

Four butterflies were frozen on a large yellow sunflower. They looked no bigger than four inches each. She recognized the wood, *bamboo*. The wings were so delicate and finely carved they were translucent. It was the most beautiful thing Mary Alice had ever seen. *Four beautiful souls, like my four beautiful children.*

Moving around the room, she admired the other wood carvings; rabbits, *maple*, owls, *pine*, racoons, *balsam*, and even a small spotted fawn standing beside a magnificent four-foot-high doe, *cherry*. Each piece was more beautiful than the next. The only sound was the shuffle of their shoes on the stone floor. When Mary Alice finally pulled her eyes away from the creations to look at her children, she was met with shining, moist eyes.

"Mom, these are unbelievable," Evan said. "Papa would be so proud."

Those words were enough to unleash the tears pooling in Mary Alice's eyes. "I know. I was thinking the same thing."

A small brass plate was engraved with the name of each piece and the artist's name.

Hope C. Pendleton.

Mary Alice's heart swelled with pride.

She made the rounds again and ended up back at the butterfly sculpture. Ellie came up and stood beside her. "It's exquisite, isn't it?"

"Yes," Mary Alice said, almost reverently.

The hostess came up beside them. "Do you see anything you like?"

"They are all wonderful. But this piece. . ." Mary Alice paused.

"We'll take it," Ellie said, gripping Mary Alice's shoulder. "Happy Birthday, Mom."

The hostess's eyes lit up.

"Oh no, no," Mary Alice held her hands out. "It's far too expensive. I don't need gifts, you know that."

Evan came up beside her. "Then Ellie and I will split it, if that makes you happy. But you obviously love it. And why shouldn't you have it?"

Mary Alice was speechless as the hostess lifted the sculpture off the base and carried it to the counter to wrap it up.

Ellie handed Mary Alice her gift. "Thank you" was all she could muster. The words were not sufficient.

From there, they went to Babies-R-Us and picked out a beautiful crib, *maple*, for Bethany. But Mary Alice's heart was still back at the gallery, filled with thoughts of Hope.

Once home, Mary Alice carefully unwrapped the sculpture and placed it on the mantel next to Charlie.

"Do you see this Charlie? Do you see what our daughter created?"

I see, Mar. I see.

The temptation to call Hope was overwhelming. She wanted to tell her . . . tell her what? That she thought she was the most magnificent sculptor in the world? That she was sorry? That she is taking it all back — that she did want a relationship with her?

She didn't pick up the phone. She didn't say any of those things.

The family was over for Sunday brunch when the phone rang. It was Char.

"Hi, Mom," she said. "Is everyone there?"

Mary Alice smiled at the sound of her voice. It was strong, more like the Char she knew. "Of course, sweetie. We are all here. Let me put this on speaker phone so everyone can say hello."

She fiddled with the phone for a moment and then held it out, Charlene's voice crackling through the speaker.

"Hey, everyone," Charlene said. "I miss all of you so much."

"What's it like in there?" Bethany asked. Ellie gave her a cross look.

"Lonely. The first two weeks were the worst. Withdrawal is a bi.... is tough. But it's better now. The therapists are good. Baby steps. That's what they tell me."

"Hey, sis," Evan said. "We miss you."

"Yeah, oh! I've got to tell you about the baby stuff I got for Christmas!" Bethany jumped toward the phone and leaned in close, rattling off every baby present she received until she

235

was out of breath.

Mary Alice held her breath.

"That sounds so nice, Bethy." Char's voice came out sweet and gentle. Char kept talking with Bethany. She didn't have a single judgmental comment. Mary Alice let herself breathe again.

Perhaps those therapists were making some progress with her after all. When Bethany had her fill of talking, she skipped back to her seat with everybody else and the conversation rolled on from there.

"Is she there?" Charlene asked. The conversation came to a screeching halt. All eyes turned to Mary Alice. "No ,Char. She is not. I've kept my promise."

Mary Alice didn't need to look at her family to know the air had been let out of the balloon.

"Oh, well. I've got to go," Char said. "There are others waiting to use the phone. We'll talk again soon. And I can have visitors now." Char's voice was softer. Was that remorse? Was she sorry she made that ultimatum? She hadn't retracted it.

"We love you, Char." Mary Alice said as the others chimed in. Hanging up the phone, Mary Alice looked at her family, trying her best to put on a smile and a brave face. "Well, wasn't that a nice surprise? She sounded good, don't you think?"

Heads nodded.

"Mom, she could still change her mind about Hope," Evan said.

Mary Alice shook her head and waved a hand for him to stop. "We're not going over this again. I need a minute."

She rose from the chair and dashed to the sanctuary of her bedroom. Sinking into the softness of the mattress, she let the tears flow. The pain was physical. Her chest tightened and she put her hand to her heart. Was she crying for Char because she was locked away?

Was she crying for the lost daughter she almost had?

Was she crying for Charlie, who should have been there to comfort her?

She didn't know.

Maybe she was crying for all three.

Thirty-Five

2018

The Wednesday after her birthday, Mary Alice met with the girls around their reserved table at the back of Scarcella's. Mary Alice caught them up to date on Charlene.

"Well, I got a call from her counselor a little after that. The evaluation ordered by the judge was to keep her one hundred and twenty days."

"Oh, I'm sorry about the extra time. But that's good you got to talk to her," said Gladys, laying her tawny hand over Mary Alice's pale white one. "I know it's hard to have her away. You know this is all good for her. Don't you? She's needed help for a long time. Look at it like a blessing in disguise."

Sophia and Mary Alice nodded.

"I'm trying to think that way," Mary Alice said. How much more could a woman take? Between Bethany, Hope, and Char, it was so overwhelming. "She asked if Hope was there when she called. Of course, I told her no."

Sophia and Gladys both nodded. "Hmm. Have you heard from Hope?" Sophia asked.

Mary Alice shook her head. "Nothing, I thought maybe she'd call . . . but she hasn't."

"Have you checked your email?" Gladys asked.

"No, I unplugged it," Mary Alice answered.

"If you want to hear from her, I suggest you turn it back on. This isn't 1963 anymore. People communicate through email, especially when it's hard subjects to face. Email is more, I don't know, safe. No one can see you cry or whatever," Gladys said. "And by the way, you look like hell.""

"Gladys!" Sophia said.

Mary Alice knew there were dark circles around her eyes. Even her new sweater did nothing to brighten her face. Had she remembered to even put make-up on? She didn't know or care.

"I suppose. And what if I do and there isn't anything there from her? Does that mean she's given up on me? That is what it sounded like at the time. She said, 'I'm not waiting any longer.' I think I acted hastily. But what do I do? Go against Char? I promised. I don't want to lose either one of them." She hung her head and they sat in silence for a few minutes.

"Ellie and Evan took me to her gallery. They bought me one of her sculptures. It's the most beautiful thing you have ever seen." Mary Alice lifted her head, "Somehow, I have to undo this. I was wrong to let Char sway me like this. I feel like every decision I make is wrong."

"It's an impossible situation," Sophia said. "But you'll figure out the right thing to do. The final decision has to be yours, and yours alone. Not Char, not even us."

"That is assuming Hope would even give me another chance. I got another brainstorm too."

"Oh boy," said Gladys. "What are you up to now?"

"Well, I was thinking that I really need to sell Charlie's shop. The kids don't want it and even though the building is free and clear, I still have the taxes, insurance and utilities to pay. But . . . after thinking about it, I might have a child interested in it. I have Hope. It would make a perfect gallery and workshop for her. So, I am thinking about gifting it to her."

"Wow," said Gladys. "That is a lot to consider. But I can see how it would work for both of you. The big IF is whether you can get Hope to come back around.

"Hey," said Sophia. "This is us. No pretenses, remember? We've got your back no matter what happens." She raised her left hand and made a V with her index and middle finger, crossing it with the index finger of her right hand. "Crittenton girls, together forever, remember?"

"Speaking of, how's Bethany feeling?" Gladys asked.

"Good," Mary Alice said with a half-smile, glad to be off the subject of Hope and Charlene. "She loves the Home. The girls call it the FC. Her grades are back up and she's much more appreciative of what Ellie and Greg are doing for her. Things are much better between them. Whatever they are teaching her there at the 'FC', it seems to be working."

"Well," said Sophia. "She is one of us now - a Crittenton Girl. Should we teach her the secret hand signal?"

"I don't know about that," Mary Alice said. She glanced between her friends and her heart swelled. Despite all the sadness she had recently encountered, her friends could still manage to lift her spirits.

She watched Sophia nab Gladys' wine glass and tip it back, saw Gladys' nostrils flare before she snatched it back, smiled at the way Sophia stuck her tongue out. For a moment, their wrinkles disappeared, their hair shone with color, and for a second, Mary Alice remembered. They were always there. Before any of them hit eighteen, and long after that. Always. There were no words to express her love and gratitude toward them.

"Hey," Sophia said brightly. "Let's throw a baby shower for Bethany when Charlene comes home. When is her due date?"

Mary Alice snapped back to the present and cleared her throat. "May 15. That's very sweet of you. Bethany would love it; she's been planning one herself — you know how excited she gets. Ellie had mentioned it, but I know she'd love your help. The ultrasound showed she is having a boy."

Gladys raised her glass of red wine and waited for the others to follow. "To Bethany and new beginnings."

"Hear, hear." Sophia and Mary Alice said in unison. Mary Alice sipped her drink and pulled out her little pocket calendar. "How about Saturday, April 14th? And it's going to be at my house, no arguments."

"Agreed," said Sophia. Gladys nodded.

Thirty-Six

2018

Mary Alice sat in her car for a long while after lunch. She meant to start it and drive home, but then she didn't. She sat there. She didn't want to go home. She wanted . . . she wanted to resolve this mess she'd made with Hope. She wanted to invite her to the baby shower. She wanted to give her the shop and shed the weight from her shoulders — the weight that went away around company and snuck right back on when she was alone, like a sneaky shadow.

Email her. She could. She should. But then there was a chance that Hope wouldn't answer it, or worse, she wouldn't even open it. *The final decision has to be yours and yours alone. Not Char, not even us.*

She saw Hope then, in her head. The way she'd looked at Mary Alice on that day, her eyebrows drawn down, her lip curled, her voice even and cold. She looked so angry. She looked so hurt. Mary Alice had let her walk right out of that door, out of her life, and back into a life where nobody was around to love her.

Mary Alice had been waiting for Hope to call her, but Hope was the one who had gotten left in the cold. She would always be too scared to try and open the door after it had been shut. And Mary Alice knew this as surely as she knew her name because she was exactly the same.

She blinked. Her child. She squared her shoulders. Email wasn't good enough. Not even a call would do. She had to see Hope. She couldn't let Char stop her. She wanted to see her daughter and that was that. She'd apologize. She'd beg if she had to get her back in her life. No more cowering in fear. She'd come clean with Evan about her financial situation, and that ended up working out fine. This could too. Charlene would have to understand — or get over it. If she didn't want to know her sister, that was her prerogative.

Mary Alice didn't have to take responsibility for Char's actions anymore. She couldn't keep Mary Alice away from her own daughter.

She would not leave Hope. Not again. No one had control over her life, not anymore. Not her parents, not Charlie, and most certainly not Charlene. She almost laughed at herself. I am woman. I am strong. Hear me roar.

She started the car. She drove. All the while, imagining that Hope was right around the corner, waiting for her. She didn't think about what she might say. She drove downtown and into the parking garage, then she wrapped a scarf around her neck and marched toward the Rockford Art Gallery. She had every right to visit the gallery, every right to see her daughter. Mary Alice crossed the strap from her handbag across her chest and walked faster.

After a few blocks, she saw the door.

After a few minutes, her fingers kissed the cool metal. She didn't move. Her resolve was melting like the shrinking piles of dirty snow along the sidewalk. Was she doing the right thing?

She shivered and stepped inside. A nervous tick worried her left eye. That was new. Calm down.

"Good morning." It was the same hostess who had greeted her when she had visited with Ellie and Evan. Her name tag said Ms. Dawson. "I remember you. Welcome back."

"Thank you." Mary Alice could feel the heat on her cheeks. She's never stalked someone before. It felt wrong. "I can't seem to stay away."

"Didn't your children buy one of Hope Pendleton's

pieces for your birthday."

Hearing her name aloud tightened the cold grip of fear on her heart. "Yes," Mary Alice paused. "Is she doing an in-person show soon?" She'd work her way up to asking for her.

"No, nothing scheduled. But she still has some lovely pieces for sale. You seem to have a keen interest. Are you also an artist?"

"Heavens no. Not an ounce of talent in me. Do you have any idea when she will have the new pieces ready?"

Ms. Dawson shook her head, her gaze now settled on a bumblebee, *rosewood*, resting on a daffodil, *elm*.

"To be honest," Mary Alice blurted out. "We are family. But we've been estranged for a while. I was hoping to see her today."

The smile vanished from the young girl's face and she stopped walking. Mary Alice thought she would tell her to get out. She gripped her purse strap so tightly that the leather squeaked.

"Well . . ." The girl lowered her voice. "I probably shouldn't be saying this . . . but Ms. Pendleton hasn't been well."

A bolt of alarm raced through Mary Alice's mind. "Not well? Nothing serious I hope?" Please, please don't let it be anything serious.

Ms. Dawson fingered her name tag. "I really shouldn't say. I spoke out of turn."

Mary Alice stepped closer and clutched Ms. Dawson's arm. The hostess froze.

"If you know something, you must tell me. Where? Where is she?"

The hostess stammered and shook her head.

"Please. Please tell me where she is. She's my daughter."

"The Fresenius Medical Center on Belmont."

Mary Alice dropped her arm like it burned. She didn't say thank you, she didn't apologize for grabbing her, she spun on her heel and dashed out of the shop.

Mary Alice rushed to the privacy of the car before the tears let loose. Sick. Something was wrong. Hope could be hurt.

She turned the car and shifted into gear, rocketing out

of the garage at a good five miles faster than the speed limit. Once she got past the exit, she shot down the street. The green light at the corner of Belmont and Lexington, turned yellow. She pressed down on the pedal.

Red. She stomped the brake and stopped short of the passing traffic lane. She drummed her fingers on the steering wheel. What could have possibly gone wrong? What if it was serious? What if she didn't get better. A horn blew behind her. She jumped. How long had she been sitting through that green light? She glanced in the rearview and waved an apology at the man behind her. He responded with a raised finger.

Mary Alice ignored him and shot across the street, her stomach churning. She wasn't far away from the place, but it felt like a city away. There was a sign for Fresenius Medical Center two blocks away, straight ahead. She gunned it.

She threw the car in park and sprinted through the door. "Excuse me," Mary Alice panted and clutched the white counter. "Do you have a Hope Pendleton here?"

The receptionist was a gray-haired woman, heavy-set and square, and her Tweety Bird scrubs were faded. She didn't look up from the computer screen she was staring at. "One moment please," she said, her voice flat and uninterested.

Mary Alice tried to remain calm. Deep breaths. In and out. In and out. She stood there staring at the woman for what must have been five minutes.

"Please," she tried "Hope Pendleton. Is she here?"

"Williamson, you say?"

"No, Pendleton. Hope Pendleton." Was she even listening? "Please, can't you look to see if she is here?" The tick in her left eye was getting worse.

A thin woman with dreadlocks strode out of a set of swinging double doors, her white lab coat fluttering behind her. She looked right at Mary Alice and smiled. Then she started walking toward her with a determined gait.

"Hello." She stopped right in front of Mary Alice and held out her hand.

"Hello." Mary Alice grabbed the woman's hand. Finally,

some help.

"I'm Amanda, your dallas nurse. You muss be Cat'rine, my new patient." Her strong Jamaican accent made it difficult to understand her words.

"Dallas?" Mary Alice dropped her hand. "What is a Dallas nurse? Wait, never mind. I'm not a patient. I'm checking on someone else who may be here. Can you please help me?" Mary Alice's voice pitched an octave higher than normal.

"Dallas," the woman repeated, a little louder, as if saying it in volume would help. "This be the Fresenius Kidney Dallas Center. Are you in the right place, dalin'?"

The word finally registered. She was saying dialysis, not Dallas. "A dialysis center? That's for kidney failure, isn't it?" Maybe she wasn't in the right place. Maybe Ms. Dawson told her the wrong medical center. "Please, is Hope Pendleton here?"

"Hope, yes, yes, lovely girl." Her voice was melodic. "She's here. Station 4B. Our patients don't usually have visitors while they receive treatment. Are you family?"

Mary Alice hesitated for a fraction of a second. "Yes, yes, I am her mother."

"Ah, don' worry," the angel of mercy said, her face lighting up with a smile of pearly whites against her dark skin. ""Mama's git special treatment 'round here. I'll tell her you here. Please sit." She waved toward the chairs and retreated behind the swinging doors.

Dialysis. Kidney failure. Terms she'd heard many times in TV shows and on the news, but never regarding anyone she knew — not family. What did it all mean? Could Hope die? People were on dialysis when they were waiting for a kidney transplant, she was pretty sure. She fidgeted with the clasp on her purse, straightened her hair with her hand, pressed her lips together. She wished the tick in her eye would stop. Would Hope see her? How would she look? What did dialysis even look like?

After an excruciatingly long time, Nurse Amanda reappeared, but she wasn't smiling. "Ma'am." All pleasantness was gone from her voice. "We gonna hafta ask you ta leave. Ms.

Pendleton say her parents both be passed on. I don't know what kind of game you playin' h'ea, but we at Fresenius treat our patients with the utmost care." She crossed her thin arms across her chest. "We won't be having this kin' of behavior."

Mary Alice felt her cheeks flush. "But I didn't lie. I'm her biological mother. It was her adopted parents that passed away. Please, tell her it is Mary Alice."

Nurse Amanda didn't budge, and Nurse Tweety Bird came from behind the desk and joined forces, arms crossed across her amble bosom. They were forming a human wall to keep her from going through those doors.

"Do I need to call security?" asked Tweety Bird.

"No, no. I'll go. I wanted to see her." She fought the tears that threatened to fall. "To be sure she's all right. I didn't know she was sick. I didn't mean any harm, honest. We only found each other after fifty years. I thought . . ."

What was the use? They didn't understand. And Hope obviously didn't want to see her. She got to her feet. Her knees felt weak.

"Wait," Nurse Amanda said. "I didn' know. I's 'dopted meeself. If my biological mama was look'in fer me, I'd wanna to see her. I'll ask her a'gin. Mary Alice, you say?"

Mary Alice nodded, wiping a rogue tear from her cheek with the back of her hand. "Thank you," she whispered.

Tweety Bird didn't seem as accommodating and kept vigil at the double doors.

A moment later, Amada reappeared. "She say she see you. Follow me."

Mary Alice gave a triumphant smile to Tweety Bird and slipped past her.

Station 4 had six reclining hospital chairs with long wooden armrests. A computer monitor, a keyboard, metal poles holding IV bags, and complex-looking machines dotted both sides of each chair. Amanda pulled the curtain between the other chairs and disappeared behind them.

Mary Alice's stomach twisted in knots. Four of the six chairs were occupied. She offered a weak smile to the man in the first chair, marked A on the wall above his head, but he was engrossed in something on a small, attached TV and he had headphones on. Hope was in the B chair. Her arm was strapped to the arm rest and two tubes were sticking out of her forearm. Her face was a little pale and she was covered in a soft blue blanket.

Mary Alice stood a little straighter and her jaw ticked, everything she wanted to say bubbling in her chest, too many words to pick a handful. Before she could speak, though, Hope gave her a weak smile. It was the most beautiful thing that Mary Alice had ever seen.

"Hi," Hope said. "I guess you found out my secret."

"Hope, why didn't you tell me? Are you okay?"

Hope shrugged a single shoulder. "Good as I can be with renal failure. These wonderful folks here are keeping me kicking."

Mary Alice moved next to the chair. "How long has this been going on?" She motioned to the equipment at Hope's side.

"Four years," Hope said. "Three times a week."

"Are you getting better?" Mary Alice fought the urge to swoop her up in her arms. Hope was strapped to the chair by her arm, she'd probably hurt her.

"Not really, no." Hope shrugged, "It's put a real dent in my work. But, . . .how did you find me? When Amanda said you were here, I couldn't believe it."

Mary Alice held Hope's free hand. "I went to the gallery. I couldn't stop thinking about you. I wanted to—I had to see you."

Hope pursed her lips and opened her mouth, closed it, then looked at her lap.

Mary Alice moved closer, almost hovering over Hope. "I needed to see you. I've taken a stand—for you. I want you in my life. Even if Charlene isn't ready to accept that, I can't lose you . . .again. Then Ms. Dawson told me you were sick."

"She shouldn't have done that. It was personal." Hope muttered.

"I'm personal, don't you think? I'm your mother." She leaned down and kissed Hope's forehead. Hope didn't push her away. Mary Alice cupped the back of Hope's head and pressed her nose into her hair. Again, Hope didn't push her away. She studied the bleep, the rise and fall of lines on the monitor, the machines, the IVs. "I'm so sorry about what I said. I was wrong to listen to Charlene. I'm so, so sorry. I won't lose you. I won't."

After a moment of complete stillness, Hope sagged and leaned into the touch. "I'm sorry too, I blew up on you. Your daughter needed more time to process, I should have been patient."

"No, no, Hope, you have nothing to be sorry about." Mary Alice said, releasing her. "You were right, I was letting somebody else decide for us. You were hurt — I hurt you, and I cannot apologize deeply enough for that. I will never make you feel like that ever again."

Hope's cheek twitched. She pursed her lips again. Then, Mary Alice realized that she was trying not to smile. Like her own mother. Yes, she could see it now, same mouth. There was a little bit of her mother, right there in Hope.

Mary Alice bent down and caught her daughter's down-turned eyes. "I mean it. I want you in my life, I've wanted you in my life since the day you were born."

This time, Hope did smile. It was small, and it was wobbly, and it was followed by a little hiccup of a sob, but it was a smile. She was happy. She wanted Mary Alice in her life, too.

Mary Alice dabbed the corners of her own eyes with the heel of her hands and sniffed. She could not start crying right now. "Look at us." She shook her head and smiled past another sniffle, "aren't we a mess?"

Hope laughed then and swiped at her own wet cheeks.

"Are you waiting for a kidney? Isn't that what they do? Do a transplant or something?"

"Yes, but I'm somewhere on the bottom of the list. Some people have been waiting for ten years. Some even more."

Ten years. How could somebody survive on machines for ten years? And what if the machines weren't good enough, what if ten years was too long? A knot formed in her belly. In her head, she watched Hope waste away.

"Hope, couldn't one of us, your family, be a match for

you. Maybe I could give . . ."

Hope shook her head. "It's probably too late. You're over the age limit. I tried to find you years ago. When I first found out I had . . .this . . . chronic kidney disease." Her eyes swept over the room. "But, like you, I discovered all the records at the Crittenton Home were destroyed in that fire."

"I don't understand. You were looking for me before? Before I placed that ad on the Facebook Reunion page?"

"Yes, four years ago. So, I couldn't believe it when it actually happened."

"Is this why you wanted to find us? To ask for a kidney donation?" Please don't say that was the only reason. That she was only looking for a donor, not a mother.

Hope shifted her eyes away from Mary Alice, staring at an invisible something on the green curtain separating the patients. "Yes, it was probably my only hope. But after we met, I couldn't bring myself to ask." Her eyes trailed back to Mary Alice. "I didn't tell you because I didn't want you to think I had ulterior motives. Because now, it was more than a kidney I wanted. I wanted you . . . a family . . . our family."

"And then I cut you out of our lives, before we even got started." Oh God, how could she have been so heartless?

"Yes," Hope whispered.

"But it's not too late. I could be tested. See if they'll let me do it." Her daughter was sick. She needed her. Need had to trump want. Char would have to accept that.

Hope shook her head. "Mary Alice . . . Mom. You don't have any idea what all is involved. First there's a blood test to see if we are even a match. Then they'd have to check to see if our blood is compatible, even if it is a match. There is a psych exam, electrocardiogram, X-rays, CT scans."

Mary Alice held up her hand and Hope stopped talking. "I don't care. I'll do it. I'll do it all."

Thirty-Seven

2018

Mary Alice's mind was spinning in a million directions. What had she committed to? She didn't know what was involved. She didn't know if she'd pass the tests, either. Once home, she turned Charlie's computer on before she even removed her coat. She typed in kidney donor in the search bar.

Oh, my goodness, this was complicated. She'd have to see her own doctor and consult with Hope's team of specialists, the nephrologist, surgeon, nurses, social workers, even financial counselors. So much . . . but it would be worth it if she could save Hope's life.

Five hours of intense reading later, she was much less confident. If she couldn't go through with it, Hope would feel betrayed. If she didn't go through with it, Hope might get sicker. She turned off the computer.

"Laparoscopic nephrectomy," Mary Alice said aloud. She hefted a heavy sigh and walked out of the office, her feet scuffing all the way to the kitchen. She looked at the box on the mantle, almost passing, but she stopped and stood there.

"Charlie, I am going to do this. It's time I make my own decisions. I am not responsible for Char's decisions, or even Hope's. It feels like, no, it has been, a lifetime that I have let other people, even you, Charlie, tell me what to do. I gave in. I let others run my life. Not anymore. And if it costs me my life, well, I guess I'll get to see you a little sooner."

It felt good being decisive. It was the right decision. If the doctors cleared her, she would donate a kidney to her daughter. And God willing, she'd be around to rebuild relationships with all her children.

Having the family over for Sunday dinner was nothing new. True, she didn't do it as often as when Charlie had been alive, but no one questioned the motive for the invitation. She'd had days to think about how to break the news, days to scour the internet for more information, days to talk herself out of it. But she was doing this.

"I went to the Rockford Gallery the other day," Mary Alice passed the potatoes.

"Aw," Bethany whined. "You promised to take me. Mom and Uncle Evan got to go on your birthday. Did you see her?"

Ellie scowled at Bethany. "No whining. Your grandmother doesn't have to take you everywhere she goes." She turned to Mary Alice. "But did you see her?"

Expectant eyes all turned toward her.

"Yes, I saw her."

"Are we going to meet her, finally?" Evan asked.

"Did she ask about us?" Bethany chirped.

"How did you feel about that?" Ricky asked.

Mary Alice lifted a hand to silence them all. "Wait. I'll tell you all about it."

"Charlie, help me out here."

Say it Mar. They'll understand.

Mary Alice took a deep breath. Start out with the hospital. Make it a story, make them understand. That was the plan. "I want to give Hope my kidney."

Plans rarely go according to plan.

Everyone around the table was silent. Even Bethany was quiet and blinking owlishly at her.

"Um." Ellie cleared her throat. "What?"

"That came out wrong." Mary Alice braced her hands against the table. "I went to the gallery, and the hostess told me that Hope was sick, but she wouldn't say with what. She told me where she was, I ran over there, and I found Hope hooked up to a dialysis machine. She said that some people wait for ten years for a kidney, and she's at the bottom of the list."

Mary Alice watched her family as they processed. They were still looking at her like they'd seen a ghost. "I want to give her one of my kidneys." She said again, calmer this time.

Evan's shocked expression faded. "Mom, that's a huge decision. We've never even met this girl."

"This girl is your sister, remember? And she's hardly a girl. She's in her fifties." Mary Alice crossed her arms.

"Yes," Evan said. "but one I don't even know. I'm sorry. I can't get my head around this. Basically, you are going to risk your life for someone you just met?"

"Evan. I didn't just meet her. I gave birth to her and I am hardly risking my life. People do this all the time."

Evan looked at Ellie and back to Mary Alice. It was unsettling the way they seemed to have unsaid conversations going on between them. "Mom," Evan said. "Is that why she wanted to connect with you? To use you as a donor? I think I'm liking her less and less."

"Stop it, Evan. What's gotten into you?" Mary Alice didn't want to answer that. Best to deflect.

"Evan is not the one being unreasonable here," said Ellie. "You are. This is dangerous. And think about your age."

"My age, my age. I'm sick of hearing about how old I am. I'm healthy —for a woman my age." She made air quotes. "The doctors won't approve it if there is too much risk. And it's not like it's happening tomorrow. First, there is a lot of prep. Tests to see if I'm compatible, physical exams, psych evaluations. But if they will let me, and I'm a match, I'm going to do it. Honestly, I thought you'd all be behind me on this."

"I don't think anyone is against you," Greg said. "But this is a huge decision. Don't you think you should get to know her a little more before you start offering your body parts?"

Mary Alice stood and tossed her napkin on the table. "You all have valid points. And I appreciate your concern, but this is not open for discussion. She is my daughter." She looked at Greg. "Wouldn't you do it for Bethany?" She turned to Ellie.

"And you can't tell me you'd even give it a second thought. I know you would. Because it's the right thing to do." She let her gaze circle the room, pinning each one of them with her eyes. "All my life I've let other people make decisions for me. First my parents when I gave Hope away, then I willingly let your Dad make decisions for fifty years. And I let Char talk me out of a relationship with Hope. No more. This is my decision alone, well, mine and about a dozen professionals. I am telling you this because I want your support, not your approval."

"Of course, Mom." Evan held up his hands and stood up slowly. He moved his way around the table until he was standing beside her, pulling her into a gentle hug. "We do support you. In anything you do. We want to know you're safe and that you're not making a hasty, emotional decision."

"What else would I base it on? She's my daughter. Your sister. Don't you think I'd do the same for you or Ellie or Char? Don't turn this into something sinister."

"Okay, okay. Calm down." Ellie said. "No reason to get yourself all worked up."

"And now you get to tell Char." Evan said, patting her on the back before releasing her. "Good luck with that."

"I'll go talk to Char in person. But first I'll call her counselor and run it by her first." The table conversation went silent.

Thirty-Eight

2018

Mary Alice worried a path in the living room carpet. She had called the counselor and got the okay to visit, but she didn't ask about Char. She froze up. Before she knew it, she had scheduled a time and a date. Today, five hours from now. Luckily, flights from Youngstown to Cincinnati were quick and inexpensive.

Next came the hard part — actually telling Char. Planning it was one thing, actually looking her in the face and giving her the news was another. She felt like she was telling her mother about her first pregnancy all over again.

The conversation with the family last night went well. Unfortunately, Mary Alice knew to expect the opposite from Char. There had to be a way to make her understand this had nothing to do with the love Mary Alice had for her. Surely the counselor could help her understand that.

She drove to the airport, nibbling on her nails. It was a habit she thought she had gotten rid of a long time ago, but apparently not. At the airport, she bounced her knee as she waited for the plane. Her flight was called. Her legs felt wobbly as she boarded the small two-engine plane for the two-hour flight. It had been ten weeks since she had seen Charlene. How would she look? Would Charlene be happy to see her?

She tried to distract herself with thoughts that had nothing to do with Hope, but the question eventually came back around every time — what would her reaction be when Mary

Alice told her?

The rehab facility was an obscure, gray brick building that looked like it could be an office or a warehouse. Mary Alice climbed out of the taxi and closed the door, staring up at the building, her stomach fluttering. She couldn't take her eyes off of the building. Char was in there somewhere. She had this. She needed to remember that she wasn't asking. Mary Alice took a deep breath and walked. Her long strides were rushed, and before she was really ready, she was at the front door. There was a sign next to it that instructed her to announce herself into the small intercom. She took another deep breath, exhaled slowly, and pressed a shaky finger on the buzzer.

A woman's voice buzzed from the speaker. "May I help you?"

"Yes, my name is Mary Alice Goodson. I have an appointment . . .with Charlene Goodson."

"Yes, come in." A buzzer sounded and a lock clicked.

She pulled on the heavy door and entered a small lobby. A woman was sitting behind a waist-high counter. She handed Mary Alice a clipboard with papers and a pen.

"Please fill this out and provide some identification. Any metal objects on you?"

Mary Alice stepped back. "No." Did they think she was going to carry a weapon in to see her daughter? She took the clipboard and sat down on a metal folding chair. The forms were simple. Name, address, phone. Who was she here to see? Did she have an appointment? A second form was the standard HIPPA disclosure. She signed and dated the forms and handed them back to the receptionist. It wouldn't hurt for her to be a little friendlier.

"Ms. Williams will be with you shortly."

Mary Alice checked her watch. She was twenty minutes early. She picked up a People magazine. The cover read Blake Shelton - Life after Miranda. The date was October 2015. Mary Alice dropped it back on the table.

At precisely 10:30 a.m., a door opened at the far end of the room. A striking young woman, right around Charlene's age, stepped out. "Mrs. Goodson?"

Mary Alice stood and shook the woman's hand.

"I'm Barbara Williams, Charlene's counselor. I'm so pleased to meet you." Her smile lit up the room. They needed a friendly face like that behind the counter.

"How do you do? How is Charlene?"

The woman didn't answer. Instead, she turned and waited on Mary Alice, who followed her quietly through the doors and into a wide, brightly lit hallway with soft carpeted floors and sunny yellow paint.

She didn't answer the question. Did that mean Char wasn't good? Mary Alice swallowed a lump lodged in her throat.

Ms. Williams opened a door to a private office. A large desk, *oak*, sat beneath a wide expanse of windows that looked out to a courtyard with stone paver walkways surrounded by bushes and plants in an array of budding color. Spring was coming earlier to Cincinnati than to Youngstown, 280 miles north. Mary Alice could picture Charlene out there enjoying the spring sunshine. "How lovely."

"Yes, we try to make things comfortable for our guests here. Now that the weather has finally improved, I'm sure the garden will get a lot of use. Please have a seat."

"Thank you, Ms. Williams."

Mary Alice looked around the room. A loveseat in a soft green chenille was positioned across from two wing-back chairs in a matching toile print. Fresh flowers graced a small oval table, *mahogany*, and an 18th century print of London filled the wide expanse of wall. All very charming, very soothing. Maybe it was all strategically placed to help in the counseling. She took a seat in one of the chairs.

"Please, call me Barbara." The counselor sat beside Mary Alice in one of the wingback chairs, leaving the sofa unoccupied. "I wanted a few moments with you before I called Charlene in. Is that okay?"

Mary Alice felt an uneasy twist to her stomach. "Of course. She is okay, isn't she?"

That nice smile again. "Yes, Charlene is making great progress. although she is a bit antsy to get out of here. The reason for this meeting, Mrs. Goodson . . ."

"Mary Alice."

"Yes, Mary Alice. So, of course, our job is to help Charlene transition back into the real world. I was so glad that you called, because this gives us a unique opportunity to do some healing in the office. Even with healing exercises, once she gets out, she is going to need the support of her whole family."

"We've always been supportive of Charlene. Even when she didn't want it." Was she sounding defensive?

Barbara nodded. "Charlene shared with me that she told you about the incident in college and the abortion. I know she believes that is what started her problem with alcohol. But I suspect the reasons go back much farther than that."

"Farther? How could that be?" Her eye began to tick.

"Let's call Charlene in now and see if we can get to the root of the problem, shall we?" Barbara rose and pressed a button on the intercom on her desk. "Mildred, can you send Charlene in now please?"

Mary Alice fidgeted with the clasp on her purse. What did Barbara mean, 'get to the root of the problem?'

The door opened and Charlene stepped into the room. She was dressed in jeans and a light-weight pullover sweater in heather gray. Her blond hair was swept into a ponytail and she wore only a dab of lip gloss. But it was her eyes that pulled Mary Alice from her chair, dropping her purse on the floor. Charlene's eyes glistened with unshed tears. Her cheeks were red and blushing. So unusual to see Charlene cry. Char was the rock, the icicle, sometimes it was easy to forget that she felt anything at all.

"Oh, Char." Mary Alice wrapped her arms around her.

Char returned the embrace, holding tightly, her face buried in Mary Alice's neck. "I'm sorry, Mom. For everything."

"Sh, sh. It's okay now, baby. You are going to be okay."

Barbara cleared her throat. "Shall we all have a seat?"

Char took Mary Alice's hand and pulled her toward the loveseat, where they sat together. Barbara lifted Mary Alice's purse from the floor and set it on the table.

"Great. Why don't we begin? I am going to pose some

questions to both of you. I'd like you to answer them to each other, not to me. Understood?"

Charlene nodded and squeezed Mary Alice's hand.

Mary Alice gulped down the knot stuck at the base of her throat. She wasn't expecting a psychoanalysis. She noticed the pitcher of water and glasses on the table for the first time. "May I?" She gestured toward them.

"Of course." Barbara leaned forward and poured three glasses of water.

Mary Alice gulped down half her glass. "Thank you."

"What was life like at home when Charlene was growing up?"

Mary Alice and Charlene looked at each other.

"It was good," Mary Alice said. "We weren't wealthy by any means, but the kids had everything they needed. We were a typical middle-class family from the suburbs."

Charlene did not reply.

"Do you agree with that scenario, Charlene?" Barbara asked.

Charlene nodded but a tear escaped and dropped onto her clasped hands.

Mary Alice felt a grip on her heart. "What? What is it darling?"

"I always felt like I was in a competition, and I was always losing."

"You mean with Ellie and Evan? You know the twins were a lot to handle and took up a lot of my time when they were little, but I . . . we . . . certainly didn't favor them over you. You must know that."

Charlene shook her head. "Not Ellie and Evan. That was the problem. I didn't know who I was competing with. But I felt like everything was being measured. And I always failed."

Mary Alice couldn't help but feel a little indignant. "That's ridiculous. Who would you have been competing with?"

As soon as the words were out of her mouth, Mary Alice knew the answer. No, no, that couldn't be. She slapped her hand over her mouth.

"Mary Alice," Barbara intervened. "Charlene told me that you found the daughter you gave away when you were sixteen. Is it possible that on some level, you were always comparing Charlene to that child?"

"No, no, of course not." As she said the words, memories flooded back. Charlene's first word: 'Daddy.' Hadn't she and Charlie even voiced aloud the question: 'I wonder what the baby's first word was?' "The baby." Between the two of them, they had always called her that, Hope, the baby they gave away. Charlene's first step, her first day of school, her first date. It was true. Every time Char had a milestone, the question of "the baby's" milestone loomed in their minds. Was it possible that Charlene had picked up on that? That she felt the comparison, although it was never voiced?

"Oh goodness. If I, we, your father and I were comparing you, we weren't doing it consciously. Did you really think we somehow loved you less? It's not true. We were so happy when you were born."

"I didn't know what was wrong. I only knew that I was wrong." Char pulled her hands away from Mary Alice and buried her face in them. Huge racking sobs shook her shoulders. "When you told me there was another child, I knew then that it hadn't been my imagination. I had been right all along my whole life. And when I found the letter, I knew. I've never been the child you wanted. That child is the one that was supposed to be in my place."

Mary Alice clasped her hands to her heart. She felt ill. What had she done? Did she, did Charlie, really do this to her? "I never meant . . . we never meant . . ." Her voice trailed off. What could she say now to make it better? How could she undo fifty years of pain? She loved Charlene. She'd always loved Charlene. She had to make her understand that. "I was only sixteen when I had her. It was a different time. I never had a choice about what happened to my baby. And I couldn't help but wonder what she was doing. Was she happy, safe, loved? I never meant to hurt you. I never meant to compare. I didn't have anything to compare to. Honey, I'm so sorry."

She had failed her daughter, and she hadn't even

known it. What kind of mother can't see that? The tick in her eye pounded harder against her skin. It wasn't so different from how Mary Alice's mother never really heard her. And, like mother, like daughter, Mary Alice had never really heard Charlene.

Barbara handed out tissues. Mary Alice took one and held it to her mouth, her lip quivering. Char started openly sobbing, and then Mary Alice couldn't hold it any longer. She started to sob too.

"The important thing here is for both of you to recognize that nothing was done on purpose to hurt anyone. Charlene, your mother is human. She made a mistake. But there was never any intention of malice. Try to put yourself in her shoes for a minute. Your parents carried a heavy burden. When they had you and the twins, wouldn't it only be natural to wonder what that missing child would have done at those landmark points in her life?"

Charlene sniffled and wiped her nose. "I guess so. When I couldn't make any sense of it, I turned to God. That's why I took theology in college, why I teach it. I was looking for answers. I asked God to forgive me for not being the daughter you wanted. I thought if I could be righteous enough, good enough, I'd win His love and yours. I know now that is why I reacted so violently to the news of finding "the baby", of finding Hope. I knew you'd never give her up again and I felt like I'd lost you completely now."

Mary Alice pulled Charlene into an embrace. "No, no. This breaks my heart. You've always been a handful. We didn't know it was your way of crying out for help. We failed you. I'm so sorry. Please believe me. Even if we did wonder what "the baby" was doing, it didn't mean we loved you less. Parents have an infinite amount of room in their hearts for their children. We loved all of you the same: you, Evan, Ellie, and yes, Hope. There are no degrees to our love. Can you forgive me?"

Charlene shrugged, then nodded. "I'm trying. What about Hope? Have you connected with her? Is she everything you always dreamed about?"

"Ah, Char,"" Mary Alice said. "It's not like that. I told

her I wasn't going to go any further with the reunion. I cut off all communication with her."

Charlene looked up through her tear-streaked face. "You did? You did that for me?"

"Well . . ." Mary Alice didn't mean to say it like that. The way Char was looking at her, so relieved and touched, was going to make it hard to admit otherwise. "I tried. I wanted to keep my promise to you. But . . ."

Char's head dropped to her chest. "But you couldn't do it, right?"

"Kind of. I told myself that if I could see that she was happy, working, creating new pieces, that she was okay, that I could let her go. But when I went to the gallery, I received some shocking news."

"What gallery?"

Oh, shoot. That's right. Char had missed all of that; the trips to the gallery, seeing Hope's sculptures. She'd been in here the whole time. How did Mary Alice forget that?

Char made a snort. "Sounds like the two of you were getting real chummy while I was in here."

"No, it's not like that." Mary Alice backpedaled. Everything she did got twisted into something sinister. "Hope is a sculptor, a wood sculptor. She has Papa's talent with wood."

Hope pinched her brows. "She does?"

"Yes, and she plays piano like Evan . . . and she has your eyes."

"Why didn't I know any of this?"

"You wouldn't listen, remember? When I came to your house to talk to you about her, you cut me off."

"That was months ago. Phones still work in here. So does email, or snail mail. In all the times we talked, you didn't think it was important to mention any of this to me?"

"I . . ." Mary Alice stammered. "I don't know. I'm sorry. I thought you didn't want to discuss it. I thought you had enough to deal with right now."

"Without all the facts." Char waved her hand, dismissing the subject. "What were you saying about shocking news?"

Mary Alice took a deep breath. "Her kidneys are failing.

I saw her in the dialysis center. And I . . . I want to help her. I want to donate one of my kidneys."

When Char didn't respond, no questions, no objections, Mary Alice kept talking. "I want to do this donor transplant, and your blessing is important to me. I know this is a lot to absorb. And maybe today wasn't the best timing, but I have to start all the testing right away."

"Whoa," Barbara said. She made the time-out sign. "Charlene, are you okay? Need a break?"

Charlene shrugged.

"Mrs. Goodson . . . Mary Alice, why don't you wait out in the lobby while I have a little chat with Charlene. This is a lot of information to absorb all at once. These things take time to process."

Mary Alice stood. Should she hug Char? Walk out without commenting further? She hesitated, then leaned down and pecked Char on the cheek. "I didn't mean to upset you."

"Please give us a few minutes," Barbara said.

Mary Alice left the room and found a seat in the lobby. She felt Mildred's formidable eyes boring into her, but she didn't look. Maybe Char had told them about her, maybe Mildred thought she was an awful mother.

Mary Alice stared at the wall. She shouldn't have said any of that to Char. That look on her face . . . Char was in no condition to process something like this right now. She shouldn't have brought up the donor part. Then again, if Mary Alice hadn't told her and did it anyway, that would have been much worse—exactly what she didn't want. This was all so complicated, and it shouldn't be. Would Char even still talk to her? Would the counselor send Mary Alice home?

What felt like an eternity later, Mildred cleared her throat and pointed to the office door. Mary Alice sent a quick, silent prayer to whoever was listening and made her way back to the office. Her mouth was as dry as a desert.

When she opened the door, Char's blotchy face was the first thing she saw. The second was the small pile of tissues on her lap, little shreds of them gathered like dust bunnies around her ankles.

"Char wants to talk about how she feels about this," Barbara said.

Char cleared her throat, pulled more tissues from the box on the table and wiped her face. She kept the tissue folded in her hands, her fingers shredding them up piece by piece. "I'm afraid. I thought I was making progress . . . we were making progress. I was beginning to understand what happened to you and why I felt so lost. What if you do this thing . . . for her . . . and you die? What if I lose you all over again?"

Charlene's face pinched and she got up to walk to the windows. She ran her hands over the ledge. Her shoulders trembled, silent sobs wracking her frame. Mary Alice rose and joined her at the window. "Charlene, I'm not going to die. And I'm not going to leave you." She wrapped an arm around her shoulders. "Honey, this procedure is done thousands of times a year. Nothing is going to happen to me. If you needed a kidney, don't you know that I would do this for you too, without blinking an eye?"

How could she convince Char that it was going to be fine when her own tiny speck of doubt crept in? Everyone had done such a good job, now even she was questioning the sanity of this. No, she had to stay strong, and convince her family, all of her family, including Char that this was the right thing to do.

Charlene turned and faced her. "You're going to do this whether I like it or not, aren't you?"

Mary Alice nodded. "As long as I pass all the tests." She cupped Charlene's cheek. "But it would feel so much better if you were sitting by my bedside praying for me."

"Mom, I don't know. How can you ask me to bless something that could hurt you? I don't even know this woman and you're ready to put your life on the line for her? Can you see why this sounds so insane to me?"

"Char, she's not a stranger. She's your sister. Your full-blooded sister. Like Ellie. What other choice do I have? Please, I need you beside me on this."

Char looked her in the eyes, a new light shining in them. "You need me?"

Mary Alice stared wide-eyed at Char when she broke

out into a fit of sobs again. Was that the wrong thing to say?

"Those . . ." Char sniffed and tried to talk through her tears, "Those are the most important words I've heard all day."

Mary Alice smiled and pulled her daughter close. It had been so long since she'd held Char.

Okay." Char sniffed. She nodded against Mary Alice's shoulder. "I'll try. That's the best I can offer right now. I want to support you, but I'm not quite there yet. I love you, Mom."

Thirty-Nine

2018

As she rode the plane home, her thoughts wandered. To Char, to Hope, to anything, and eventually, as she stared out the window, she realized that she still had two more people that she needed to tell.

She was only home long enough to grab her keys, and then she was driving to the Lake Park Cemetery on Midlothian Blvd. She hadn't been there in years—since 2006, to be exact. There was a double plot reserved for her and Charlie in there next to his parents, but she hadn't been ready to put him in the ground yet. She drove through the winding road, around tall mausoleums and small tombstones. The grounds were well maintained. Pretty, even.

It had been so long that she almost forgot where to turn. That was wrong. She should have come sooner.

It was the mid-February and after a hard winter, they were getting an early spring. Small buds of crocus and daffodils were sprouting in front of many of the tombstones. Growing up, she had helped her father plant flowers on her grandparents and great-grandparents grave every spring.

She parked her car at section C10. Her eyes scanned the grounds, hunting for the double stone marked with Cranston. Taking three long breaths, she opened the car door and got out, holding a small folding stool. She climbed the small hill until she was standing in front of the large headstone. Two names were engraved beneath. Robert Howard Cranston, May 16, 1916 - January 27, 2006. Beside it, Margaret Hasting Cranston, August 28, 1918 - January 17, 1997.

Mary Alice unfolded the stool and sat down in front of the stone. She reached down and pulled some weeds from around it. "Hey, Mom, Dad. Sorry it's been so long since I've been out here. I'm sorry I haven't kept up with the flowers. But the groundskeepers do a good job, don't you think?"

"Life's been . . . difficult, to say the least." She pulled a long blade of grass and peeled it apart with her fingernails. "I found her, you know. I think you would have liked her. She's smart, and talented, and beautiful. For the longest time, I was angry at you for making me give her away. For pretending she never existed. I never told you that once she was gone. But you wouldn't have expected me to, would you?"

"There were expectations to live up to. I wasn't the perfect, obedient daughter. I am sorry I let you down. But you let me down too. I needed you back then. I was afraid and so very naive. All you wanted to do was white-wash it away." She stared at the stone, ran her fingers across the etchings. "You know, life is funny. I thought I was coming out here to tell you that I won, that I have her back. But there is no winning or losing, is there? You were a product of the times. In your own twisted way, you really did think you were doing what was right. I see that now. And I don't feel any anger toward you anymore. I feel sorry for you. And I forgive you."

She paused. It was a peaceful sort of quiet out here. She closed her eyes and forced the likeness of her parents into the world so she could look at them. She expected them to look like she always remembered them, but they didn't. They looked calm, they looked like they were looking at her and not through her. Like they were listening.

"Did you ever wonder about her? Your first grandchild? Did you wonder what she was like, was she happy, safe? I did. Almost every day for half a century. Now I have a chance to do something for her. It's the least I can do, don't you think? She's sick. She needs a kidney or she will die. If we had kidney

Joanne Simon Tailele

disease in our family, I never knew it. I pray I didn't give this to her. Or Charlie. Of course, the kids are concerned. They think I'm too old. But this is my decision. For once, I'm going to stand up for myself and do what I think is best. I hope that doesn't mean I'll be seeing you sooner than I expected. But maybe this will make you proud of me."

She opened her eyes and ran her fingers along the engravings. She felt . . . light. She felt okay.

"I'll see ya." Mary Alice picked up the stool and turned to walk away. Then on second thought, she turned back, kissed her fingers and touched them to the tombstone. "I love you."

Back at the car, she sat in the silence for five minutes, ten, fifteen, she wasn't sure. Then she reached for her phone and called Hope. As soon as the phone was picked up, before Hope could say 'hello,' Mary Alice said, "Hope. I'm doing it."

"Oh." Hope sucked in a breath. "Are you sure you want to do this?" Her voice had a little tremble in it.

"Positive. Why does everyone keep asking me that? I'm seeing my family doctor on Wednesday and if I pass, my next stop was to see a nephrologist. So, yes, I'm sure. And I think it's time for you to meet your family."

Hope gasped. "Really? Have you talked to them about me?"

Mary Alice laughed. "I'd say you are about the biggest conversation we've had since we found out about Bethany's pregnancy."

"What about Charlene? Is she on board too?"

"She's not home yet, but I've been to see her, and she understands what I want to do and why. And as soon as she gets out, you'll get to meet her too. Let's start with the others. How about brunch on Sunday?"

"Sure. Oh my God. You have no idea how happy this makes me. I'm so nervous. What if they don't like me?"

"They'll love you. No question about that. Be your beautiful self."

266

Forty

2018

Mary Alice fussed over the brunch preparations. She set the dining room table with her grandmother's good linen table-cloth and the fine china. No, that was all wrong. Too fussy. She pulled it all off and reset the table with a red gingham cotton cloth and the everyday china. She floated a spray of yellow cro-cuses in a glass bowl and placed it in the center of the table. There. That was good, pretty but low enough that it didn't block the views across the table. She checked the quiche in the oven and smoothed the stray hairs away from her face. She'd altered the recipe to make it kidney friendly, leaving out the onions and salt. Would the kids even notice? How would they react to Hope? She'd warned them not to bring up the kidney donation. This brunch was to get to know each other. That's all.

"*Evan wouldn't say anything after I warned him, would he, Charlie?*"

Don't be silly Mar. Evan would never do anything like that. You know better.

"*I hope you're right, Charlie, I'm so nervous. I wish you were here.*"

I'm right beside you, sweetheart.

Ellie, Greg and Bethany, now almost seven months pregnant, arrived first. Her granddaughter waddled through the door on swollen feet and she looked radiant. She wrapped Mary Alice in a hug.

"I can't wait to meet Auntie Hope." She giggled. "That sounds so strange."

Mary Alice gave her a kiss on the cheek. "You know, none of this would be happening if it wasn't for you. You and your social media idea. You made it happen. Thank you, Bethy."

Evan and Ricky arrived right behind them. "Is she here yet?" Evan asked. "I didn't see any extra cars. Is she still coming?"

"And hello to you too, son." Mary Alice planted a kiss on his freshly shaved cheek. "No, she's not here yet. But she's coming."

Evan was quick to dart into the kitchen. Mary Alice hurried after him and got there as he pulled open the oven door. "Hmm, smells great, Mom."

"Get out of there." Mary Alice swatted at his wrist. "It's not done yet. You're going to ruin it. Make yourself useful and mix some mimosas."

Ricky raised an eyebrow. "Mimosas? Alcohol? Since when do you drink?"

"Well," Mary Alice blushed. "I thought it was a special occasion."

"It is indeed," Ellie said from the doorway. "Pour me a double."

Mary Alice accepted a glass and moved to the living room window, in time to see Hope's tan Nissan Rogue pull in behind Evan's sports car. "She's here," she said softly, more to herself than to anyone else. Her heartbeat pulsed in her ear. They would love her, wouldn't they?

Everyone rushed to the window and watched as Hope, dressed in off-white slacks and a matching pullover sweater, exited the car. To Mary Alice, Hope looked like an angel. She carried a bouquet of hyacinths. Hope hesitated at the car door for a minute before heading up the walkway. Was she nervous too? How could she not be?

Mary Alice raced past everyone and opened the door before Hope had a chance to ring the bell. She wrapped her in an embrace. "Come in, come in. Everyone is here and can't wait to meet you."

Hope held out the flowers.

"Thank you. They are beautiful. I'll put them in a vase right away."

When Mary Alice turned around with Hope linked in her arm, five faces in a semi-circle stood staring back at them from the living room doorway. Hope let out a little gasp.

"Well, can we at least get out of the doorway before I start introductions?" Mary Alice said with a laugh.

"Of course," Ellie said.

"Sorry," Evan mumbled.

They parted like the Red Sea and Mary Alice led Hope between them into the living room. They gathered in front of the fireplace but still, no one took a seat. They formed the same semi-circle of expectant faces with perhaps a few extra feet of breathing space.

Mary Alice sighed. She wished they didn't look like they were about to devour her. "Now, Hope, this is your family." She took a few steps toward Ellie, who seemed to be holding Greg's arm for support. "This is Elinor . . . Ellie, and her husband, Greg."

Ellie stepped forward and offered an awkward hug, eyes brimming with tears. "Hi. Pleasure to meet you."

Greg shook Hope's hand and nodded a silent hello.

"And this is their beautiful daughter, Bethany."

"Auntie Hope!" Bethany threw herself at Hope so hard, she stumbled backward. Bethany pulled back and held her aunt by the shoulders, looking into her amber eyes. "Gram, look. She looks like me. Well, except for this." She pointed to her belly.

That seemed to break the ice. Laughter erupted from all of them. Evan stepped out of the semi-circle and blew an air kiss passed her cheek, barely touching her. "Hi. I'm your brother Evan." He pulled Ricky beside him. "And this is Ricky, my husband."

Mary Alice's heart swelled as she watched the exchange between her children. The tension had left the room. She needn't have worried. No one was going to offend Hope. Everyone began talking at once, asking questions.

"Yes, I'm excited to meet you too," Hope said. "No, I can't

believe this is happening either. Yes, it is a bit overwhelming."
She raised a time-out sign and gulped at the air. "I'll answer all
your questions and more. My goodness, this is a big family."

Was that flush on Hope's cheeks from excitement or fear?
Not that anyone could blame her. They practically attacked her.

Everyone laughed. The only thing better than this would
have been if Char and Charlie were there with them. Mary
Alice clapped her hands. 'Okay, okay. Give Hope a minute to
breathe. Into the dining room. Brunch is ready.'

The gang followed her into the other room. Bethany
plopped down next to Hope before anyone could object.

"Char would never let us start eating without saying
grace first." Greg said. "Who wants to say it?"

"I'll say it," Mary Alice said. She bowed her head, and
everyone followed. "Dear Lord, thank you for bringing Hope
into our lives. For protecting and caring for her all these years
when her father and I could not. Thank you for this loving
family around this table and keep Charlene safe until she can
be home with us. Bless this food and love and protect us all. In
Jesus' name, Amen."

"Amen," everyone said.

Mary Alice bit into the quiche. It was bland. She hoped
no one would bring it up.

"Did you know you were adopted, Auntie Hope?"
Bethany asked.

Greg shot her a warning look.

Hope glanced at Greg, then smiled at Bethany. She set
her fork down and looked around the table. "Let me say how
happy I am to be here. And I want all of you to feel free to
ask me anything. We have so much to learn about each other."
She turned to Bethany. "I've always known I was adopted. My
parents told me from the very beginning, they called me their
chosen one. I was very blessed to be raised by two wonderful
people who loved me very much."

"Weren't you curious about your real family?" Bethany
asked.

"To me, they were my real family. And to tell you the
truth, I never gave it much thought until my parents both got

sick around the same time. When I thought about being all alone in the world, that's when I began to wonder if I had another family somewhere. Well, at least I imagined one."

"Your adoptive parents both got sick at the same time?" Ellie asked. "I can't imagine that happening to my mom and dad."

"Yes, they did. And they died within six months of each other . . . about two years ago now."

"Oh, I'm so sorry," Ellie said.

"Are we at all what you imagined?" Bethany said.

"That, and so much more. Being an only child, I couldn't imagine much more than maybe one sibling. But look at all of you." She beamed. "Look at all of you."

"You have no idea what you're getting into," Greg said, poking Ellie in the ribs. "We can be a loud and crazy bunch."

Hope beamed. "I think I got a little taste of that. Sounds like heaven. I know a little about each of you from your mom." She smiled at Mary Alice. "But it was only the beginning. I want to know everything."

"We'd be glad to answer any questions about us for you." Mary Alice said. She refilled coffee cups and mimosa glasses.

"What about your kidney disease?" Evan asked.

Mary Alice froze. He had promised he wouldn't go there. She gave him her best I'm-your-mother-and-I-told-you-not-to-bring-it-up look. "We don't need to talk about that now."

"I think we do," Evan said.

"It's okay," Hope said. She looked at Evan straight-on. "When I was eight, my parents learned I'd been born with renal dysplasia. My kidneys didn't develop normally."

Mary Alice's heart stilled. Born with it? Was this terrible disease something she gave to her? Charlie? Was it their fault?

Hope looked at Mary Alice. "No, it's not what you think. All kidney disease is not hereditary. Including mine. Some people are born with it."

Mary Alice attempted a smile. "How did you find out?"

"I was tired all the time. My mother took me to see a doctor for a complete check-up. It was in the blood tests. Then, it progressed to chronic kidney disease when I was about fif-

271

teen. For a long time, we were able to control it with medication and diet. But about four years ago, the medication quit working. I had to go on dialysis. I started out on peritoneal dialysis at home several times a day. I thought not having to go to the clinic would be good, but I had less time than I expected. I felt alone all the time."

"Why?" Ricky asked.

"I couldn't do things other people could do. My disease interfered with every aspect of my life. Every spare minute was taken up with my dialysis. I was exhausted all the time. It was hard . . . and lonely. So, I started going to the clinic, because I only have to go three times a week. It felt good to be around others who understood the dialysis, the fatigue, loss of appetite. It is kind of like a second family."

"I get that," Bethany said. "That's how I feel at the FC. That's the Florence Crittenton home. I was really sad and afraid when I found out I was pregnant. Then Gram took me to the FC, and I am finishing high school there and learning how to be a good mom, and I've met a bunch of other really neat girls in the same situation. It's awesome."

Hope wrapped an arm around Bethany's shoulder. "I'm sure you'll be a great mom, Bethany. And you are very lucky to have this big loving family around you."

Bethany nodded. "Ooo. Yes. They're throwing a baby shower for me. Can you come? It's on Saturday, April 14th."

Hope looked around the table. "Well, I don't know."

"Yes, yes. You must come. We are all one family now." Mary Alice said, looking at Hope. "If things had only been like this when I was pregnant with you, you could have been raised by Charlie and me and been a part of the family from the very beginning."

"I bet Char would say that everything happens for a reason." Ellie said.

"I would have to agree," Hope answered. "I believe I was meant to be raised by the mom and dad I knew. They gave me so much, spiritually, emotionally, and physically. And I believe I gave something back to them as well — a child to love and care for. They kept me well fed, in a beautiful, safe home. Always made sure I had my meds. I wanted for nothing - except for a normal life without kidney disease. I believe this too. . ." She waved a hand around the room to encompass them all, "is all happening for a reason as well."

"So you can get a kidney?" Evan asked.

Mary Alice put her own fork down. "Evan."

"It's okay," Hope said. "He has every reason to speculate. Yes, I did originally want to find you to ask for a donor. But things changed after I met your mom. I knew that having all of you, even if it was for a shorter life span, was more important than a longer life without you. I didn't want to chance it, so I never mentioned it."

Mary Alice looked down at the table and fidgeted with her napkin. "Then I cut you off and you thought you lost both — your family and a donor. I'm so sorry, Hope."

"But that's not the end of the story, is it? Now I have all of you, and whether or not we ever do the donor transplant, no one can take you away from me. And that is the most important thing in the world."

Everyone nodded, everyone except Evan. He studied Hope, squinting at her when he thought nobody was looking. But Mary Alice saw him. So unlike him to be so pessimistic. Ellie raised her mimosa. "Here's to a family united."

"Hear, hear," everyone echoed.

Forty-One

2018

March flew by without any trauma. Mary Alice had passed the physical with her family doctor and received good news from the nephrologist. He put her on a regime of vitamins and immune suppressants. He said they would need to double check her immunizations and keep her on a high protein diet. But that was it until the day of all the testing. Thank God. Today was the day. The baby shower. The day Char came home.

As pleased as Mary Alice was that Char was finally out, and in time to attend the shower no less, it had been a long sprint. This would be the first introduction between Char and Hope.

Mary Alice sat up and tried to assume a meditative pose, but old legs don't bend that easily and she settled for sitting at the edge of the bed, her legs dangling over the side. She rested her hands on her lap. Deep breaths in, deep breaths out. Her meditation turned into more of a plea.

"Help me Charlie. This day could make or break relationships forever."

You've got this Mar. Both Charlene and Hope are good people. It will all work out.

She slipped off the bed and headed for the shower. Mary Alice chose a simple cotton shirt dress with spring flowers an hour later. It was going to be a good day. It was going to be the beginning of a wonderful new family dynamic. Maybe if she kept on saying it, she would believe it. The party was scheduled for two, but Gladys and Sophia arrived at noon. They were beside themselves with excitement over the shower.

"Stop." Mary Alice laughed as Gladys hauled in two more armloads of decorations. Little blue plastic baby buggies for party favors, blue and white streamers that read It's a Boy, a huge cardboard stork with a baby wrapped in a blue blanket that stood five feet tall. "Where am I going to put everything?"

Mary Alice's house seemed to be slowly filling up with every imaginable baby blue decoration her friends could find.

"Don't you worry about it," Sophia said, following Gladys through the door with a bag full of blue paper plates, napkins, and cups. "We'll do all the decorating. Your job was the three dozen sandwiches and cupcakes." She pulled a sleeve of little blue teddy bears from her bag. "Look at these cute toppers for the cupcakes."

"The presents are in my trunk," Gladys said and headed back out the door. Three trips later she had everything in. "I still need to wrap a few of them, so where can I put them for now?"

Mary Alice pointed up the stairs to her bedroom. "Up there. Seriously, Gladys, didn't you go a bit overboard?" She picked up the huge box with a picture of a highchair. "He won't be needing this for at least a year. And I think Ellie was planning on getting a highchair."

"Well, then she can have one to keep here," she said as she headed up the stairs.

Sophia came from the guest bedroom. "Is that why there happens to be a crib in your spare bedroom, Mary Alice?"

"Well, he'll need a place to sleep when Bethy comes over," Mary Alice said.

Gladys smiled at her friend. "And I suspect you're hoping that is quite often."

"Of course. My first great-grandchild. You bet I want her and the baby here a lot. It's been a long time since we've had the pitter patter of little feet around here." She carried the rest of the packages into the bedroom. "Now, take a break. I'll put the kettle on."

275

Sophia plopped into a chair at the kitchen table. "Whew. Good idea. All that shopping wore me out."

Mary Alice filled the electric teapot and set three mugs on the table, along with a tin of freshly baked snickerdoodles. Gladys came down and joined them. "What's happening with Charlene?"

"She's home. Said she needed some alone time. But she'll be here for the shower."

"Does she know that Hope is coming?"

Mary Alice nodded. "I told her over the phone. It will be the first time they meet."

Sophia grimaced. "Oh, boy. How do you think that will go?"

Mary Alice poured the hot water into the mugs and handed them each a tea bag. Earl Grey for Sophia and Raspberry Herbal for Gladys. A plain Lipton bag went into her cup. "I'm hoping for the best. It seems like she's accepting things ever since the talk with the counselor. At least she didn't say she wouldn't come if Hope was there. I told them both to come an hour before everyone else. I think the three of us will need a little time alone before we're thrust into the crowd of Bethany's FC friends and the rest of the family."

"Agreed." Sophia nodded at Gladys. "We're here to herd any early arrivals into the family room. You should use the den since it has a door to close for privacy."

"Thanks," Mary Alice said. "What would I ever do without you two? You're the best."

"FC girls forever," Gladys said, crossing her fingers with the secret V symbol.

Mary Alice stirred her tea without taking a sip, twirling gray curls at the nape of her neck with her left hand.

"Maybe you need a double shot of whiskey in that," Sophia said.

"Oh yeah, that will help," Mary Alice scoffed. "Alcohol and sleep deprivation. That should make a good combination for a feather-weight like me."

"You've done all you can," Gladys said. "The groundwork has been laid. All you need to do is let it play out. Give them a little space, and a little credit. They're both smart girls."

"That's what Charlie said."

Mary Alice kissed her friend on the cheek. "If we're not out of the den by two o'clock, or you hear things being hurled across the room, come and save me."

"Deal," Sophia said. "Right now, you should be out there to greet them at the door. Then I'll usher them into the den."

"This all feels so sinister," Mary Alice said.

Gladys motioned toward the door. "Not sinister, delicate. And you've got this."

Mary Alice watched as Charlene pulled into the drive at 12:20 p.m. She opened the trunk and lifted out a blue-and-white wrapped box. She closed the trunk but didn't move. Was she having the same trepidations as Mary Alice? Meeting a sister you never knew you had for the first time had to be weird, if not a bit scary.

Charlene gathered her arms tighter around the package and repositioned the strap to her purse on her shoulder as a tan Nissan Rogue pulled in beside Charlene's Lexus.

Oh, no. Hope. Should she rush out? Introduce them? Mary Alice's feet wouldn't move. No sound came from her moving lips as she tried to call out to Sophia and Gladys.

Hope exited her car. Charlene didn't move from her spot between the two cars. The two sisters looked at each other. With Char's face turned away from Mary Alice's view, and the darn weather-efficient windows closed, she couldn't tell if Charlene was talking. She watched Hope's face for some kind of reaction.

Hope smiled, but seconds later the smile faded.

Oh, no. What was Char saying to her?

Hope appeared to be talking calmly. She took a step forward and raised her arms like she was going to hug Charlene. But Char stepped back. She shook her head and her blond hair swished across her shoulders. Mary Alice's heart sank. Still, Char didn't walk away and the conversation did not seem over.

Char shifted the package in her arms and extended a handshake. Hope accepted it. At least that was a start. Nobody was swinging punches. Mary Alice would take that as progress.

Gladys walked into the room and looked out the window. "Oh my God. They are out there together?"

Mary Alice could only nod.

"How long have they been out there?"

"I don't know, a couple of minutes I guess," Mary Alice mumbled. "I wanted to run out there, but I couldn't move."

Sophia walked into the room. "What's going on?"

"Hope and Charlene are out there getting acquainted," Gladys said.

"What?" Sophia rushed over to the window. "Holy shit." She slapped her hand over her mouth. "Sorry. Can you tell if it's going well?"

Mary Alice shook her head "They're still talking. Should I go out there?"

"No," Sophia said. "I think this is for the best. Let them work it out. They'll come in when other cars start pulling up."

"Boy, I'd love to be a little bird out there right now," Gladys said.

Mary Alice nodded.

Outside, the conversation seemed to be winding down. Hope went back to the open door and lifted out the plastic-wrapped package with a huge blue bow at the neck. Char waited for her and together, they made their way up the walk.

Mary Alice jumped when the doorbell rang. Her feet moved that time. She darted toward the foyer, Sophia and Gladys at her heels. Before Mary Alice could grab the door handle, Sophia lurched forward and pulled it open. "Sorry about the doorbell, my hands were full," Char said. Gladys reached out and grabbed the package. "No problem. Welcome home." Sophia planted a kiss on Charlene's cheek. "You look great."

"I do?"

"Fantastic, darling," Mary Alice said.

Char turned to Hope. "I met someone in the driveway."

Mary Alice moved forward. She gave Charlene a quick hug. "So I see. Not exactly the way I had it all planned out."

Hope's eyes were misty. Not crying, but almost. Were those happy tears or distraught tears from something Char had said?

"Hope, these are my best friends, Sophia and Gladys."

Hope offered a nervous smile. "Nice to meet you. This is kind of heavy," Hope shifted the unusual package on her hip. "Where can I set this for Bethany?"

"Oh, I'm so sorry." Mary Alice reached out. "Let me take that for you."

"I've got it." Hope said. "Point me in the direction it goes."

Everyone headed into the family room. Sophia set Charlene's gift on the card table and Hope placed hers on the floor in front of it. Hope pointed to the black plastic bag. "I tried wrapping paper, but it tore. So, I had to settle for this."

"No problem. All the more mysterious," Mary Alice said. She looked at her watch. "How about the three of us have a little talk in the den before the other guests arrive?"

Charlene shook her head. "No, I don't think so. We're good." She nodded to Hope. "Right, Hope?"

Hope didn't meet Charlene's eyes, but responded with a forced smile. "Of course. We have plenty of time for serious conversations. It's time for a celebration."

What did that mean? If only Mary Alice could have been privy to their conversation. Did that mean they were going to be civil to each other or actually begin a relationship? Perhaps now wasn't the time to get into it. She should be glad they were friendly and leave it at that. "Okay, then," Mary Alice said. "How about the two of you help us set out some more folding chairs? I'm not sure how many of Bethy's friends from the Home are coming."

The doorbell rang moments later. Sophia waved them off. "Gladys and I have the chairs, you guys man the door."

"It's okay." Hope said, already walking toward the kitchen, "I can help."

The sound of the front door banging open could only mean that it was one of Mary Alice's kids, thankfully. Sure enough, Ellie appeared minutes later, her arms loaded down and her daughter waddling behind her. "Gram, everything looks wonderful," Bethany clapped her hands as her head swiveled around the room. "Ahh, look at those little baby buggy party favors. Sooo cute."

"Yes, and they still need to be filled with mints. Can you handle that?" Mary Alice asked.

"Got it," Bethany said. She made her way into the kitchen.

Gladys pointed up the stairs. "I've still got some wrapping to do. Ellie, can you mix the punch?" She nodded toward the large crystal punch bowl on the card table. It was sandwiched between ginger ale and blue Gatorade. "Of course," Ellie said.

With all of the extra hands, it took no time at all to set up. They were done by the time Hope set the last chair. She pushed it toward the wall and looked up at Mary Alice. "Anything else I can do?"

"I think we're all set." She glanced at Char and Ellie, then back at Hope. She smiled. All of her daughters were in one room. "Shall we sit?"

Charlene chose a wing-back chair. Mary Alice and Hope sat at either end of the sofa. An awkward silence filled the room.

"The place looks great, Mom," Ellie said, pouring ginger ale into the bowl.

"Sophia and Gladys did most of it."

"How nice to have such great friends," Hope said.

"They've been friends since high school," Charlene said. "They've been more like family to us."

"Are you girls talking about us?" Gladys breezed into the room, her arms stuffed with newly-wrapped packages.

"I was telling Hope how you've been friends with Mom since high school," Charlene said.

"Over fifty years," Gladys said as she came down the stairs.

The doorbell rang. Bethany hurried from the kitchen, yelling "I'll get it!" The sound of excited squeals soon filled the house. Mary Alice didn't realize how much she missed having a gaggle of teenaged girls around until they were crowding her living room and cooing at all of the decorations.

And the girls kept coming. It seemed that the doorbell

rang every five minutes, and slowly, the guests filled up the house. Mary Alice stayed on the sofa and kept an eye on Hope and Charlene, trying to determine exactly what was going on between them. Hope appeared at ease, smiling at all of the new guests individually, drawing out the shy FC girl who huddled in the corner with questions about the Home, and complimenting Mary Alice on the decorations. Charlene was reserved, which was totally out of character for her. At some point, she moved from the wing-backed chair to a spot near the punch bowl. She stood alone, not saying a word, though she nodded and smiled along with everyone as the presents were opened and the silly games were played. It was obvious that she had other things on her mind. Mary Alice had to get her alone, if only for a minute.

The snack table was dwindling. Perfect. "Char, can you help me with more sandwiches in the kitchen?"

"I can do it," Ellie offered.

Mary Alice gave her a pointed look and a quick head shake.

""Sure," Charlene said, drifting to the kitchen as Mary Alice pulled herself off the couch. She walked to the kitchen and stopped shy of the threshold, watching the back of Char's head. She stood perfectly still and faced the sink.

Mary Alice hesitated, only for a second, before she walked to Charlene. She placed a gentle hand on her daughter's arm. "Honey, are you okay?"

"Sure," Charlene said. She didn't look away from the sink. "It's weird. Being back home. Everyone knowing where I've been. Her here."

"Did the two of you have words out there in the driveway?"

"She thinks she can walk into our lives and we'll welcome her with open arms. I'm not buying it. She's using you, Mom, to get your kidney. How can you not see that?"

"You're wrong. She wasn't even going to ask. I found her at the dialysis center. She wasn't going to tell me."

"You're naïve, Mom. You always think everyone is honest and innocent. Papa liked taking care of you because of that. But he's not here anymore. We—me, Ellie, and Evan have to do that now. And I don't trust her."

"Give me a little credit, Char. I know what's happening here. I'm getting my daughter back, and I'm going to save her life. This isn't up for debate. We've already been through this."

Mary Alice pulled more sandwiches from the fridge, arranged them on a plate, and handed them to Charlene. "Give her a chance, Honey. Keep an open mind. That's all I ask."

Charlene mumbled something incoherent and left the room with the plate.

I guess she's not as adjusted to this as I thought. I'll have to take more time with her, make her understand this reunion is good for everybody, even Charlene.

Mary Alice took a few deep breaths, plastered on a smile, and headed back to the party.

Back in the family room, FC girls in various stages of pregnancy oohed and aahed at the tiny sleepers, onesies, and bibs.

"I love these tiny zebra jammies," one said.

"What about these tiny tennis shoes? I couldn't resist when I found them," another said.

Bethany looked up. "Gram. You're back. Now I can open YOUR present."

Mary Alice had thought long and hard about what she wanted to get her granddaughter. She could have gotten her anything and Bethany would have loved it, that's how she was. But Mary Alice didn't want to give her just anything. It had to be more. Something that Charlie would have given her as well.

Mary Alice opened the den door and reached inside, grabbing the worn wood and dragging it out on the carpet. The big blue ribbon bobbed with each movement.

Bethany's eyes grew big and she pressed her hands to her lips. "Gram." She stood up and waddled to Mary Alice, her hand reaching out reverently to touch the wooden armrest.

She ran her fingers down the smooth wood and sank into the seat. "You're really giving me Papa's rocker?" Her voice warbled.

"Papa would want you to have it."

"Ah, Gram."

"One more gift," said Hope.

All eyes turned to her. She set her punch down and lifted the large plastic-wrapped package, bringing it across the room. She set it on Bethany's lap. "Sorry about the wrapping."

Bethany untied the blue bow around the top and gasped when she pulled the plastic down. It was a wooden sculpture of a young woman cradling a baby in her arms.

Mary Alice inhaled. *Pine.* It was exquisite, each detail perfect, the tiny fingers and toes of the baby, the endearing eyes of the mother clearly showing the love for the child.

"Oh my gosh. Charlie. Look at that. It's beautiful."

"I . . . I don't know what to say," Bethany said. "This is the most beautiful thing I've ever seen."

Everyone moved closer to look at the sculpture. Everyone except Charlene, who sat cross-armed in a folding chair in the corner.

If Mary Alice could send telepathic messages, she would have told Char: Can't you see she's a good person? She only wants to be part of our family.

Charlene didn't meet her eyes. Instead, she shot to her feet and busied herself with cleaning up dishes and running them into the kitchen.

Mary Alice planted a kiss atop Bethany's head and left the group to follow Charlene, who was bustling along with an arm load of dessert plates. "Honey, you look upset."

"I'm fine." Charlene said, dropping the dishes in the sink. "Why wouldn't I be? You have your perfect little family now, don't you?" She headed back into the family room before Mary Alice could answer. Mary Alice followed her back to the guests.

The party was winding down now, and one by one, the FC girls were leaving.

"I'd say that was a big success," Sophia said. Char took a spot behind the rocking chair and peered over Bethany's shoulder. Probably so Mary Alice couldn't corner her to continue the conversation.

"Oh my gosh, yes. Look at all this stuff," Bethany

exclaimed, fondling a soft blue baby blanket.

"Bethany, your friends are so nice," Hope said. "They're all from the Florence Crittenton Home?"

Bethany nodded. "Yea, they're the best. It's so much easier knowing other girls are going through the same thing as me."

Sophia agreed. "For sure. I don't know how I ever would have made it without Gladys and your grandmother."

"Wait. What?" Ellie pinned her eyes on Mary Alice before looking between the two of them. "You were pregnant too? When Mom was in high school?"

Mary Alice sank onto the sofa next to Sophia and gave Ellie a guilty smile. It hadn't been her place to say anything about Gladys and Sophia. She glanced at Gladys and raised her eyebrows. Gladys nodded.

"Sophia and Gladys were my roommates at the Home. That's where we met." Mary Alice folded her hands on her lap and saw Charlene stop dead in the doorway, arms full of dishes. A saucer slipped from her hand and dropped onto the carpet. She swiveled on her heel. "What? All three of you were unwed mothers? I thought you were high school friends."

"I said we've been friends since high school," Mary Alice said. "I never said we went to the same school."

"Semantics," Char said.

"Wow," Bethany said.

Char carefully placed the dishes back on the table and walked toward the nearest chair before sinking into it. She looked a little dazed. "Why didn't you ever tell us?"

"Yes, I don't understand why we're hearing about this now," Ellie said.

"There was no reason for you to know," Mary Alice said. "It was their business, not yours."

"No, it's fine," Sophia said. "We've had each other's backs ever since and wouldn't want it any other way."

Ellie smiled. "Thank you for that. We're glad to have you in our lives too."

Bethany looked at Sophia, then to Gladys. "What happened to your babies?"

"Same as with all the babies at the Home back then," Sophia said. "They were put up for adoption. I found my child, a girl, about twenty years ago. But she didn't want a relationship with me, so I respected that."

"I had a boy, but I never saw him, not even the day he was born. It was best that way," Gladys said.

"I'm sorry," Hope said, staring down at her hands.

Gladys shrugged, collapsing next to Mary Alice on the couch. "Nothing to be sorry for. It was a long time ago."

Mary Alice reached over and squeezed Gladys' hand. "The important thing is we had each other, and it saved us. Together, we learned to handle everything."

With her free hand, Mary Alice flashed the V sign.

Forty-Two

2018

The following Wednesday, when Mary Alice arrived at the Fresnius Medical Center, Amanda, the nurse who had been so kind to her when she'd gone to visit Hope, greeted her at the front desk.

"G'morn'in," Amanda said with a toothy smile. "The nephrologist will be here jes' a minute. We'll get you started with some blood work, okay?"

Mary Alice nodded and followed Amanda through the double doors. They passed the room where she'd seen Hope getting her treatment. The room they entered was smaller with inexpensive still-life prints hanging on the soothing light green walls. "Did you bring the paperwork that we mailed to you?" Amanda asked.

Mary Alice opened her purse and grabbed the packet, handing it off to Amanda. Her fingers quivered when she let go. "Yes, all done."

Amanda scanned through the papers. Mary Alice had a doozy of a time filling out the in-depth questionnaire.

Amanda nodded to herself and flipped through the papers until she found the letter from the family physician. She scanned it, nodded again, and then looked up at Mary Alice with a bright smile.

"Okay. Let's get started. Have a seat there, please."

Mary Alice clutched her purse and sat in the leather

chair the nurse was pointing at. Amanda pulled out a leather band and got to work.

The rubber hose was tightened around Mary Alice's upper arm. She didn't like needles, but the draws were fairly painless, and they were over before she knew it.

Mary Alice turned her face away as electrodes were affixed to her body and an IV inserted in her other arm. She had been happy with "passing" the interview with the nephrologist, but this step made her queasy.

"We're going to do a Dobutamine Stress Test," Amanda said. "It will make your heart respond as if you were exercising very hard. You will feel out of breath. That's all normal. Then we'll have an echocardiogram to see how your heart and blood flows"

When that was done, Amanda moved her to another room. "Next is a pyelography test. We can use the same IV, so no new needles. We're shooting a dye that reaches the kidney through the bloodstream. The X-ray will show the structure of your kidney, ureter and bladder."

A CT scan and X-rays came next, and before she knew it, half the morning was gone. Her stomach growled in protest. Thank God, Amanda appeared with a cup of orange juice and some biscuits. Bless her. Mary Alice scarfed down the refreshments, instantly feeling the strength return to her body.

"The cardiologist, Dr. Erwin, will see you next and go over the results of this morning's tests. Then we have you scheduled with the psychologist at 1, the social worker at 2, and finally the surgeon at 3. Ah you up for all dat?" Amanda's eyes sparkled like the tiny diamond stud on the side of her nose.

Mary Alice raised her cup of orange juice. "As long as you keep these coming."

After seeing the cardiologist who gave her the all-clear, she was taken to Dr. Preston, the team psychologist. He was a stout man with wide glasses and a neat grey beard. Everybody she'd seen thus far had been incredibly kind and warm. Upon first glance, the psychologist seemed anything but. However, when he looked up from his folder, his little smile lit up the entirety of his stoic face and Mary Alice felt herself smiling back.

"Please, have a seat Mrs. Goodson."

"Call me Mary Alice."

"Okay, Mary Alice." He folded his arms on the desk and leaned forward. "This is a very admirable thing you are doing here; can we talk a little bit about that?"

Why else was she here? "Of course."

Dr. Preston pressed his fingers together into a tent. Mary Alice half expected him to wiggle his fingers and "show all the people."

"I understand that this is a newly found reunion between you and Hope. Tell me a little about that."

Mary Alice started at the beginning, telling him about how she was forced to give Hope away, all the way through to finding her half a century later. He didn't say anything, he simply watched her as she talked. Sometimes he smiled, sometimes he nodded very seriously, but he never interrupted. When she was done, Mary Alice glanced at her watch. That took her all of twenty minutes. Imagine that — her entire life whittled down to less than half an hour.

"How does the rest of your family feel?"

Mary Alice was tempted to lie, but his eyes were too focused. He'd been watching her the whole time, probably reading her body language or something. He would probably know it if she lied. "Well, almost everyone is thrilled."

"Almost?"

"My oldest, well, our first born after we married, Charlene, did not take the news very well. Charlene has her own personal problems and I think she feels threatened by Hope."

"Hmm. Why do you think that?"

"Well," Where to start? "Char doesn't have children of her own. Or she would understand. Mothers have an infinite amount of love in their heart for their children. By finding Hope, she thinks it's taking my love away from her. She's a grown woman, a philosophy professor, you'd think she would get that. But I don't think she does." A lump formed in the back of her throat. She gulped it down.

Dr. Preston reached under his desk and produced a bottle. "Water?"

"Yes, please." She chugged half the bottle before coming up for air.

He nodded and tapped his fingers together again. "And how are you handling that?"

"Oh, I'm fine," she said, probably too quickly. I told her that this was something I am doing with or without her consent. Of course, I'd love her blessing, but she is not going to change my mind. All my life I've let people make decisions for me. I had a wonderful husband and he kept life very simple for me. But Hope needs this kidney. What kind of mother would I be if I didn't help her? It would be like deserting her all over again."

"Interesting. Is that the way you feel—that you deserted her when she was put up for adoption?"

How did she get backed into this corner? Yes, she did feel that way, but was that the answer he was looking for? Would he think she felt obligated or forced to do this?

"Umm, yes. . . I mean no. I know I had no choice in the matter. But I think every biological mother would feel that way. I know I don't have to do this. This is something I want to do."

He stared at her for a moment, his eyes darting all over her face. Mary Alice held her breath. Finally, he nodded.

"Very well, Mary Alice. I believe you. I think we are done here. I'm going to send you over to our financial team now, okay?"

That was it? Did that mean she'd passed the test? Mary Alice exhaled, "Yes, yes, of course."

She was whisked away, through winding corridors and down two different elevators. When her escort dropped her off on the administration side of the building, it felt like success.

A young man greeted Mary Alice and welcomed her into his little cubby, tucked behind a row of filing cabinets.

"Mrs. Goodson, I'm Craig Simon. This will only take a few minutes."

"Thank you." She didn't offer her first name. He looked too young. This man was going to discuss finances with her?

289

"Ms. Pendleton's insurance will pick up the majority of the cost for the surgery and hospital stay. It will also cover all costs here for testing. If you are accepted as a donor, your only financial obligations will be your routine appointments with your GP and any medications over and above what you are taking now."

"I see. I have good insurance with a reputable company. And I'm also on Medicare."

"Yes, I see that. I am here to answer any other financial questions you may have. Are you still working? According to Dr. Newman, you will most likely be in the hospital for anywhere from two to seven days, assuming there are no complications. I'd count on closer to seven, given your age."

There it was again. Her age. It was beginning to rankle her. Yes, she was old for a donor. But she wasn't dead. And if she was, she'd still want to give Hope her kidney. Still, she smiled and answered all of the young man's questions before shaking his hand and heading for the exit. She couldn't wait to get to the nearest fast-food establishment for a big, juicy cheeseburger.

The following Monday, Dr. Newman, the surgeon and head of the nephrology team assigned to Hope, called.

"Good morning, Mary Alice. All of your tests are in," he said. "Our team met this morning, and I am recommending we go ahead with the kidney transplant for Hope."

Mary Alice whooped loudly into the phone. "Doctor, that's wonderful. When can we get this done?"

Dr. Newman laughed. "That's the best response I've heard in a long time. Your surgery will be laparoscopic and will only take about an hour. You should be back to your old self within a week or two. Hope's procedure will take considerably longer, as will her recovery period. Our scheduling department will be giving you a call to put it on the books. We're looking at some time in the next thirty days. Thank you, you are doing a wonderful thing for your daughter."

Mary Alice hung up and danced around the room. It was going to happen. Should she call Hope first, or wait to hear from her? Surely, Dr. Newman was calling her with the good news right this very minute. The kids. She should call Ellie and Evan, and of course, Charlene. No, Bethany should be first. She was the one that had made this all possible. If anyone was saving Hope's life, it was Bethany.

Bethany picked up on the first ring. "What's wrong, Gram? You never call me unless I'm in trouble."

"Not this time, sweetie. In fact, something is very, very right."

Forty-Three

2018

"It's happening." Ellie said into the phone. "We're at the hospital with Bethy."

"The baby? Oh my." Mary Alice glanced at the clock. Thank goodness it wasn't at some insanely late hour. "Do you want me to come?"

"No, I wanted you to know. You know how these things go, Mom, and I wouldn't want you to be here for hours on end. She's a little scared, but she's being a real trooper."

It brought back memories. Not with Mary Alice's own deliveries, but when Ellie went into labor with Bethany. The twelve-hour stay in the waiting room had been worth it to get a few minutes with her newborn granddaughter.

Ellie practically squealed. "Just think, I'm going to be a grandmother real soon. Didn't seem real until right now."

"Becoming a grandma is special. And you will make an awesome one. I'm so proud of how you've handled this whole thing. Bethany is very lucky to have you and Greg by her side."

"Thanks Mom. We'll call you as soon as there is more news."

"Okay. Give Bethy a big hug and kiss for me. I'm sure it will all go well." Mary Alice tapped the phone off. *You got this, Bethany*. She looked up at the ceiling. Lord, please watch over our girl.

The phone rang minutes later. That was fast. Mary Alice

reached for it and dropped it on the floor.

"Ellie?" she said when she retrieved it from the carpet.

"No, Evan. Where is she? I tried calling the house. Nobody's answering. And she's not picking up her cell either."

"They're at the hospital."

"With Bethany?" Evan laughed, "Wow. I'm going to be an uncle. I can't believe that. Shouldn't we be up there?"

"Ellie said no. I think they want to keep this an intimate family moment."

"What are we, chopped liver?" Evan said.

"It's kind of a mother-daughter thing. Greg's probably pacing the halls. Ellie's the birth coach, so she's in for the long run."

"Want some company?" Evan said. "Ricky's out of town."

Mary Alice smiled into the phone. "Is my boy feeling lonely? Come on over. We can wait for the news together. How about a game of Scrabble?"

"You're on."

Evan's car rolled in at the same time she set a fresh sheet of chocolate chip cookies on the cutting board to cool. He pecked her on the cheek and grabbed a mug from the rack.

"Hmm, you smell good," she said. One thing she could count on with Evan was that he was always well dressed, perfectly groomed, and smelled good enough to eat.

"Any word?" Evan poured himself a cup of coffee.

"Not yet. I think I'll send Greg a text."

"I'll do it," Evan said. He pulled his phone from his back pocket and Mary Alice watched his thumbs fly across the screen.

His phone beeped almost immediately, and Mary Alice peeked at the phone.

It's close, Greg messaged. I'm going nuts here.

Mary Alice put on a new pot of tea for herself and coffee for Evan.

"Does this bring back memories of when we were born?" Evan slurped at the coffee. "I bet this one makes you think about

Hope's birth."

Mary Alice twirled the liquid with her spoon. "It couldn't be more different. I'm so glad things are better with Bethany. She is a lucky girl to have the support of her whole family like this."

"We wouldn't have it any other way. I can't wait to get my hands on that little guy."

"Me too."

They passed the time in each other's quiet company, mindlessly shuffling Scrabble tiles across the board. Hours ticked by, but Mary Alice didn't notice. Evan fell asleep on the couch at some point and Mary Alice watched him as he dreamed. Although he was grown, she could see the round-faced little boy he used to be when he slept.

They both jumped when Evan's phone rang. Evan rubbed his eyes and looked at the phone. He sat up straight, his eyes suddenly bright and alert. "It's Bethany. She's on FaceTime."

"On what?"

Evan pressed a button then turned the phone toward her.

"Hey Gram," Bethany said. "Want to meet your great-grandson?" She turned a little blue bundle around. The baby's eyes were wide open. Phooey on the notion that babies can't see at birth. He was looking right into the phone.

"Hi, little guy," Mary Alice got so close to the phone that it almost touched her nose. The baby blinked back at her and Mary Alice smiled. "We've been waiting a long time for you. I can't wait to hold you. Oh Bethy, he's beautiful. Does he have a name yet?"

Bethany turned the phone back to her face. Her hair was limp and her skin glistened with old sweat, but her smile was radiant. "Yes, I named him Charles Gregory, after Papa and Dad."

Tears swam in Mary Alice's eyes and she could barely hold them back. She raised her hand to the phone, like she could reach through and run her fingers through the baby's soft hair. "Charlie, my dear sweet Charlie."

Forty-Four

2018

Bethany and little Charlie were home and doing great. She was getting the hang of being a mother a lot quicker than Mary Alice had. Then again, Charlie was a much easier baby than Char had been. He even slept through the night sometimes.

It was a reminder that life came as easily as it went. And more and more, Mary Alice found herself wondering if her surgery would go wrong. She was more at peace with the possibility than she thought, but not so at peace that it didn't worry her. She had little Charlie to help look after now, she had Hope to make up for a lifetime of not being there, she had Char that still needed to heal. Her plans didn't matter, she knew that. Only God's.

Since Charlene was still in town, the timing was perfect.

I need to call a family meeting. She typed her group message and hit send. She was getting pretty good at this texting stuff.

Sure, when? Evan texted back.
Something wrong, Mom? Charlene texted.
Bethany is feeding the baby. Can you wait until she is done?
Why not give her some time alone with her son.
Just your generation this time.

"Well, look at you, getting here early." Mary Alice planted a kiss on Char's cheek. "I think this is a first."

"I was already in town at an AA meeting."

Good for her. "You're looking well, Char. I'm proud of the progress you've made. And I'm glad you're here first. I wanted to talk to you alone about something."

Char pursed her lips and drew away a little. "What's this all about Mom? You know I hate it when you say that. "Talk to you alone sounds so . . . well, bad."

She strode to the kitchen like she was running away. All these years and she still walked off like she was in trouble. By the time Mary Alice reached her, she was pouring herself a cup of coffee.

Char sat down at the table. Mary Alice sat beside her.

She reached across the table and took Charlene's hand. "I'm sorry. I didn't mean to scare you. But in case things don't go well with the transplant —"

"Stop." Char held up her other hand. "Don't even say it. Nothing is going to go wrong."

"I know, but . . . I need to say this. Okay?"

Char rubbed the top of Mary Alice's hand. Mary Alice noticed how papery thin her skin looked. *I guess I am old.*

"In case," Mary Alice began again, "things go wrong. I owe you a huge apology. I'm sorry that I haven't told you enough that I loved you. You need to believe me. You were never a replacement for Hope. It was never about not loving you. You were such an autonomous little thing—like you didn't need anyone or anything. You were the strong independent one, so different from Ellie and Evan, who demanded my attention 24/7."

"I wasn't strong at all. It was all an act." Charlene pulled the band from her ponytail and twirled blond strands of hair through her fingers "Mom, I get it. You don't have to do this."

"I do. And I'm not making excuses. You were a child. I was the adult. I should have seen what I was doing—comparing you to a little girl I could only imagine, a little girl you never knew existed. I was selfish, caught up in my own sorrow and guilt."

"Mom, stop."

"Please, Char. Let me get this out. If I could live my life

over, I'd do it so differently. I'd be honest, I'd be brave, I'd be a better mother." The words stuck in her throat like peanut butter. She took a sip of tea to wash it down. "But you don't get do overs in life, not usually, but this is Hope's second chance, and mine, to do better."

Tears brimmed in Charlene's eyes and she nodded. "I know, and I love you for it."

"I was a coward, Char. I didn't stand up to my parents to keep Hope."

"Don't be so hard on yourself. You were only sixteen. You weren't given a choice. No one could have done any different."

Mary Alice shook her head. "I didn't try hard enough. This is my one chance to make it up to her, to show her that I'll fight for her life this time. That I'd give up my life for her. Do you understand? It's time I make a stand for Hope and for myself. And for you."

Char put her mug down and looked ahead, focusing on something far away as she blinked her tears back. She took a deep breath before she turned her head to look at Mary Alice. "I understand, Mom. It's taken me a long time to see it, but I do now. I was too judgmental. It was easier to fling accusations at you than to face my own problems. If anyone owes someone an apology, I owe you one. I'm sorry I said those awful things about you and Hope."

Mary Alice tried to smile. "I knew you didn't mean them." She swirled the spoon in her mug. "Can I be honest? The reason I'm saying all this is I'm a little afraid. What if your brother is right? What if I am too old? Something could go wrong in there. And what if you are right, that Hope is only using me?"

"I don't believe that anymore. And neither do you. The doctors never would have cleared you for this if there was any real danger." She took both of Mary Alice's hands in hers. "But I'm the same blood type as you. I will take your place if you want. We can stop this right now and I'll go through all the testing. Hope can wait a few more weeks."

Mary Alice looked into Charlene's eyes. The same as

Charlie's and Hope's. Did she mean that? Was this the same girl that called Hope a bastard and made ultimatums? What was happening here? Had the mountain that kept them at arm's length for Char's whole life suddenly crumbled? Were the walls finally down?

Mary Alice allowed the wall to dissolve in her tears. It felt like the end of a lifetime of regret, replaced by a connection to her daughter that seemed so fresh and new. She didn't try to wipe them away. "Ah, honey. That is so kind . . . and very brave of you. But you'd never be approved. You know, with your dependency issues. But I am very proud of you that you would even offer."

"Oh," Char looked down. "Right. Well, I would if I could. And not just for you. I'd do it for Hope too."

"Thank you for saying that. It means so much to me." More than she could possibly understand.

Char turned fully in her seat, her knees brushing against Mary Alice's chair. She wrapped her arms around Mary Alice and held her tight. Mary Alice turned in her chair, too. She tried to freeze the moment in her head so that she could remember it always. The warmth of her daughter's arms, the smell of her blonde hair, the way Char's heartbeat against her chest. Mary Alice pulled her a little tighter, cheek-to-cheek. Their heart beats fell in sync. Their tears blended together. No matter what happened from here on, she had all her daughters. She could face anything now.

The sound of a car pulling up broke the spell. Char pulled away and Mary Alice dried her eyes. Char slipped away without a word, swiping furiously at her face as she made a beeline toward the bathroom in the hall. The front door creaked open, and Evan's voice rolled down the hall. Ellie was right on his tail.

"Mom?" he called. "Char?"

"Don't yell, oh-smart-one, they're probably in the —" Ellie breezed past the kitchen and pulled up short when she caught sight of her mother. Evan skidded to a hard stop behind her.

"I saw Char's car is here already." Evan stepped into the

kitchen and planted a kiss on his mother's cheek.

Charlene came out of the bathroom seconds later and rejoined Mary Alice at the table. Evan punched her in the arm affectionately. "You, early? What have you done with my sister?"

"Ha, ha," Char replied. "Yay, so I was early. It's a first. Where's my prize?"

"In the oven," Mary Alice said. "Everyone, sit. Everything's ready. Go sit in the dining room."

At the mention of food, all three of them bolted out of the room. Mary Alice could see them from the kitchen claim the same seats they'd sat at since they were children. And still, there was the vacant chair that belonged to Charlie.

Mary Alice shook her head and grabbed the apple pie from the oven before making her way into the dining room. She set the dish down and six hands vied for the first slice. Mary Alice sank into her chair and waited until they began eating so they wouldn't have the chance to talk over her.

Mary Alice doled out equal slices to each person. "I called you all because I have an idea I want to run by you."

"Are you changing your mind about the transplant?" Evan's fork hovered in front of his mouth, his expression a little too hopeful for Mary Alice's liking.

Mary Alice looked at Charlene, then back to Evan. "No, the transplant is still on. But this is about Hope."

"Go on," Ellie said.

"You know I have been trying to figure out what to do with Papa's shop. The accountant suggested that I sell it. But I was thinking maybe it would be a good location for an art gallery."

Evan's eyes lit up. "For Hope? That's a great idea!"

"Yes, she can put her gallery in the front and work in the shop like Papa did. I can see it already." Ellie said.

"I hoped you'd be on board. I couldn't see any other good use for it. I know I'm being sentimental, but I hated the idea of selling it. Of course, if I deed it over to her, she'd be responsible for the taxes and utilities. But then, it wouldn't be mine to deed to you when I am gone."

"We don't care about that and Papa would love the idea." Ellie said. "Imagine having all those wood scents back in the shop. It'll be almost like having Papa back there."

"Well, almost." Mary Alice said. A pang of longing crept toward her heart.

"Then it's settled," Ellie said. "When are you going to tell Hope?"

"I think after the transplant. Let's get through one big event at a time. I got a call from the scheduler. We are set for Tuesday, the 22nd, but I need to be there on Monday."

"So soon? Okay then. I'll pick you up next Monday for the trip to Columbus," Evan said. "We'll all be there for you."

Evan drove with Ricky by his side, Ellie and Mary Alice in the back seat. It was a little less than a three-hour ride from Struthers to the Ohio State University Transplant Center on the OSU campus. The closer they got, the more Mary Alice began to doubt her decision. What if Evan was right—what if she was too old? She hated hospitals and the very idea of anyone cutting into her, let alone removing part of her body. Was it too late to back out? She ran a hand through her hair.

"Mom?" Ellie asked. "You okay?"

Mary Alice tried to force a smile, "Oh, sure," she lied. "Just thinking about Hope and hoping this goes well for her. Sometimes bodies reject the transplant, you know."

Good job Mar, diverting the focus away from you.

"I hope, Charlie. I don't want them to know I'm scared."

Ellie patted her hand. "Hope's going to be fine. The OSU transplant facility is one of the best in the whole nation. I read that they do over 400 transplants a year. It should be a piece of cake for them by now."

"Yes, that's nice." Mary Alice really wasn't listening. They exited I-71 and turned onto 315 South.

"Looks like spring is rapidly turning into summer." Ricky said. "The crocuses and daffodils have already been replaced by pansies and daylilies."

Ricky was right about all the vibrant colors. Each turn brought more flowers, and neatly trimmed lawns, as green as

Mary Alice imagined she looked.

You're going to be fine, Mar. And so are things with Hope. This is good - all good.

"I hope you're right. Charlie."

"I'm going to drop all of you off at the entrance, then go park," Evan said. "Don't go whisking away where I can't find you. This campus is humongous."

"We won't," Ricky said. "Besides, we're a half hour early. We'll check her in and wait for you and Char."

Inside, a nurse checked Mary Alice in and strapped a green band around her wrist and told her someone would be out for her soon.

"Do we get to go back with her?" Ellie asked.

The nurse smiled. "Yes, once we get her settled, you can all be with her until they take her into surgery. Hope is already here being prepped. You can see her as well."

"Uh, sure," Evan said.

Mary Alice gave him a silent warning. Now was not the time for any judgment.

Char bounded through the door moments behind Evan. "Hey, so this is it, huh?" She plopped into a chair beside Mary Alice. Her hair swirled softly around her face and across her shoulders. The stress lines around her eyes were gone. It was the first time Mary Alice had seen her with full make-up since who-knew-when. She looked happier and more chipper since before rehab.

Mary Alice fidgeted with the plastic ID bracelet on her wrist. "You're in a good mood today. Happy about your mother going under the knife?"

Char's smile disappeared. "Mom, no. I—"

"I was kidding. Gosh, don't take me so seriously. I could use some of your good energy right now."

"I do feel good. And I've got a good feeling about this. It's all going to go great." Char sat down beside her. "But it's still all up to you. Are you scared? I think you can change your mind up to the very last minute."

"Maybe a little," Mary Alice admitted, maybe a lot more than a little, "but I'm not changing my mind."

"It's a good thing you are doing here, Mom. I'm so proud of you." Charlene bumped shoulders with her.

"Mrs. Goodson?" A nurse came with a clipboard. "We're ready to get you prepped. Once you're settled, your family can come in. And we'll wheel Hope in to see you as well, before you both go nighty-night."

Seriously? Nighty-night? What are we—five? Nurses could be so annoying.

Mary Alice was taken to pre-op, where she changed into a hospital-issued fashion statement. The nurse said that Hope would join her, but she was getting some last-minute testing done. Nothing to worry about.

Easy for her to say.

The family was called in and they hovered around the bed. Nobody said much, probably as nervous as Mary Alice. The door swung open again shortly after she was settled, and Mary Alice sat up when she saw a bed peeking past the corner.

It was Hope. She looked so happy.

A nurse wheeled the rest of the bed inside and parked it beside Mary Alice. "Hi," Hope said. "Am I interrupting something?"

"No," Mary Alice said. "We're waiting for you - the star of this dog and pony show. Char was offering to take my place."

Hope's eyes met Char's. "You'd do that?"

Charlene straightened to her full height, shoulders back, determination set in her jaw. "Yes, Hope. I would if I could. For Mom and for you. I've been wrong about you. I didn't give you a fair shake. But we're family now and family sticks together." She looked at Mary Alice. "Right, Mom?"

"Right. And no one needs to take my place, because I'm ready. Let's get this show on the road."

The rest of the pre-surgery went quickly in a flurry of surgical staff. A nurse came by to talk to the family about the process. Next came the anesthesiologist who once again explained the possible complications.

"Are you sure this is what you want to do?" he asked first Mary Alice, then Hope.

Both gave an enthusiastic yes.

Mary Alice reached for Hope's hand. The last thing she remembered as the sedatives were administered was the warmth of Hope's hand in hers.

When Mary Alice woke, she looked around for Hope.

"She's not down yet," a nurse said from beside her bed. "Don't worry. The transplant was a success."

Good. That was all she needed to know before she fell back asleep. Mary Alice drifted in and out of consciousness. Each time she looked for Hope. Each time she was assured everything was fine. But then, where was she?

When Mary Alice opened her eyes again sometime later, she asked for Hope. The nurse nodded and wheeled Mary Alice's bed across the hall.

Hope was awake and smiling at her.

"We did it," Mary Alice said. "I had to see you for myself."

"Hey," Hope was a little groggy, and her smile was weak. She wiggled her fingers hello before she shut her eyes and fell back to sleep. "You both need to rest." The nurse pushed Mary Alice back to her own recovery room. Mary Alice hummed an agreement and shut her eyes again.

Later that evening, they wheeled Mary Alice to a room on the post-op surgical floor. The kids were all waiting for her.

"You look great," Ellie said. "How are you feeling?"

"Fine, I think. What happened with Hope? I kept looking for her in recovery. It seemed like a long time — of course it could have only been a few minutes. I kept drifting in and out."

Evan placed a hand on her shoulder. "We don't know, Mom. Only that you were in recovery first. Maybe that's standard practice. It's a bigger operation for her. The doctors will tell us. You need to rest and not worry about her."

"I'll see if I can find out anything," Char said. "I have a few connections here."

"Thanks, honey." Mary Alice leaned her head back and closed her eyes.

"Charlie, are you watching over our girl?"

She's fine Mar. Get some sleep.

303

It was dark outside the window the next time Mary Alice opened her eyes. Evan was asleep in the chair in the corner. Char, Ricky and Ellie were nowhere in sight.

A team of doctors bustled through the door as soon as she sat up. Mary Alice recognized some of them from their nephrology team, but the others she had never seen before. Oh yes, this was a teaching hospital. God knows how many people watched the procedure.

"Hello," Dr. Newman said. "Things went well. We were able to remove your kidney laparoscopically as planned." He walked over to Mary Alice and lifted her gown to look at the small bandage on her right side.

Evan sat up and rubbed his eyes. "Oh, hey. Sorry. Didn't mean to doze off there."

"No problem. The lady needed her nap. No reason why you shouldn't too."

"So, everything's good? How long will Mom and Hope have to stay in the hospital?"

"We would like to monitor your mother for two or three days, then she should be able to go home. Hope's going to stay with us a little longer. We placed Mary Alice's kidney above Hope's malfunctioning one. It will take a while to see if her body accepts it. The body considers it a foreign object, and its job is to remove those things. The transplanted kidney doesn't know how to regulate the metabolism like a regular kidney. It has to be taught through medication and diet. But the good news is, no more dialysis. And the prognosis is good for a long, healthy life."

This was information that had been explained to Mary Alice before the procedure. Mary Alice got the feeling this was for Evan's benefit.

"Why was Hope in surgery so much longer than me? She was, wasn't she?" Mary Alice asked. Things were still a little foggy.

"We had a little trouble connecting the ureter to the new kidney. It took three tries for us to get it to hold, but everything is fine now. We will watch it closely to make sure it stays intact."

"I don't know how to thank you," Mary Alice said, tearing up. "You saved her life."

Dr. Preston smiled. "I think that was you."

Mary Alice stayed with Charlene at her condo for the first week after her discharge, three days after surgery. She didn't want to be that far away from Hope, but it was for the best. Charlene insisted she take the only bedroom. Normally Mary Alice would have objected, but this time she was grateful for the comfortable queen-size bed. She couldn't actually say she was in pain—discomfort was a better word. Like the worst gas pain she'd ever had. Pulling her knees up to her chest alleviated most of it, and she sheepishly gave in to taking the pain meds she had refused the first day. Who was she kidding? A martyr for pain she was not. Thank God there was an elevator in the building. School had recessed, so Char was available to help her out the door and to the hospital every day to see Hope.

Today, Char and Mary Alice brought a tin of cookies. Char had been the one to bake them—Mary Alice's famous snickerdoodle cookies.

Mary Alice knocked on the hospital door. Hope softly called out for them to come in. Char helped Mary Alice across the room and into her usual chair before handing the tin to Hope.

"Hey," Hope said, grabbing the tin and eyeing it. "Thank you, what is it?"

Char shrugged. "Snickerdoodle cookies. I don't guarantee they'll be as good as Mom's, but I swear I followed the recipe to the T."

Mary Alice beamed. Char was speaking to Hope as if she'd always been her sister. This was the best medicine any mother could ever need.

"Any word on when you can go home?" Mary Alice asked.

"Soon. Doc says everything is staying attached. No signs of rejection. Food's going to be a little challenging. They've got me on a rigorous schedule of medication and diet, and I need to stick to it very closely. You'd think they'd want me out of here pronto because of my immune system. If you aren't sick before you go into a hospital, good chances are you will by the time you go out. But I'm trying to be a good patient. Any diet and schedule have got to beat four hours of dialysis three times a week. I already feel so much stronger."

"I'm so glad," Mary Alice said, leaning over and planting a kiss on her cheek. "I had an ulterior motive."

Hope raised her eyebrows.

"Call it restitution—for abandoning you when you were born. I feel like I got a second chance to give you life."

"Ah, you didn't owe me anything. You had no choice at sixteen, and I had a wonderful life. No regrets, no guilt trips. Promise?"

Mary Alice gulped down another floodgate. Would she ever be able to talk about this without losing it? She swallowed hard and nodded at Charlene to go ahead.

"There's something we, well, Mom and the rest of us have been talking about," Charlene said. "We have an idea for your art studio."

Hope's eyebrows shot up. "Really? What?"

Mary Alice and Charlene exchanged a knowing look. "Well, Charlie, I mean, your dad's, showroom and workshop has been sitting empty ever since he passed," Mary Alice said. "We own the building. I didn't know what to do with it. It could make a wonderful art gallery for you, with plenty of room for you to create in the workshop in the back. If you are interested, that is?"

Hope's mouth formed a perfect O. "Um, wow. That is amazing. My very own studio? Where is it?"

"It's downtown on Chalmers Street, in Youngstown," Charlene said. "Papa bought the building fifty years ago, when Y'town was booming. Not a lot of foot traffic now, but it's not far from the university."

"Wait. I think there's already an art gallery there," Hope said. "If I remember, it's called the Soap Gallery. They have events there."

"Yes, I know that place," Char said. "Ricky has friends who own it. I guess you'd have to check to see if they had a no-compete clause. It wasn't an issue for a cabinet shop."

Hope's eyes were dancing. "I'll look into it as soon as I get out of this place. Maybe a little competition would be good. Give people a reason to go downtown again. We could turn it into another art district like the Short North in Columbus."

The nurse came in and shooed Charlene and Mary Alice out. "Visiting hours are over. Our girl needs to get her rest." More plural speaking nurses? It irked the heck out of Mary Alice.

"Okay, we're going." She leaned over and gave Hope a peck on the cheek. "See you tomorrow."

Forty-Five

2018

On the night of the grand opening gala, the sign above the door read, "The Hope Gallery."

Mary Alice stood by the bar and smoothed her hands along the folds of her silk, chartreuse evening gown. Everyone was dressed in their finest. Handsome servers in tuxedos offered Champagne on silver trays. The lighting was perfect, soft sconces on the walls, spotlights on each sculpture. Evan sat at a baby grand in the corner, playing softly. Close to a hundred guests moved in a slow circle from piece to piece in the spacious showroom, oohing and aahing over each new discovery. Hope, dressed in a floor length silver gown, moved through the crowd with ease and grace, stopping to chat with each guest.

She looked fabulous. Was it her impeccable make-up, or did she look healthier? It was less than three months since the transplant, and she looked like a new woman. Mary Alice's heart swelled. She couldn't take her eyes off her.

"This is amazing, isn't it?" Sophia said as she and Desmond approached, Gladys right behind.

Mary Alice smiled at her friends. "Yes, Charlie would be so proud. You all look fab."

Sophia squeezed her husband's arm. "Yea, he cleans up pretty good."

Desmond's eyes twinkled as his gaze traveled down Sophia's slinky black gown and settled on her dipping decollate. "Not so bad yourself, Babe."

"And look at this bombshell." Sophia twirled Gladys in a circle, her leopard print caftan blooming around her.

"Stop," Gladys said. "I can hardly stand in these heels, let alone twirl."

Ellie and Greg joined them. "Did you see how many sold tags there are already? She's doing very well. This is a perfect location for her," Ellie said.

Mary Alice nodded. The cabinet shop's showroom had been completely transformed, but the back room was where the magic still happened. Where wood met artist and was turned into works of art.

Bethany squeezed into the growing group, little Charlie wrapped snugly in a soft blue blanket. His amber eyes were wide open, seeming to be taking it all in. Even Estelle and a few of the girls from the FC were there. Mary Alice led their little group around the gallery — it definitely wasn't her first rotation. Bethany was drawn away by some of her FC friends, and soon it was only Mary Alice and her children drifting from one piece to another.

"What's the story behind that piece?" Ellie nodded toward the front of the room where a tall bronze stand held something covered in a black velvet cloth.

"I don't know," Mary Alice said. A dozen or so guests were clustered around the mystery piece, talking softly among each other. "It must be some special reveal. She is certainly building a lot of interest with the intrigue."

Hope breezed across the room and grasped Mary Alice's arm. "Can you guys join me up front for the reveal?"

Ellie grabbed Evan and Char, smiling brightly at her older sister. "Finally. I've been waiting to see this all night." The three of them quickly made their way toward the covered piece while Hope and Mary Alice took their time in following. They didn't speak, they didn't have to. Mary Alice couldn't remember a night that felt as beautiful and utterly right. When they got to the end of the room, Hope released Mary Alice and stepped up on a felt-covered black box next to the sculpture. A man with a tray of champagne appeared right next to her, holding up the tray with one hand and a silver fork in the other. Hope smiled at him and took a flute, raising it above the crowd. She tapped the fork against the glass until everyone quieted.

"Ladies and gentlemen, first I want to thank all of you for attending the grand opening of the Hope Gallery. Your support is greatly appreciated." She smiled down at her family. "This is a dream come true. There are no words to adequately express thanks to my family or my joy at having this gallery where my father created his own magic." She paused and smiled at her sister. "This last piece is my most recent. It is not for sale. Charlene, will you join me, please?"

Charlene raised her brows and opened her mouth wide. She looked at Mary Alice, who nodded for her to go ahead. She stepped forward, looking bewildered and a little embarrassed by the attention.

"This piece has special meaning to me," Hope said. "I have named it Equal Love. Charlene, this is a gift for you." She pulled the black cloth from the sculpture.

Everyone gasped. Mary Alice's hand flew to her mouth. The sculpture was a woman, standing tall, arms outstretched, a tiny baby cradled in each hand. Perfectly balanced. Equal Love.

"Oh, Hope, it is beautiful." Mary Alice said. She was glad she was in front of the crowd.

Charlene swallowed hard, and when Hope stepped down and wrapped an arm around her, the floodgates opened. Mary Alice had never seen her daughter openly cry in public, yet there she was, wiping at her perfect eye makeup. "I don't know what to say. Thank you hardly feels adequate."

"Nothing to say," Hope said. "It's meant to show the equal love our mother has for both . . . no, for all of us."

Mary Alice moved closer to the sculpture. The scent of the wood encompassed her. *Cedar.* Charlie's favorite wood. She closed her eyes and breathed in deep. It was almost like having him there. Charlie. So many memories together in this room.

Hope raised her voice above the crowd. "Hors d'oeuvres and cake are now being served in the back room. Please stay and enjoy the refreshments."

The guests drifted toward the workshop, looking at the

other pieces in the room. The family stayed together admiring the piece. Everyone agreed it was perfect. Mary Alice couldn't tear her eyes away from it.

Eventually, the event wound down. At the end of the night, the photographer gathered the family together. They pressed in tight together, surrounding the sculpture like it too, was part of the family. Mary Alice stood to the right with baby Charlie in her arms. Bethany stood beside her. Charlene and Hope were on the other side of the sculpture. Ellie and Greg stood behind Charlene and Hope. Evan and Ricky stood behind Mary Alice and Bethany.

The photographer snapped a few photos then lowered his camera, frowning down at it. "I'm sorry folks, we may have to do this elsewhere in the room. There's the oddest shadow that I can't seem to get rid of."

Mary Alice smiled, a warmth running through the entirety of her body. "Don't worry about it, dear. I'm sure they look perfect."

Of course, Charlie would not be left out.

We did this, Mar. We made this beautiful family.

"Oh Charlie."

"Wait. One more photo," Mary Alice said.

She shooed most of the group away and gathered Sophia, Gladys, Bethany and Hope around her. "Okay, now you do your fingers like this, yes, and cross that finger in front

It only took a moment for Hope and Bethany to catch on. Each of them raised their hands, holding their fingers in crossed V shapes, smiling into the flash of the camera.

"The Crittenton Girls."

Epilogue

2020

The children are all around me as we place Charlie's ashes into the ground. It is time. Life moves on and so must I. Grateful is not a strong enough word to describe how my life has turned out. All four children stand arm-in-arm and my heart soars with joy. Bethany is hopelessly trying to keep the reins on rambunctious two-year-old Charlie during the brief service. I don't mind. Let him run. I'd run right alongside of him if I had any chance of keeping up. Life is for running and laughing and forgiving and learning. I have learned that finding my voice does not take away from someone else's opinion and in the long run; I am respected and stronger for it. It's too bad it took me over a half a century. I guess some of us are slower learners.

Praise for The Crittenton Girls

Exceptional dramatic family saga that pulls your heartstrings from love, loss, shame and despair in search of hope and redemption. Masterful storytelling with a chain reaction of psychological intrigue and suspense. Five stars.

Fast paced, satisfying and unforgettable characters with universal themes for wide audiences.

James Masciarelli
Author of Beyond Beauport

The Crittenton Girls is a moving story of the evolution of the women in a family over half a century. Mary Alice gains the strength to share her secret and demonstrates that a mother's love for her children can overcome enormous obstacles that once seemed insurmountable. A must read for women of all ages.

Dr. Dolores Burton
Award Winning Author

The Crittenton Girl chronicles one woman's struggle to find her own voice while weathering complicated and turbulent relationships with her daughters, and herself. An inspiring, touching story about how we love each, how we hurt each other, but most importantly, how it's never too late to grow.

Lidija Hilje
Book Coach and Author

The Crittenton Girls is a moving dual-timeline story about a girl without a voice, and her journey in reclaiming it sixty years later. The protagonist, Mary Alice, has a tale that spans from the gates of the Crittenton Home in the puritan sixties all the way to the present. As a psychology enthusiast, I could appreciate the primary character's childhood conditioning, and as a woman in her twenties, I finally understood why — and how — the experiences that shaped the women of the past made them so different from my generation, and yet still fundamentally the same in our need to protect, nurture, and fight. Nowhere is that more clear than in this story when Mary Alice is forced to come face-to-face with her own reflection in her granddaughter, take a leap of faith to find the daughter that she lost, and stand her ground against the daughter she raised. TCG is a story of family, sacrifice, and forgiveness, but most importantly, it is about finding your voice in a world that would rather you stay silent.

Arra Boles
Castle Book Coaching